THE
BRIDGE
AT QUÉBEC

RAILROADS PAST AND PRESENT

EDITED BY GEORGE M. SMERK

THE
BRIDGE
AT QUÉBEC

WILLIAM D. MIDDLETON

Indiana University Press / Bloomington and Indianapolis

This book is a publication of Indiana University Press,
601 North Morton Street, Bloomington, IN 47404-3797 USA

http://www.indiana.edu/~iupress

Telephone orders 800-842-6796
Fax orders 812-855-7931
Orders by e-mail iuporder@indiana.edu

The paper used in this publication meets the minimum requirements of
American National Standard for Information Sciences—
Permanence of Paper for Printed Library Materials, ANSI Z39.48-1984

Manufactured in the United States of America

Library of Congress Cataloging-in-Publication Data

Middleton, William D., date.
The bridge at Québec / William D. Middleton.
p.   cm.
Includes bibliographical references and index.
ISBN 0-253-33761-5 (cl : alk. paper)
1. Pont de Québec (Québec)—History.
2. Bridges, Cantilever—Design and construction.
3. Railroad bridges—Québec (Province)—Québec—History.
I. Title.

TG27.P66 M53 2001
624´.35´0971428—dc21   00-061394

1 2 3 4 5   06 05 04 03 02 01

CONTENTS

PREFACE

I FIRST LEARNED ABOUT THE EXTRAORDINARY STORY OF THE QUEBEC BRIDGE FROM a high school science text more than a half century ago, and it quickly became a subject that has fascinated me ever since. Surely it is a remarkable tale of determination and perseverance in the face of daunting obstacles and tragic failure, ending in the final triumph of the successful completion of one of the world's great bridges. This epic struggle to build a bridge of unprecedented scale across the St. Lawrence River incorporates all of the elements of man's unending and stubborn quest for technological advance: the determination to go higher, farther, or faster than anyone has ever gone before; suffering grievous failure; learning from it; and trying again until success is finally achieved.

Much has been written about the story of the bridge, particularly of the collapse of the first bridge. Too much of this, unfortunately, has been inaccurate, and some of it downright wrong. In this book I have endeavored to tell the story as accurately and objectively as I could. I sincerely hope the knowledgeable reader will be able to say that I have succeeded.

There is an intriguing legend that goes with the story of the Quebec Bridge that I cannot omit to mention. Many years ago I was told about the unique iron ring worn by Canadian engineers. According to the legend, the iron ring—presented to newly graduated engineers as a reminder of their obligation to maintain high professional standards—is made of metal from the collapsed first Quebec Bridge. It seemed such an appropriate way continually to remind an engineer of the responsibility of his or her calling. Alas, as I've learned more recently, the story isn't true, even if it ought to be.

"Remnants of a legend that iron rings were made from the collapsed bridge still exist," I was told by G. J. Johnson, professional engineer and secretary of Camp One, Toronto, one of twenty-four Camps across Canada that conduct the Ritual of the Calling of an Engineer, as the iron ring ceremony is called. The first Ritual, Johnson told me, was held in 1925 using an Obligation wording written by Rudyard Kipling that is still in use today. Rather than using metal from the bridge, he assured me, the early iron rings were made by World War I veterans as part of an occupational therapy program at a Toronto veterans' hospital.

Throughout the book I have generally used the French spellings and punctuation for all place names in Québec, using the English version only when it appears in an English name, such as, for example, the Quebec Bridge Company. In direct quotations, of course, I have left spellings and punctuation as I found them.

In recounting the story of the Quebec Bridge, I have been aided by an exceptionally rich historical record. Given the heroic scale of the structure, its planning and construction were the subject of exceptionally detailed coverage in the engineering press of the time. The Royal Commission that investigated the collapse of the first Quebec Bridge did so with uncommon thoroughness and objectivity; and its report is a model effort of its kind that leaves little doubt about what happened or why. The Government Board of Engineers that guided the design and construction of the second bridge concluded its work in 1918 with a handsomely prepared report that provides a remarkably complete and detailed account of every element of the project. In a general account such as this it is impossible to explore fully the many complex engineering issues involved in the design and construction of a great undertaking such as the Quebec Bridge. For the technically minded reader with a further interest in such matters, these publications will provide a rewarding source. These and the many other sources that have contributed to the story are summarized in the bibliography.

My exploration into the long history of this extraordinary project has been aided immeasurably by the willing assistance of a great many institutions and individuals, without which it would not have been possible.

In Canada I have enjoyed the use of the splendid resources and the assistance of the able and helpful staffs at the National Archives of Canada and the National Library of Canada at Ottawa, the National Archives of Québec and the libraries of Laval University and the Provincial Parliament at Québec, and the McGill University library at Montréal. At Québec, President Jaques Jobin of The Coalition for the Quebec Bridge provided extensive information about his organization's plans for lighting the bridge. Director Kanatakta, librarian Alexis Shackleton, and photographer Martin A. Loft at the Kanien'kehaka Raotitiohkwa Cultural Center at Kahnawake (old Caughnawaga) all provided much assistance with the story of the Caughnawaga ironworkers. Louise Filion at Canadian National media relations in Montréal answered a variety of questions related to the former National Transcontinental Railway, while Rocco Cacchiottio and Alain Martineau in CN's engineering organization provided extensive details about the current renovation program for the Quebec Bridge. Also at Montréal, Jo-Anne Colby of the Canadian Pacific Archives, Glenn Brown at the McGill University Archives, and archivist Pierre Lavigne at l'École Polytechnique de Montréal supplied valued biographical information, while the McCord Museum made available some notable photographs of the bridge from the Notman Photographic Archives.

In the United States significant reference material and illustrations concerning the bridge were located in the division of engineering and industries at the Smithsonian Institution at Washington, D.C., with much assistance from museum specialist William W. Worthington, Jr. Also at Washington, the American Society of Civil Engineers provided information concerning the designation of the Quebec Bridge as an International Historic Civil Engineering Landmark. Valuable reference materials and photographs were located in the Phoenix Bridge Company holdings of the Hagley Museum and Library at Wilmington, Delaware, where archivist Christopher T. Baer and Barbara Hall of the pictorial collections were particularly helpful. At Phoenixville, Pennsylvania, Lois Donovan, archivist for the Historical Society of the Phoenixville Area, kindly made available extensive material and photographs concerning the Phoenix Bridge Company. The archives at my alma mater, Rensselaer Polytechnic Institute, provided copies of drawings of the Serrell suspension bridge plan of 1852 and John Roebling's sketch of a proposed suspension span at Québec from its Roebling collection, and I am indebted to assistant institute archivist Gretchen Koerpel for her help in exploring these extensive holdings. Elaine Pichaske Sokolowski of the Peoria (Illinois) Public Library's reference department went far beyond the call of duty to locate materials concerning Peoria-born engineer Arthur Birks. The staff at the Linda Hall Library at Kansas City have been ever prompt and efficient in response to my numerous requests for copies from the library's holdings in technical journals. At Charlottesville the staffs of the University of Virginia's Alderman Research and its Science and Technology libraries, and the library's interlibrary loan staff, have proved unfailingly helpful.

In Great Britain Michael M. Chrimes, librarian for The Institution of Civil Engineers, located extensive biographical information concerning Max am Ende and James Brunlees, while Richard C. Packer, photographer for the Department of Civil and Environmental Engineering at the Imperial College of Science, Technology and Medicine at London, kindly supplied a print of the classic view of Benjamin Baker's demonstration of the cantilever principle.

A number of individuals have contributed to the book in diverse ways. In Canada Peter Wright at the University of Toronto and Roger Dorton, a noted bridge engineer and former partner of Philip L. Pratley, have been most helpful in my search for biographical information about the key Canadian engineers involved with the bridge. G. J. Thompson, a professional engineer in Toronto, kindly enlightened me on the history and meaning of the iron ring ceremony.

In the United States David L. Waddington drafted the splendid drawings of early bridge proposals which carry his credit line, while artist Werner K. Sensbach has produced the handsome drawing of the caisson launching of 1901 for the first bridge. *Railroad History* editor Mark Reutter brought to my attention George Mitchell's wonderful piece from *The New Yorker*, "The Mohawks in High Steel," which I would surely otherwise have missed. French scholar Charles Rice at the University of Virginia has expertly translated a number of important materials from French. The late Martin J. Havran, professor of history at the University and a fervent Canadian, very kindly read and offered valued advice on portions of the manuscript concerned with Canadian political issues of the time.

Finally, I thank my wife Dorothy for her usual careful review of the manuscript that has saved me from much grammatical and punctuation error. As always, however, I must accept full responsibility for any lapses which she may have overlooked.

WILLIAM D. MIDDLETON

THE
BRIDGE
AT QUÉBEC

PROLOGUE:
THE GREAT RIVER

J ACQUES CARTIER, THE FRENCH EXPLORER WHO DISCOVERED THE ST. LAWRENCE, is said to have called it "the River of Canada." It is an apt description, for it was the St. Lawrence which afforded a route to the interior of North America for generations of the French and British explorers, fur traders, missionaries, and soldiers who opened much of Canada and the American West to exploration and settlement. As others followed in their path, it then became a great artery of commerce between Europe and the new nation.

Second in North America only to the Mississippi-Missouri system, the St. Lawrence ranks among the great rivers of the world. Flowing generally to the northeast, connecting the Great Lakes basin with the Atlantic Ocean, the river lies between the Appalachian and Adirondack Mountains and the Laurentian upland or Canadian Shield in a triangular depression that was carved by receding glaciers some 6,000 years ago.

For some 600 miles between Montréal and the Gulf of St. Lawrence, the middle and lower reaches of the river flow through the St. Lawrence Lowlands, forming a broad passage between the Gulf and the ports along the river or far beyond on the St. Lawrence Seaway system. Every year the hundreds of oceangoing vessels and lakers that ply its waters transport some 55 million tons of grain, iron ore, coal, iron, steel, and other commodities. Between Montréal and Québec, the river is a formidable stream generally close to two miles wide, with a channel dredged to a depth of 35 feet. The great river moves toward the sea at a rate that grows to an average of some 450,000 cubic feet of water every second as it flows into the Gulf of St. Lawrence. Ocean tides reach as far upstream as Trois-Rivières, some 77 miles above Québec. Below Québec the river becomes a tidal estuary, gradually widening to as many as 70 miles before it merges with the Gulf of St. Lawrence.

Strictly speaking, the St. Lawrence proper is only some 750 miles long, extending from the foot of Lake Ontario, opposite Kingston, Ontario, to the Gulf of St. Lawrence. But in reality the St. Lawrence reaches much further than this, for its drainage basin encompasses all five of the Great Lakes and the rivers and streams which feed them. Thus, the true headwaters of the St. Lawrence lie at the source of the St. Louis River in the Mesabi Range of northern Minnesota, some 2,400 miles from the sea. This enormous area drained by the St. Lawrence comprises a total of some 457,000 square miles, and it includes within it the largest body of fresh water anywhere in the world.

Although other Europeans were probably there earlier, the first recorded European exploration of the St. Lawrence was by Jacques Cartier, the great Breton pathfinder commissioned by Francis I of France to explore what he grandly called New France. Cartier first sailed along the coast of what is now Newfoundland and into the Gulf of St. Lawrence on his first voyage of 1534. A year later he returned to further explore what he believed to be the Northwest Passage to China so eagerly sought by explorers of that time. On this second voyage Cartier sailed beyond the Gulf and into the St. Lawrence River, traveling far into the interior of the North American continent before he was halted by the Lachine Rapids at the native settlement at Hochelaga (where Montréal is now located). Cartier's journals describe the rich, lovely, and unspoiled land he found along the St. Lawrence:

> The whole country on both sides of the river up as far as Hochelaga and beyond is as fine a land and as level as ever one beheld. There are some mountains visible at a considerable distance from the river, and into it several tributaries flow down from these. The land is everywhere covered and overrun with timber of several sorts and also with quantities of vines, except in the neighborhood of the tribes, who have cleared the land for their village and crops. There are a large number of big stags, does, bears, and other animals. We beheld the footprints of a beast with but two legs, and followed his tracks over the sand and mud for a long distance. Its paws were more than a palm in size. Furthermore, there are many otters, beavers, martens, foxes, wild-cats, hares, rabbits, squirrels, wonderfully large [musk-] rats, and other wild beasts. The people wear the skins of these animals for want of other apparel. There are also great numbers of birds, to wit: cranes, bustards, swans, white and gray wild geese, ducks, drakes, blackbirds, thrushes, turtle-doves, wood-pigeons, goldfinches, tarins [siskin or finch], canaries, linnets, nightingales, sparrows, and other birds the same as in France. Again this river, as has been already stated in the preceding chapters, is the richest in every kind of fish that any one remembers having ever seen or heard of; for from its mouth to the head of it, you will find in their season the majority of the [known] varieties and species of salt and freshwater fish. Up as far as Canada, you will meet with many whales, porpoises, sea-horses, walruses, and *Adhothuys* [beluga or white whale], which is a species of fish that we had never seen or heard of before. They are as white as snow and have a head like a greyhound's. Their habitat is between the ocean and the fresh-water that begins between the river Saguenay and Canada.
>
> Moreover, you will find in this river in June, July, and August great numbers of mackerel, mullets, maigres, tunnies, large-sized eels, and other fish. When their [spawning] season is over you will find as good smelts as in the river Seine. In spring again there are quantities of lampreys and salmon. Up above Canada are many pike, trout, carp, breams, and other fresh-water fish. All these varieties are caught, each in its season, in considerable quantities by these people for their food and sustenance.[1]

Cartier established France's claim on the New World, and in time others followed in his path and beyond to explore and open up much of North America. Important among them was explorer Samuel de Champlain, who came almost seventy years later bearing a commission from King Henry IV. Champlain's first journey, in 1603, took him up the St. Lawrence as far as the Lachine Rapids; and from the Indians he learned something of the rivers, valleys, and lakes that lay beyond. Five years later Champlain led a party of French colonists up the St. Lawrence to found Québec, the first permanent settlement in New France; and in later years he explored much of the territory that lay to the west and north.

Champlain was followed into this new French empire in North America by still other explorers, fur traders, soldiers, and missionaries. For all of them the waterway formed by the St. Lawrence and the Great Lakes was the pathway that led to the interior. They traveled on the great river and its tributaries and on the lakes, in canoes and flat-bottomed bateaux that could easily be portaged around the rapids, becoming the first to explore and map much of the interior that would later become the American West.

Gradually the region was settled, and commerce developed along the St. Lawrence. The Lachine Rapids was as far as oceangoing vessels could reach; and Montréal, established near there in 1642 on a long island in the river, soon became a major port and a competitor to Québec. Above Montréal, canoes, bateaux, and small lake vessels transported the traffic, with much transshipment of cargo around the many rapids. By the 1840s the completion of a system of locks and canals made it possible for small ships and barges to operate all the way from Montréal to the Great Lakes; but it was not until the St. Lawrence Seaway opened in 1959 that larger oceangoing vessels could navigate to the furthest reaches of the Great Lakes.

While the St. Lawrence provided a great natural pathway for Canada's waterborne commerce, the river also had some formidable shortcomings. For four months or more every winter, ice closed the river to ship traffic and made passage from shore to shore an exceedingly risky venture. Small boats and canoes had to make their way among great ice floes, or their occupants portaged across successive floes until they finally reached the opposite shore. Sometimes the river froze solid, and travelers could only make the river crossing in sleighs or carrioles or on foot. The ice bridge, as it was called, that sometimes formed between Québec and Pointe-Lévy was usually lined with wooden refreshment huts and shelters erected around fishing holes cut in the ice. The annual breakup of ice as the weather warmed in the spring was always a dramatic event that signaled the resumption of communication with the Old World. Weakened by the warmer air, the great sheet of ice usually broke with a roar into huge blocks that were carried down the river by the current, sometimes forming enormous ice jams as they encountered obstacles.

Through one of the characters in her novel *The History of Emily Montague*, eighteenth-century Canadian writer Frances Brooke described the annual breakup of ice between Québec and Pointe-Lévy:

> From the time the ice is no longer a bridge on which you see crowds driving with such vivacity on business or pleasure, every one is looking eagerly for its breaking away, to remove the bar to the continually wished and expected event, of the arrival of ships from that world from whence we have seemed so long in a manner excluded.
>
> The hour is come; I have been with a crowd of both sexes, and all ranks, hailing the propitious moment: our situation, on the top of Cape Diamond, gave us a prospect some leagues above and below the town; above Cape Diamond the river was open, it was so below Point Levi, the rapidity of the current having forced a passage for the water under the transparent bridge, which for more than a league continued firm.
>
> We stood waiting with all the eagerness of expectation; the tide came rushing with an amazing impetuosity; the bridge seemed to shake, yet resisted the force of the waters; the tide recoiled, it made a pause, it stood still, it returned with redoubled fury, the immense mass of ice gave way.
>
> A vast plain appeared in motion; it advanced with solemn and majestic pace: the points of land on the banks of the river for a few moments stopped its progress; but the immense weight of so prodigious a body, carried along by a rapid current, bore down all opposition with a force irresistible.
>
> There is no describing how beautiful the opening river appears, every moment gaining on the sight, till, in a time less than can possibly be imagined, the ice passing Point Levi, is hid in one moment by the projecting land, and all is once more a clear plain before you; giving at once the pleasing, but unconnected, idea of that direct intercourse with Europe from which we have been so many months excluded, and of the earth's again opening her fertile bosom, to feast our eyes and imagination with her various verdant and flowery productions.[2]

Indeed the St. Lawrence was a great river.

BOOK ONE:

THE FIRST BRIDGE

The great escarpment of Québec looked like this from the south bank of the St. Lawrence in 1860. The view was captured in a painting from the Pointe de Lévy shore by artist Richard Principal Leitch. National Archives of Canada (Neg. C4900).

CHAPTER 1

A BRIDGE AT THE
NARROWING

As Canadian commerce developed in the nineteenth century, the St. Lawrence River took on an ever-expanding importance as the principal trade route linking the Canadian interior with the Eastern Seaboard and Europe. But as long as waterborne traffic used the St. Lawrence, trade was effectively cut off during four months or more every winter when the river was iced over. This placed Canadian merchants at a severe disadvantage to their American competitors to the south, where a well-established system of railways and canals linked the interior with the ice-free ports of Boston and New York.

By the mid-nineteenth century, the development of railways in Canada offered the opportunity to maintain traffic year-round by creating new trade links with such ice-free ports as Halifax, Nova Scotia; Portland, Maine; and Boston. Montréal was well ahead of Québec in adopting this new technology to strengthen its position as the leading Canadian port. Canada's first railroad was the Champlain & St. Lawrence, which opened in 1836 as a land link in the St. Lawrence–Lake Champlain–Hudson River waterway system, providing an alternate route for Canadian trade through U.S. ports. A much more important route began to take shape in 1845, when the St. Lawrence & Atlantic was chartered to build a railway from Montréal through St-Hyacinthe and Sherbrooke to the U.S. border, where it would be linked with an American counterpart to complete a route to Portland, Maine. Construction began in 1846, and by 1853 the entire line was complete between Longueuil, across the St. Lawrence from Montréal, and Portland.

In 1852 a new project was organized to build the Grand Trunk Railway west from Montréal to Toronto and Sarnia in Upper Canada (now Ontario). Within a year the Grand Trunk had incorporated the St. Lawrence & Atlantic into a grand scheme for a railway that would extend all the way from Sarnia to the ice-free port at Portland. Its declared strategy was to draw trade from the American Midwest into Canada for shipment through Montréal or, during the winter, through Portland.

Québec was left far behind by all this development. The city's first railway link was the Quebec & Richmond, incorporated in 1850, which extended from a waterfront station at Pointe-Lévis, on the south bank of the river opposite Québec, to a connection with the St. Lawrence & Atlantic at Richmond, Québec. A steam ferry made the connection between Lévis and Québec. The line finally opened in the spring of 1855, by which time it had already been incorporated into the fast-growing Grand Trunk system. Québec, however, was still without a railway link to the west, and it would be almost twenty-five years before this critical gap would be filled. Local promoters obtained a charter to build the North

Shore Railway along the north shore of the St. Lawrence between Québec and Montréal in 1854, but it was not until 1879 that this line was finally completed.

At both Montréal and Québec, the St. Lawrence River itself represented a formidable barrier to the movement of railroad traffic between the Canadian interior and the ice-free Atlantic ports. During the navigation season, freight could at least be ferried across the river. This became increasingly difficult, and finally impossible, as the river began to fill with ice. Only when the river froze solid could traffic cross on the "ice bridge," and this was at best a risky and uncertain business. The only sensible solution to the problem at either city would be a bridge.

Once again, Montréal got a long head start on its downriver rival in solving the river-crossing problem. The idea of a bridge across the St. Lawrence at Montréal was being advanced as early as the mid-1840s, when several location studies were completed. The great British railway engineer Robert Stephenson, together with Alexander Ross, chief engineer of the British firm that was building the Grand Trunk, designed an innovative wrought iron tubular structure. A site upstream from the harbor was selected, and construction got underway in 1854 for what was to prove an exceedingly difficult undertaking. Although the water was relatively shallow at the chosen site, a structure nearly two miles long was required. Swift currents and the winter ice conditions added to the difficulty of the work, and it was not until 1859 that the bridge was finally completed. Named in honor of the queen, Victoria Bridge was one of the engineering wonders of its time. Railroad traffic from inland points could now move across the St. Lawrence without costly and time-consuming trans-shipment, and Montréal's primacy as Canada's principal eastern port had been greatly strengthened.

Members of the Québec business community were keenly aware that these developments were placing their city at a disadvantage, and the idea of their own bridge across the St. Lawrence was being discussed as early as 1850.

As difficult a project as the Victoria Bridge at Montréal proved to be, a crossing of the river anywhere below Montréal would be an even more difficult undertaking. Almost everywhere between Montréal and Québec, the river was close to two miles wide, the water deep, and the current strong. Moreover, any bridge would have to provide adequate vertical clearances for the oceangoing vessels that traveled as far up the St. Lawrence as Montréal.

Fortunately, one of the best locations for a bridge anywhere below Montréal was right at Québec. The St. Lawrence is both narrow and deep as it passes Québec, where the Laurentians and the Appalachians close in on the river to confine it to a gorge-like formation about three-quarters of a mile wide and eight miles long. Indeed, the name Québec is said to be an Algonkian word meaning "a narrowing."

The narrow passage would shorten the overall length of a bridge, while the height of the escarpments on either side would make it easier to attain the height required for navigational clearances. Nevertheless, it was still anything but an easy site. The extreme depth of the water, as much as 190 feet at the center of the river, made the construction of intermediate piers infeasible over much of the width of the river. The current velocity reached about 8 or 9 mph at ebb tide, and the range of spring tides was about 18 feet. The winter ice formations at Québec were heavy, and the ice tended to pile up, or "gorge," in the narrow passage, sometimes rising to a height of 50 feet.

In 1850 no bridge of the scale or difficulty required for such a crossing had yet been built anywhere in the world. But the advocates for a bridge at Québec were aware of a project underway in the United States that would at least approach the dimensions required at Québec. This was a planned crossing of the Niagara River gorge just below Niagara Falls that would establish a new railway link between the United States and Canada.

At the point below the Falls chosen for the bridge, the Niagara gorge was about 800 feet across and more than 200 feet deep. This was far too great a span for the railroad bridge-building technology of the time; and the turbulent rapids, together with enormous ice jams in the winter, made the construction of piers or falsework impractical.

Only a suspension bridge seemed feasible for a span this long. The suspension bridge had been used in a primitive form for centuries, and a Pennsylvanian named John Finley had developed a practical suspension design for vehicular traffic as far back as 1801. Finley's design, patented in 1808, employed a flexible chain of wrought iron links and a stiffened deck structure.

As early as 1826, British engineer Thomas Telford had completed his Menai Straits suspension bridge with a clear span of 579 feet between towers. Elsewhere in Europe suspension bridges spanning as much as 870 feet were built during the next decade. In America Colonel Charles Ellet, Jr., a Pennsylvania-born engineer who had studied at l'École Polytechnique in Paris, completed a 358-foot suspension span across the Schuylkill River at Philadelphia in 1842. Ellet then built a 1,010-foot span across the Ohio River at Wheeling, Virginia, that was the longest suspension span anywhere in the world when it was completed in 1849. All of these early suspension spans, however, had been built for road traffic only. The only attempt to use a suspension span for railway traffic, completed for England's pioneer Stockton & Darlington Railway in 1830, had not been successful.

The idea of a suspension bridge across the Niagara River had first been put forth in 1824 by Francis Hall, a British émigré, who proposed the construction of a wrought iron chain link suspension bridge between Lewiston, New York, and Queenston, Upper Canada (now Ontario), on the model of Telford's Menai Straits bridge. Nothing came of Hall's scheme, and it was more than two decades before the idea of a bridge across the Niagara came back to life.

The Niagara suspension bridge project that caught the attention of Québec's bridge proponents had been launched in 1846 with the formation of the Niagara Bridge Company, which was to build a combined road and railroad bridge at the site below the Falls. A contract for the work had been awarded to Charles Ellet in 1847, but this was terminated the following year in a dispute with the bridge company. The contract then went to John A. Roebling, who had also submitted a proposal for the bridge. Roebling designed a bridge spanning 821 feet between towers that was supported by four 10-inch-diameter wire cables, which were to be spun in place from wrought iron wire. Roebling planned to counteract the undesirable lack of rigidity of suspension bridges by using heavy wooden trusses to carry the bridge's double-deck structure and a system of under- and over-deck wire rope stays. Construction began in 1851, and the structure was opened to traffic in March 1855.

With this ambitious project moving ahead on the Niagara, the Québec City Council in April 1851 resolved to bring civil engineer Edward Wellman Serrell to the city to study and report on the feasibility of a suspension bridge across the St. Lawrence. Only 25 years old, Serrell was already well known as a suspension bridge engineer. Born in London of American parents in 1826, Serrell had returned to the United States at an early age. He was educated in New York City public schools and then took up civil engineering under his father and an elder brother. From 1845, when he began his engineering career at the age of 19, until the Civil War, Serrell was engaged in a variety of railroad and bridge design and construction work. His railroad experience included work as an assistant engineer for the Erie Railroad, an assignment in charge of surveys for the Northern Railroad of New Hampshire, and a period as engineer for the Central Railroad of New Jersey. He also served as an assistant to the chief of the U.S. Army's topographical engineers and was an assistant engineer for the 1849 survey that located a route across the Isthmus of Panama for the Panama Railroad.

Most pertinent to the Québec bridge project, Serrell had been engaged in suspension bridge work for several years. He was one of four engineers who had advised the newly formed Niagara Bridge Company in 1846 on the feasibility of a suspension bridge over the Niagara Gorge, the other three being Ellet, Roebling, and a Canadian engineer named Samuel Keefer, who later designed the Upper Suspension Bridge over the gorge, just below the Falls.

Even as the Roebling bridge was moving ahead, Serrell had taken on the daunting task of designing and supervising construction of the first permanent bridge across the Niagara.

(Pages 10–11)
Drawings for Edward Serrell's proposal of 1852 for a suspension bridge across the St. Lawrence at Québec depicted an elegant structure of towers and turrets, crenellations, and crosses inset into the masonry. The bridge's main span of 1,610 feet would have surpassed any bridge built in the nineteenth century. Drawings by David L. Waddington from original Serrell plans in the Roebling Collection, Rensselaer Polytechnic Institute Archives.

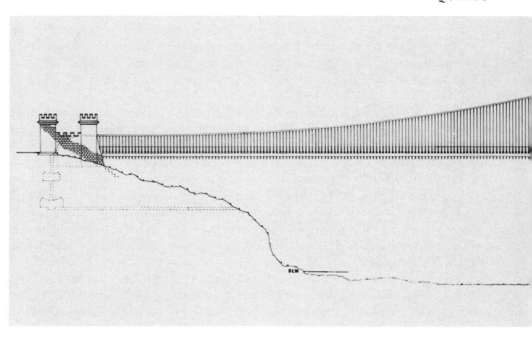

This was a suspension span for road traffic located just above the head of navigation in the river at the Lewiston-Queenston site. The cables supporting the bridge were suspended from stone towers erected near the tops of the bluffs on each side of the river. The cable span of 1,040 feet between the towers was a world record for its time, although the bridge deck itself was only 849 feet long. Work began in 1850, and the bridge was opened to traffic in March 1851.

The Québec City Council was particularly interested in a bridge spanning the St. Lawrence between Lévis and Québec proper, but Serrell considered other sites as well. One

Plans for an unprecedented railroad suspension bridge across the Niagara River at Niagara Falls inspired Québec to consider a similar structure for a crossing of the St. Lawrence. Completed by John A. Roebling early in 1855, the Niagara Falls bridge spanned 821 feet between the towers. This drawing appeared in *Ballou's Pictorial* for June 16, 1855. Smithsonian Institution (Neg. 48439).

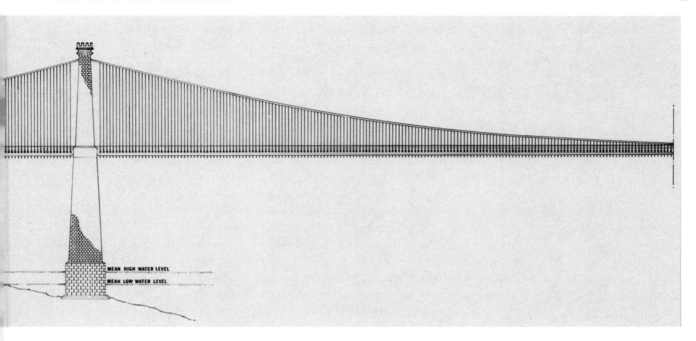

site at the north end of the long escarpment on the north shore of the river extended from the Terrace of the old Palais St. Louis in Québec to Pointe-Lévis. A second site opposite Lévis and a few hundred yards above Cap-Diamant was considered but quickly discarded because of both the extreme water depth and the greater length of bridge that would have been required.

Serrell's report, submitted to the mayor and city council in March 1852, recommended a third site about seven miles up the river, just above its confluence with the Chaudière River. Here, Serrell pointed out, the river narrowed to a width of only 2,440 feet, while the

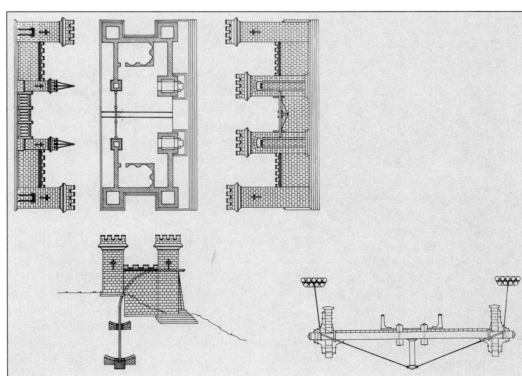

high, rocky banks on both sides of the river, 165 feet high on the north bank and 140 feet high on the south bank, made it easy to provide the navigational clearance that would be required.

A bridge at this point, said Serrell, would require an extreme length of 3,400 feet, and the drawings that accompanied his report detailed a structure that would have far surpassed anything yet imagined in bridge engineering. It was to be a wire suspension bridge with a main span of 1,610 feet between the centers of its two massive towers and side spans of 805 feet between the towers and the cable anchorage at each end. The hollow stone masonry towers, which Serrell proposed to locate where the river was 12 feet deep at average low tide, would stand 330 feet high above their bases and would be 52 feet by 137 feet at the base, tapering upwards. These would be constructed within timber cofferdams sunk into place on the rock of the river bottom with stone ballast and then pumped out to permit the masonry work. Icebreakers faced with heavy iron plates were to be constructed above and below each pier.

The span was to be supported by nine cables on each side made up of a total of some 80,000 strands of No. 10 "best bridge wire." Any movement of the cables as they expanded and contracted with temperature changes or moved under load would be accommodated by carrying them in segmental saddles of iron plates at the top of each tower. A system of cylindrical rollers placed between the saddles and a lower cast iron plate which rested on the masonry allowed for any movement. At each anchorage the wire cables were to be attached to a system of iron bars which extended down through a shaft 56 feet deep into the solid rock of the river banks.

Unlike most suspension bridges of the time, in which the cables hung in a vertical plane, Serrell proposed that those for the Québec structure would be slightly inclined. The cables on each side would be 70 feet apart at their supports on the main towers but only about 38 feet apart at the center of the span at their lowest point to form horizontal as well as vertical curves in the cables. "This arrangement will materially stiffen the entire structure," wrote Serrell; "light bracing rods are to be added to the suspending rods in such manner as to prevent heaving motions or vibrations which would otherwise arise in the very long ones from passing loads.

"The main cables are to be tied together overhead by cross ones of smaller dimensions," he continued. "This too will stiffen the work and tend to prevent pulsatory movement."[1]

The roadway for the structure was to be 162 feet above extreme high water at each abutment, rising by 8 feet to a height of 170 feet above high water at the center of the span. The bridge deck was to be 32 feet wide within parapet walls on each side, allowing room for a 10½-foot roadway on either side of an 11-foot way for a single railroad track at the center. Both the roadway and the parapets were to be constructed of oak timbers. The bridge floor was to be built of 3½-inch-thick planks supported by 12-by-15-inch transverse beams spaced 4 feet apart, and each braced underneath by a king post and iron tension bars. The parapets on each side were to be built of four tiers of 15-inch square timbers, tree-nailed together and each piece jointed with ship laps to form a continuous piece the full length of the bridge.

Serrell's drawings showed an elegant, well-proportioned structure. The two main towers and a fortress-like structure that surmounted the anchorage at each end were fitted with towers, turrets, crenellations, and crosses inset into the masonry, looking much like medieval castles.

This structure, Serrell calculated, could easily support a maximum possible load made up of a line of locomotives and tenders reaching from one end of the bridge to the other, with the roadways filled with as many people as could stand upon them. Even this load, he said, would stress the cables to less than one third of their capacity.

There were many doubts about the feasibility of any suspension bridge for railway traffic, and Serrell went to great lengths to assure his Québec clients that his design would overcome all of the problems of wind loads and vibration to which suspension bridges were believed to be so susceptible. The bridge could be built, said Serrell, for a little over $3 million. While he didn't develop detailed plans for a bridge at the Palais St. Louis–Pointe

Lévis site, Serrell estimated that a bridge with the longer span and higher towers that would be required at that location could not be built for less than $9 million and would more likely cost anywhere from $11 to $12 million.

In the conclusion to his report, Serrell laid out a rather impassioned view of the city's need for the bridge:

"If then this railway [Québec to Halifax] is constructed," he wrote, "and there is no doubt it will be, sooner or later, suitable and adequate means must be provided for connecting with it.

"The entire trade of the great upper country for nearly one half the year, must go over it.

"From the nature of the country and the width of the river, the railway cannot cross the St. Lawrence below Quebec.

"If then it does not cross here what is the alternative? where is Quebec? The entire trade with all its concomitant advantages gives your city the 'go by.'

"Gentlemen of Québec," Wellman concluded, "you must either *build a bridge or a New City.*"[2]

For all that, Serrell's bridge was not to be.

The situation at Québec was much different from that at Montréal. There the new bridge over the St. Lawrence was a key element in the Grand Trunk scheme for a through railway route from inland Canada to Portland. The project was attractive to investors, with its financing greatly aided by government guarantees on its bonds.

In 1852 there was no similar imperative for a bridge at Québec or for government support. Completion of even the railway link between Lévis and the Grand Trunk's line to Portland at Richmond was still four years away. It would be another twenty-four years before a railway ran along the south shore to Halifax and twenty-seven years before the North Shore Railway to Montréal would be completed.

Further contributing to a lack of enthusiasm for the project was the unfortunate collapse several years later of a much smaller suspension bridge at Montmorency Falls, just a few miles north of Québec. Spanning the Montmorency River just above the falls, the structure failed only five days after it had opened, when one of the anchorages gave way, pitching three people to their deaths in the 287-foot-high falls. In any event, no one was able to come up with a way to finance the $3 million project. Edward Serrell's report went on the shelf as the first in a rather long line of unfulfilled proposals for a bridge at Québec.

In retrospect, it may have been just as well that it did. Serrell's bridge, at least in the form that he had proposed it, would very likely have been a colossal failure. While John Roebling had correctly foreseen the need for special measures to assure the stiffness of his Niagara suspension bridge for railroad traffic, Serrell and other engineers had not.

Lacking adequate means of maintaining its stiffness, Charles Ellet's great suspension span at Wheeling was torn to pieces in a severe windstorm in 1854. A year later Serrell's lightly constructed Lewiston-Queenston bridge narrowly survived a similar storm, and John Roebling's wire rope company promptly landed an order for cable stays to help stabilize the bridge. Early in 1864 these guys were unfastened to prevent damage from a great ice jam in the river. The bridge workers failed to reattach them, and a few months later this bridge, too, was wrecked in a severe windstorm.

Whatever the stability problems encountered by these much smaller bridges, they surely would have been dwarfed by those of a structure of the much greater size and exposed location of Serrell's proposed Québec bridge. Although Serrell's design included his concept of providing an incline to the placement of the main cables to provide some measure of horizontal stability, as well as his several other ideas to improve stiffness, it lacked the kind of stiffening measures adopted by Roebling for his Niagara bridge. Instead of heavy stiffening trusses, only modest parapets made up of a few 15-inch timbers supported Ellet's single-level deck, and his design lacked entirely any form of wire rope stays.

For the next thirty-five years, interest in a bridge at Québec flared periodically, as one new proposal or another was put forward.

Although there is no record that John Roebling ever offered a formal proposal, his papers in the archives of Rensselaer Polytechnic Institute include an intriguing sketch for a bridge at Québec. Probably dating to the late 1850s, the sketch shows a cross section for a single-level bridge that would have had a span of 1,800 feet at Québec or 1,200 feet for the Ohio River. Evidently to improve its stiffness, the bridge's eight main cables were to be tied together with a system of lateral pipes. Two cables each would have supported four deep stiffening trusses, one on each side of two 13-foot roadways flanking a 13-foot way for a single railroad track at the center of the span.

By the early 1870s, there was a revival of interest in the bridge project. The British North America Act of 1867, under which Ontario, Québec, New Brunswick, and Nova Scotia were confederated into the Dominion of Canada, had included the obligation to build a railway link to the Maritime Provinces as an inducement to bring them into the confederation. Work had begun on this Intercolonial Railway in 1869, and it would reach a junction with the Grand Trunk's line along the south bank of the St. Lawrence at Rivière-du-Loup, Québec, in 1876. Work was progressing as well, although slowly, on the North Shore Railway between Québec and Montréal.

One idea for a novel alternative to a bridge received brief attention in 1872, when Québec physician W. Marsden privately published a pamphlet advancing his idea for a submerged tubular or tunnel bridge under the St. Lawrence to link the south shore railroads with the North Shore Railway then nearing completion. Written in the form of a letter addressed to the North Shore's chief engineer, Silas Seymour, the paper was short on details. The submerged structure, said Marsden, should cross the river between Lévis and St. Charles, providing a more direct connection between the two shores, with easier grades, than would a bridge route crossing the river at the Chaudière site upstream.

"This link or portion of a great commercial highway across this continent, the *shortest and most direct route from Great Britain to the Pacific Ocean*," proclaimed the doctor, "will be only the beginning of a great end—one that will affect the whole European policy, and particularly its trade with China, India, Japan, &c, &c."[3]

At about the same time, the Québec newspaper *Le Canadien* published a series of articles extolling the virtues of a suspension bridge to tie together the railway lines then developing in every direction from Québec and to assure the city's commercial future. The newspaper, too, saw a bridge across the St. Lawrence as something that would make Québec a key link in the shortest and most direct route to the Pacific and the Orient.

"To begin, it is needless to say that Québec is the place on the river where a suspension bridge must be built, in the very interest of the whole of Canadian trade," said *Le Canadien*. "Québec will necessarily become, before a great many years, the principal seaport and the great emporium of trade in the West."[4]

As before, nothing happened. Two years later *Le Canadien* reported that the Grand Trunk had decided to build a suspension bridge crossing at Cap-Rouge, which was near the Chaudière site recommended by Edward Serrell. The railroad wanted to do this, speculated the newspaper, to monopolize the traffic. "We don't blame them," said *Le Canadien*, "and we are convinced that Québec should help them to realize this project, which is necessary for the progress of our city."[5] The report proved premature, however; and once again the bridge project languished.

Within another decade, however, the Québec bridge project finally began to take on new life. Not only was the project becoming ever more desirable from a commercial point of view, but by this time major advances in the materials and methods of railroad bridge engineering had begun to offer some feasible alternatives to the idea of a suspension bridge for a span of this magnitude.

By then steel, stronger, tougher, and more wear resistant than either cast or wrought iron, had come into common use for bridge construction. The Bessemer process for making steel, developed in 1856 by the English inventor and engineer Henry Bessemer, had

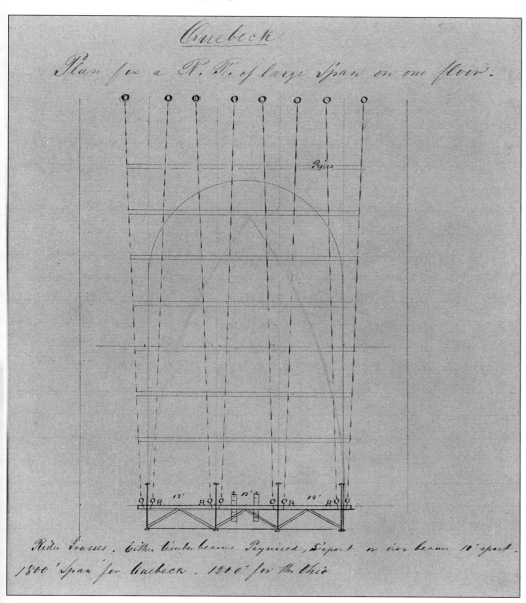

The great nineteenth-century suspension bridge engineer John Roebling considered the question of a suspension span across the St. Lawrence at Québec, as evidenced by this undated sketch from his papers. Eight suspension cables would have been linked together by pipes to help provide rigidity for the 1,800-foot span, which would have carried a single railroad track and two 12-foot roadways. If it had been built, the structure would have eclipsed Roebling's great work, the Brooklyn Bridge. Roebling Collection, Rensselaer Polytechnic Institute Archives.

made steel both plentiful and inexpensive. Engineer James Buchanan Eads had used steel for the main arches of his great St. Louis Bridge, completed during 1867–1874, and the Chicago & Alton Railroad had completed the first all-steel bridge in 1879 for a crossing of the Missouri River at Glasgow, Missouri.

With the availability of steel, simple truss bridges were pushed to greater lengths than ever before, reaching spans of almost 550 feet before the end of the century. But more important for Québec, where a span length far greater than this was needed, was the development of new bridge forms that would prove more suitable for extremely long-span railroad bridges.

The most versatile of these was the cantilever truss bridge. In its basic form, the cantilever truss was typically made up of anchor arms at each end, which were continuous with cantilever arms projecting beyond supporting piers. These two cantilever arms were then joined by a "suspended" or "floating" simple truss span at the center to form the main span of the bridge. In this arrangement the anchor arms of the bridge counterbalanced the load of the cantilever arms and the suspended span, substantially reducing the maximum bending moment at the center of the span and allowing significant material economies.

The cantilever form also offered some important advantages in erection. While the anchor arms at each end were typically erected on falsework, much like a conventional truss bridge, the cantilever arms could be built outward from the supporting pier as self-supporting cantilevers, without any falsework. Once the cantilever arms were complete, the center suspended span could be erected by continuing to build it outward from the ends of the cantilever arms as a cantilever and then converting the center structure to a simple truss once the two halves were joined. Another method that was sometimes employed was to build the center span elsewhere, float it into position on a barge, and then lift it into place.

Although the cantilever form can be found in prehistoric structures, it was first used in a modern structure by German engineer Heinrich Gerber for a road crossing of the Main River at Hassfurt, Germany. Completed in 1867, the bridge had a center span of 425 feet. The first major cantilever bridge in North America was a Cincinnati Southern Railway crossing of the Kentucky River designed by C. Shaler Smith and completed in 1877, which had three equal spans of 375 feet each. This was followed in 1883 by a Niagara River cantilever bridge crossing for the Michigan Central, designed by Charles C. Schneider, that had cantilever arms of 175 feet and a suspended span of 120 feet to create a 470-foot clear span. Within another decade this span length had been substantially exceeded by a crossing of the Mississippi River at Memphis, Tennessee, designed by engineers George Shattuck

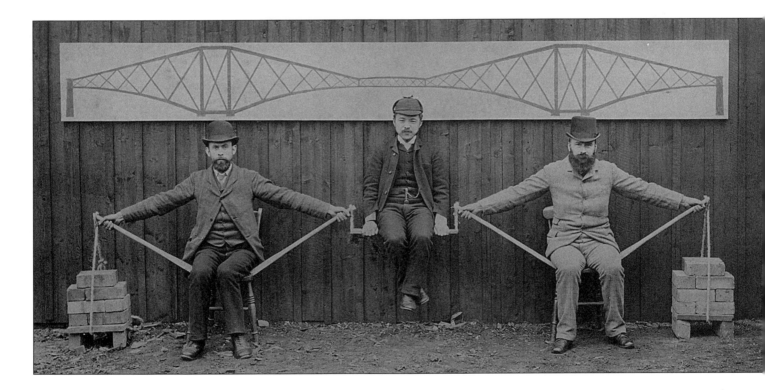

This remarkable photograph shows the Human Cantilever devised by Forth Bridge engineer Benjamin Baker to explain the cantilever principle for a Royal Institution lecture in 1887. The two men at left and right sat in chairs that represented the main piers and extended their arms, which were supported by sticks. The central suspended span was represented by the board suspended from the arms of the two men, while the pile of bricks at each end represented the counterbalancing effect of the anchor piers. When a load was put on the center span by the person sitting on it, the men's arms and the anchorage ropes came into tension, while the men's bodies from the shoulders downward and the sticks came into compression. Representing the center span load in the photograph was Kaichi Watanabe, a Japanese student of Baker and John Fowler, who was invited to participate to remind audiences of the debt owed to the Far East, where the cantilever principle originated. The History Collection of the Departmental Library, Department of Civil and Environmental Engineering, Imperial College, London.

The great Firth of Forth cantilever bridge completed by Sir John Fowler and Sir Benjamin Baker in 1890 provided an inspiring example for a similar span at Québec. Then beginning its second century of service, the Forth Bridge is seen in a view from North Queensferry in April 1991. William D. Middleton.

Morison and Alfred Noble, which had a cantilevered clear span of 791 feet over the main channel of the river.

But anything yet built or planned in North America was to be dwarfed by a new railroad cantilever bridge that began to rise over Scotland's Firth of Forth in 1883. Designed by engineers John Fowler and Benjamin Baker, this enormous structure incorporated two adjacent cantilever spans, each with a central clear span of 1,700 feet. Seven years under construction, the great bridge was opened to traffic in 1890.

With the Forth Bridge as example, there soon emerged a number of proposals for a cantilever bridge at Québec. The first of these, proposed for the Chaudière site, was developed early in 1884 at the instigation of Alexander Luders Light, the chief engineer of government railways for the province of Québec and a forceful advocate for a bridge at Québec.

The design proposal put forth by Light was developed by James Brunlees, a distinguished London consulting engineer and a former president of Britain's Institution of Civil Engineers. The 68-year-old Brunlees' engineering career spanned nearly a half-century in the location and construction of railways, dock and pier work, and bridge and viaduct construction in England, Europe, and South America; and he was then serving as the engineer for the first Channel Tunnel Company. Shortly after his involvement with the Québec project, Queen Victoria knighted Brunlees for his work on the difficult Mersey Railway, which involved the construction of a tunnel under the Mersey River between Birkenhead and Liverpool.

The Québec Bridge proposed by Brunlees bore a remarkable resemblance to the Forth Bridge. This was not surprising, for Brunlees had been a member of the advisory panel on the Forth Bridge design developed by Benjamin Baker.

The structure designed by Brunlees would have had an overall superstructure length of 2,800 feet. There would be anchor spans of 550 feet at each end, cantilever arms of 550 feet, and a center suspended span of 300 feet, providing a clear span of 1,400 feet over the river channel. Each of the tapered cantilever towers was to be 150 feet deep and about 150 feet wide at the base, rising to a height of 350 feet above the top of a pair of massive stone piers, each 30 by 160 feet. Brunlees had managed to keep the projected length of the main span to only 1,400 feet by placing the piers in relatively deep water, 27 feet on the south shore and 30 feet on the north shore. In a curious recall to Edward Serrell's suspension bridge proposal of thirty years earlier, Brunlees' drawings show a medieval castle–like structure, complete with crenellations and inset crosses, perched atop the abutments at each end of the bridge.

A much-revised proposal for the bridge, attributed to Brunlees, Light, and T. Claxton Fidler, an assistant to Light, was submitted to the Québec Board of Trade a year later. The overall dimensions of the new design were similar to those of the previous version, with a steel superstructure 108 feet wide and 2,800 feet long overall carrying two railroad tracks. The main span over the river channel was 1,442 feet long and provided a 150-foot navigational clearance above high water. The form of the structure, however, was much changed. Instead of sloping downward to the main piers, the bottom chords of the anchor and cantilever arms were to be horizontal members at the level of the bridge deck. The cantilevers rose from each end in a parabolic curve to a maximum depth of 258 feet over the main piers.

The structure's massive masonry main piers were to be approximately 130 feet deep and 150 feet wide at water level, and would have had an overall height of almost 200 feet. They were to have been carried to rock on the river bottom at a depth of about 24 feet below high water level, and would have risen 150 feet above the high water mark. To guard against the great masses of ice that came down the river during the winter season, massive masonry icebreakers rising to a height of 60 feet were planned for the upstream face of each pier. An arched masonry viaduct approach was provided at each end of the span. Masonry towers at the outer end of the approaches were designed to anchor the land end of the cantilevers to counterbalance the load of the suspended span and train loads on the center span. The estimated cost of the structure was about $5 million.

A year later, still another cantilever bridge proposal was brought forth. This was in the form of a plan and scale model developed by Joseph Tomlinson, an Ottawa bridge engineer, and exhibited at the 1886 Indo-Colonial Exposition at London under the auspices of the Canadian Department of Railways and Canals. Tomlinson's plan, developed for the Chaudière site, envisioned a double-track structure 2,640 feet long, with anchor arms of 565 feet and a center span of 1,510 feet. The cantilevers would rise to a height of 212 feet at the towers over the main piers.

The Brunlees-Light and other proposals came at a time when it actually seemed the project might become a reality. In 1882 a group headed by M. W. Baby of Québec had obtained a charter for the construction of a cantilever bridge over the river. Nothing having come of this project within the required period of two years, the charter lapsed. But by the beginning of 1884, a bill was before the Canadian Parliament for the incorporation of a company to build the bridge.

In a letter to the *Morning Chronicle* of Québec, Chief Engineer Light laid out the benefits a bridge would bring and made the case for a government guarantee of its bonds. All of the railways would benefit by the link, he maintained, while an extension of the Canadian Pacific to Québec would give that road a direct link over the Intercolonial Railway with the ice-free Canadian ports at Halifax, St. John, or St. Andrew, alleviating the fears of many in eastern Canada that the CPR was planning to send its winter business to American ports. " The City of Québec," Light wrote, "would become a large grain shipping port, the terminus of two great lines in summer, and would be on the line of business with uninterrupted railway communications to and from all parts of the Continent, instead of being, as it is to-day, a 'cul-de-sac.'"[6]

Interest in the project ran high, and early in 1884 a delegation representing Halifax, St. John, and Québec that had been organized by Mayor François Langelier of Québec traveled to Ottawa to press the case for the bridge with the Privy Council of Canada and the prime minister, Sir John A. Macdonald.

Once again, however, a Québec bridge plan went on the shelf. But finally some real momentum for a bridge was gathering, and within the next few years the long-debated project would move to a new stage.

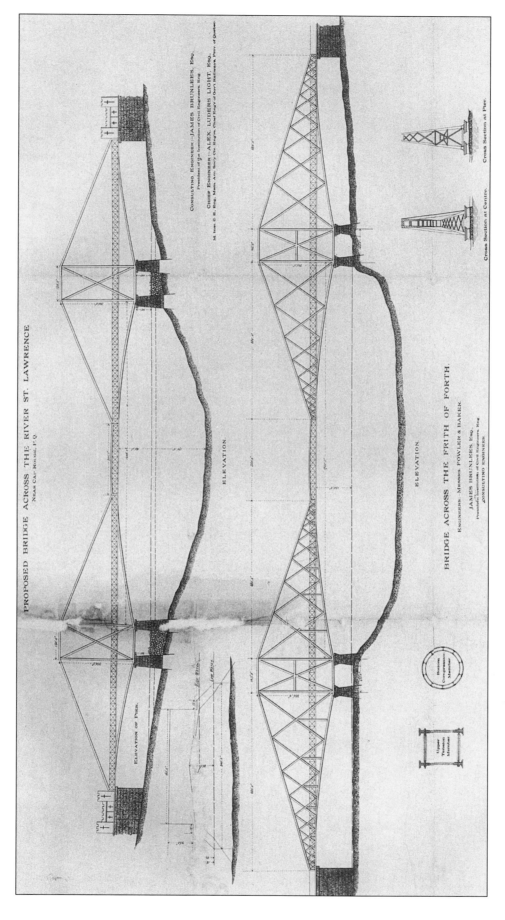

A proposal for a cantilever crossing of the St. Lawrence at the Chaudière River site put forth by James Brunlees and Alexander Luders Light in 1884 was closely based upon the design of the Forth Bridge, then under construction. This drawing compares the proposed Quebec Bridge, at the top, with the spans of the Forth Bridge at the bottom. National Archives of Québec.

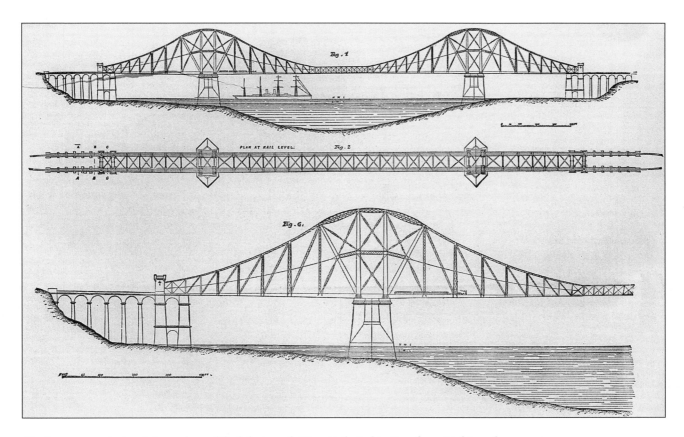

(Facing page and above) A much-modified design of 1885, attributed to Brunlees, Light, and T. Claxton Fidler, is depicted in these drawings from the May 30, 1885, issue of *Scientific American*. The new design incorporated a much different cantilever form, which had the advantage of providing a full 150-foot clearance under the structure over its full length. The great trusses for the anchor and cantilever arms rose to a maximum depth of 258 feet over the main piers. Author's Collection.

Developed by an artist for the Phoenix Bridge Company, this painting depicts the company's design that was selected by the Quebec Bridge Company for the crossing of the St. Lawrence at Québec. The view shows the bridge from the downstream, or east, side. Originally planned to have a main channel span of 1,600 feet, the design was later modified to provide an 1,800-foot main span. Historical Society of the Phoenixville Area.

CHAPTER 2

A PROJECT AT LAST

Y THE LATE 1880S, THE PRESSURE TO BRIDGE THE ST. LAWRENCE AT QUÉBEC WAS building. The lack of direct transportation links between the railroads on the opposite banks of the river placed the city and its port at a serious disadvantage, and Québec was steadily losing trade to the rival port of Montréal, 160 miles upstream.

Montréal had held a significant advantage ever since the Victoria Bridge had opened to traffic in 1859, giving the Grand Trunk a continuous rail route all the way to Portland, Maine. By 1876 the Intercolonial Railway had been completed to a connection with the Grand Trunk's line along the south bank of the St. Lawrence at Rivière-du-Loup, Québec, giving the Grand Trunk access to a second ice-free Atlantic port at Halifax. In 1886 the Canadian Pacific completed a second crossing of the St. Lawrence at Lachine, just above Montréal. Just four years later, the CPR would complete its own line across Maine to the ice-free port at St. John, New Brunswick, establishing a competitive route to the Grand Trunk.

The event that seemed finally to get a Québec bridge project moving was an enthusiastic public meeting held at the Québec Board of Trade on April 1, 1887. Reflecting the growing demand for a bridge, a group of prominent business and political leaders had petitioned Mayor François Langelier to convene the meeting, at which they hoped to consider the best means of organizing a company to build a bridge, and even to persuade citizens to buy shares in the undertaking. Noting the large and influential attendance, the Québec *Chronicle* was prompted to term the venture, " A Movement that Promises Success."

The case for the bridge was set forth in a series of what the *Chronicle* called "enthusiastic speeches," which were followed by the unanimous passage of resolutions.

One put forth:

> that the construction of a railway bridge over the river St. Lawrence at or near the city of Québec, is, in the opinion of this meeting of paramount importance for the development of the commercial and manufacturing interests of this Province in common with those of the Maritime Provinces and indeed of the whole Dominion, as it will form a complete and unbroken connection on Canadian territory between the Intercolonial and Canadian Pacific Railways, and also enable the lines building and to be built, on the North Shore, to connect with the Grand Trunk and Intercolonial and other lines on the South Shore.[1]

The bridge proponents clearly had an eye on federal financial support: "This work should be regarded as a strictly national work," said another resolution, "and this meeting considers that it should receive material assistance from the Dominion Government."[2]

There were calls for local subscription to stock in the project, demonstrating confidence in the effort that would encourage government support. Even before the meeting was over, a subscription list was opened, and several enthusiastic attendees each had signed up for as much as $1,000 in stock. The meeting ended with the election of a "Quebec Bridge Committee" of more than fifty members to pursue the project.

This enthusiastic start to the bridge project was followed by a flurry of activity.

By mid-April a smaller working committee had been organized, stock subscription committees formed, and subscription books distributed in every ward of the city and in the neighboring communities. More importantly, by mid-June the Canadian Parliament finally passed an act that incorporated the Quebec Bridge Company with a capital of $1 million and the power to issue bonds. The company was empowered to build and operate a railway bridge across the St. Lawrence River and to adapt it to the use of foot-passengers and vehicles, and it could also construct railway lines to connect the bridge with existing or future railways on each side of the river. Construction was required to begin within three years and to be completed within six years of passage of the act.[3]

Provisional directors of the newly formed company, most members of the working committee, included some of the most influential business and political leaders in the city and province. Lt. Col. William Rhodes, who was elected president of the provisional board at its first meeting on July 11, 1887, was a prominent Québec banker and businessman who had been one of the promoters of the North Shore Railway and at one time its president. James Gibb Ross, who had also been one of the promoters of the North Shore Railway, was a senator in Parliament and a wealthy and influential Québec City businessman with widespread interests in banking, commodity trading, shipbuilding, steamship lines, railroads, and the lumber industry. Richard Reid Dobell was a politically active, wealthy Québec businessman with interests in a major lumber business and in wharfage and warehousing companies, who was also active in the Québec Board of Trade and an officer of the Québec Harbour Commission. Thomas McGreevy was a wealthy Québec contractor and businessman with interests in banking, steamship lines, and railroads and had been a North Shore Railway contractor. Long active in the Conservative Party, McGreevy had been a member of Parliament since 1867. Joseph-Israel Tarte was a journalist and the long-time editor of Montréal's influential *Le Canadien* newspaper and a powerful and active member of the Conservative Party. Lt. Col. Joseph Bell Forsyth was a Québec City merchant and broker, one of the founders of the Quebec & Levis Electric Light Company, and a Québec Harbour commissioner. Still other members from the Québec business community included Gaspard Lemoine, a wholesale flour, grain, and provisions merchant who was also active in the affairs of two local railroads; Herbert M. Price, a banker and lumber merchant; Cyrille Duquet, a watchmaker and jeweler who had long been prominent in public affairs; and Eugene N. Chinic, a hardware merchant.

With a bridge company finally established, the provisional board turned its attention to the most immediate problem of financing the project. Subscription books for bridge company stock were opened on July 21, with shares at $100 each; and before the end of September, well over $600,000 had been subscribed, with the full million dollar capitalization required by the act of incorporation soon in hand. It was clear that Dominion government financial support would also be required, and much effort was now put forth in that direction. By April 1888 a deputation representing the bridge company, the Québec Board of Trade, and the city council had been organized and traveled to Ottawa to press the case for government support. The proponents "received much encouragement," according to a later account of the effort, "but were also told that nothing definite could be said until the plans of the proposed site of the bridge had been submitted to Council."[4]

The company fared a little better at the local level, where the Québec Legislature authorized a grant sufficient to help meet the costs for the preliminary surveys that would be required to establish a site for the bridge. There would soon be no shortage of proposals for the bridge company to consider, for the prospect of building what would rank as one of the world's great bridges would attract the ideas of some of the best bridge engineers in Europe and North America over the next decade.

By August 1888 the company was ready to proceed, and the board engaged Québec civil engineer Edward A. Hoare to conduct surveys and determine the feasibility of potential bridge sites. Hoare began work immediately; and early the following year, he reported his preliminary findings to Colonel Forsyth, who had succeeded Rhodes as president of the bridge company.

Considering that a bridge anywhere downstream of the Québec Citadel would draw objections for military and naval reasons, Hoare had confined his surveys to three of the most favorable sites upstream from that point. A cantilever bridge just above the citadel at a Cap-Diamant site, which would have provided the most direct connection between Québec proper and Lévis, was judged to be the most costly alternative.

"This is accounted for," wrote Hoare, "by the excessive length of heavy bridging required to span the deep water at any tide level, and the great depth of water to contend with for sinking foundations, and the consequent inestimable contingencies in connection with them, the navigable channel may be said to extend entirely across the river."[5] A second site still further upstream at Point-à-Pizeau, crossing the river between Sillery and St-Romuald, was little better for most of the same reasons.

By far the most advantageous location for a bridge, according to Hoare's report, was the same site near the mouth of the Chaudière River that Edward Serrell had selected for his suspension bridge proposal more than forty years earlier. "It is obvious, from comparison of plans alone," wrote Hoare, "that a large saving in cost can be made by adopting a crossing near the Chaudière. The deep water or channel is confined to the centre of the river, and is clearly defined, and can be bridged with a less span than at any other place, and the two main piers can be kept out of extraordinarily deep water. The remaining foundations can be built dry. The only contingency to face in this bridge will be in connection with the superstructure or cantilevers."[6] Even with its much more costly connecting lines, which included a tunnel under a long ridge on the north side of the river to reach the Canadian Pacific, the Chaudière crossing promised to be far less costly than either of the downstream alternatives.

The best alignment for a bridge near the Chaudière appeared to be just upstream from its junction with the St. Lawrence. This would necessitate an expensive crossing of the Chaudière on the south side of the St. Lawrence, noted Hoare, although further surveys might show that this expense could be avoided. "Treat the crossing of the St. Lawrence at the Chaudière as you may," commented Hoare, "its differences in cost being so marked, and the contingencies for foundations being reduced to a minimum, are sufficient reasons for enlisting a majority in its favor. And it seems as if nature had, so to speak, especially [formed] this place, and had marked it with its sign, as being the only place where the river can be bridged for a reasonable expenditure."[7]

Acting on Hoare's evaluation of the three sites, the bridge company board formally adopted the Chaudière site for the bridge on February 25, 1889. But despite its evident cost advantages, not everyone was happy with the site. A number of members of both the Québec City Council and Board of Trade would have preferred a location that provided an easy and direct link between Québec and Lévis, while the Chaudière site was a good eight miles upstream from the centers of both cities. This lack of unanimity concerning the site did the bridge company no good in its continuing efforts to obtain financial support from the Dominion government.

In April 1889 yet another deputation of local citizens and members of the city council, the board of trade, and the bridge company journeyed to Ottawa to press its case with the various government ministries. "The Government duly promised to give the matter consideration," said an account of the visit, "but the division of opinion existing on the choice of the bridge site was referred to and it was clearly intimated that until the choice of the site was generally approved of, no further action could be expected from the Government."[8] Meanwhile, still further study of potential sites and design proposals went forward.

Later in 1889 the bridge company engaged Walter Shanly, an eminent Montréal civil engineer, businessman, politician, and member of Parliament, to evaluate the three sites identified by Hoare. Shanly was well fitted for the task, with extensive work in railway location and construction in both Canada and the United States and the successful completion of the difficult Hoosac Tunnel in Massachusetts among his many accomplishments.

After evaluating the three sites, Shanly was clearly convinced that Hoare had made the right choice. "In respect of all natural difficulties the two lower sites [Citadel and Point-à-Pizeau] stand at an immense disadvantage when compared with the upper, or Chaudière, crossing," he wrote in his report. "The difference of the Chaudière project, carried out in its entirety, and that of either of the other proposed bridges, is so immense, that to speak of the two latter as rivals of the former, would be a misnomer. . . . I feel compelled to record my belief that the construction of a bridge, either on the Citadel line or Pointe-à-Pizeau line, is *practically impractical*."[9]

Edward Hoare continued his surveys and evaluation of sites. Refined cost estimates for the three sites completed in March 1890, all based upon double-track bridges and connecting lines, placed the potential cost of a Cap-Diamant crossing at almost $15.3 million, while a bridge at the Point-à-Pizeau site, Hoare estimated, would have cost almost $14 million. Even with its much more costly connecting lines, including the tunnel to a Canadian Pacific connection, Hoare placed the expected cost of a crossing at the Chaudière site at just over $9.1 million. By reducing the connecting lines to single track, and substituting a circuitous connecting route for the CP tunnel connection, the total cost of the project might possibly be reduced to no more than $5.5 million, suggested Hoare.[10]

Before the year was out, still other proposals were in hand. These were developed by Alexandre Bonnin, a French-trained engineer and professor of engineering at l'École Polytechnique de Montréal, who completed a study of a number of alternate bridge sites for the provincial government in October 1890. One of these was for a cantilever crossing of the river opposite Québec proper, which Professor Bonnin estimated could be built for $6.5 million. The remainder of Bonnin's site studies, however, involved an entirely new route across the St. Lawrence. All of these would have crossed the river by way of Île d'Orléans, a 23-mile-long island that lay in the middle of the stream just a few miles below the Québec city center, dividing the river into two major channels.

Bonnin identified two possible routes across the island. One would have crossed the south channel of the river from Pte-Martinière in Lévis to Ste-Pétronille at the west end of the island and then proceeded directly across the island to cross the north channel opposite Montmorency Falls, where it would have been linked with the Québec-Charlevoix railway. A second route would have crossed the south channel at the same location and then turned east for nearly five miles to cross the north channel between St-Pierre and l'Ange Gardien, where it would have joined the Charlevoix line. For the south channel span, which would have crossed the main shipping channel, Bonnin estimated costs for both three-hinged arch and cantilever spans that would have provided a 150-foot clearance at high water. The much shallower north channel would have been crossed with truss spans providing high water clearances of either 150 feet or 60 feet, which Bonnin suggested was adequate for this less important channel of the river. Professor Bonnin's cost estimates for the various combinations of the Île d'Orléans routing ranged from just under $4 million to almost $7 million.

Any routing across the island had serious disadvantages, reported Bonnin. The long, circuitous route would have made the use of the crossing impractical for road traffic, while the extra length of a rail connection across the river, together with the need to enter Québec by way of the St. Charles River swing bridge, which was opened about forty times every day, would have seriously delayed rail traffic.

Even though it was more costly, the cantilever crossing opposite the Québec City center was much the best solution, said Bonnin. The railway line, he recommended, would tunnel through the cliffs on the north bank to reach the very heart of the city. Both a roadway and tramway on the bridge would provide direct communication between Québec and Lévis.

Either the crossing opposite Québec or any of the routes across Île d'Orléans were preferable to a crossing anywhere further upstream in the St. Lawrence, claimed Bonnin. Inevitably, he said, the bridge would create a new center that would develop around the new junction of railway lines where the bridge line was linked with the existing rail lines, to the detriment of the city. "Québec City will only be served by a secondary line ending in a cul-de-sac," wrote Bonnin, "and part of its trade will be displaced to the newly formed town."[11]

By early 1891 the Dominion government's Ministry of Railways and Canals was taking an active interest in the problem of selecting a site for the bridge, and its chief engineer, Collingwood Schreiber, was instructed to review and report on the various proposed locations. Late in February Schreiber met with Edward Hoare, who by this time had further refined his evaluation of the Cap-Diamant, Point-à-Pizeau, and Chaudière sites and also had evaluated an Île d'Orléans alignment. Schreiber looked at them all with Hoare and came away convinced "there is not the shadow of a doubt that a bridge near Québec can be built." Schreiber agreed that Hoare had made the right choice. "In truth," he wrote to Minister of Railways and Canals A. P. Bradley, "this location strikes me as safe from any opposition."

Hoare's cost estimates clearly showed that the Chaudière site was the right choice, at least from the point of view of cost. A bridge at the Chaudière site would have an overall length of 3,420 feet, Schreiber noted in his report to the minister. The Point-à-Pizeau site would require a 6,754-foot-long structure, almost twice the length of one at the Chaudière site, while the Cap-Diamant site was almost as bad, requiring a bridge with an overall length of 5,866 feet.

After visiting with the Québec mayor, the chamber of commerce vice president, and others, Schreiber was well aware, too, that there was a strong sentiment in the community favoring location of the bridge at Cap-Diamant or another site directly opposite the city, even though a structure at one of these sites might cost at least $9 to $10 million.

For almost all of the sites, the exact conditions at the river bottom, which could materially affect the cost and feasibility of pier construction, remained largely unknown. "Before choosing a definitive location," Schreiber recommended to Bradley, "considerable exploration of the detail of the river bottom would have to be undertaken as soon as possible at the sites in question."

In proposing this additional work, Schreiber was fulsome in his praise of the work done by Hoare. "I believe that this work would best be entrusted to the care and oversight of Mr. Hoare," he told his chief, "and that his findings will be fully acceptable and trustworthy. From what I have seen of his work, I think he is a very skilled and conscientious engineer deserving of every confidence, and whom I would trust completely."[12]

Still another quarter was heard from in April 1891, this time a well-known London consulting engineer named Max am Ende. Born in Germany, Ende had studied engineering at the Polytechnic School in Karlsruhe during 1857–1860. After several years in engineering work in Germany, Ende had come to London to begin a distinguished practice in the design of bridges and other large structures, with major bridges in such widespread locations as Russia, England, and Costa Rica to his credit.

Ende decided to take his ideas for a Québec bridge right to the top. In an April 11, 1891, letter to the provincial premier, Honoré Mercier, Ende offered a proposal for a huge double-track structure that combined a 1,660-foot steel arch span with an enormous truss. Huge Gothic-like steel towers at each end of the main span were to project 250 to 300 feet into the air.

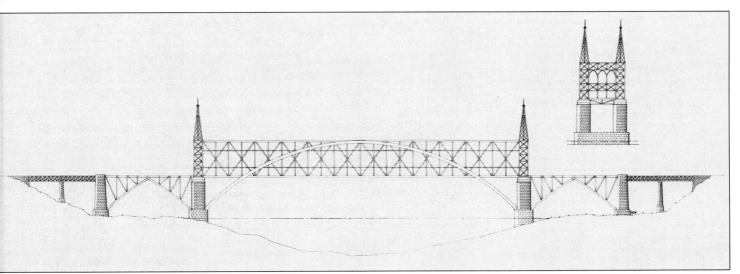

"I consider the arch superior on all accounts to a suspension or cantilever bridge," wrote Ende, "and particularly on account of economy." The structure could be built for about £600,000, he said, and built in much less time than a cantilever.[13]

"Of all the forms submitted up to now," commented the weekly Québec newspaper *La Semaine Commerciale* several years later, "it is assuredly this one that presents the most picturesque aspect. Arch bridges are marvelously handsome."[14]

Premier Mercier evidently had developed a great interest in the Québec bridge question, for during a visit to Paris early that year, he met with the noted French engineer Alexandre Gustave Eiffel to obtain his views on the project. Best known for the great steel tower at Paris that bears his name, Eiffel had also designed such disparate structures as buildings, dams, locks, and even the inner supporting structure of the Statue of Liberty in New York Harbor; but his greatest achievements were as a bridge engineer. Beginning in 1864, Eiffel had designed and built several major iron or steel railway viaducts across the deep gorges of France's Massif Central. The most notable of these was the Garabit Viaduct, completed in 1884, which carried a line across the Truyère River on a great steel arch with a span of 530 feet and a rise of 400 feet. Still in service today, this elegant structure ranks among the great achievements of nineteenth- century bridge engineering.

In response to Mercier's request, Eiffel and his staff considered the various proposals for a St. Lawrence River bridge at Québec that had been developed by Ende, Bonnin, Hoare, and Serrell. Eiffel's report to Premier Mercier, submitted early in August 1891, concentrated largely on the relative merits of the several structural forms for a bridge. In view of the pier foundation problems posed by the great depth of the river, as well as the navigational clearance requirements, Eiffel recommended the construction of a long-span bridge. This might be an arch, a suspension, or a cantilever bridge, he said, but he recommended a cantilever as the best choice for a bridge at Québec.

The need to erect an arch bridge without temporary supports, as well as the heavy masonry abutments that would be needed to resist the horizontal thrust of the arches, would make an arch structure a more costly solution than either of the other two alternatives. While a suspension bridge had the advantages of lightness and relatively simple erection, it was not the best solution either, according to Eiffel, because of the great height of the towers that would be required. The depth of water, the navigational clearance requirements, and the height above the bridge level needed to support the cables, Eiffel estimated, would necessitate towers with an overall height above their foundations of almost 400 feet.

On the other hand, Eiffel pointed out, a cantilever bridge eliminated all horizontal thrusts on the piers or anchorages, and the cantilever form greatly reduced the required

German-born British bridge engineer Max am Ende offered this proposal for a bridge at Québec to Québec Premier Honoré Mercier in 1891. The 1,660-foot span steel arches would have supported a huge truss structure framed by Gothic-like steel towers over each of the main piers. "Arch bridges are marvelously handsome," commented the Québec weekly, *La Semaine Commerciale.* Drawn by David L. Waddington from sketches in *La Semaine Commerciale,* October 9, 1896.

height of the piers. But the cantilever's principal advantage lay in the relatively simple erection that was possible by cantilevering the structure outward from the piers. "We believe that the cantilever system is the most economic," Eiffel concluded.[15]

The premier had little time to do much of anything with Eiffel's recommendations. Before the end of the year, Mercier was dismissed from office by the lieutenant governor, Auguste-Réal Angers, in the wake of a Baie des Chaleurs Railway scandal involving his administration, and little more was heard of the Eiffel report. In any event, despite all of the plans and proposals that had been put forth, the bridge project seemed largely to have come to a halt by 1891.

Having failed to begin work within the three-year period specified by the 1887 Act of Incorporation, the bridge company was obliged to return to Parliament in 1891 to obtain an amended re-enactment of the act, this time requiring that work begin within three years and be completed within six years of the July 1891 date of the new act. This provision, too, the bridge company failed to meet; and in 1897 the company would have to go back to Parliament once again for a re-enactment, which this time would extend the required completion date to June 1902.

But by 1897 the bridge project was finally in motion again, largely because of a major political shift in Canada. In June 1896, after a long period of Conservative dominance, the Liberal Party had come to power in Ottawa with Sir Wilfrid Laurier as its prime minister. Laurier was from Québec City, where a long-time protégé and supporter was Mayor Simon-Napoléon Parent. A businessman and lawyer, Parent had begun his political career early in 1890 with his election to the city council from the St-Vallier ward and, later in the same year, to a seat in the Québec Legislature. Parent was strongly supported by the Québec business community, which was anxious to promote regional development. After a group of business-supported candidates was elected to the city council early in 1894, the council elected Parent to the office of mayor, where he soon established himself as a public leader of remarkable talent and accomplishment. Over the next several years, Parent worked hard and with notable success to improve the administration of the city's affairs and to advance the development issues favored by the business community.

The implications of the 1896 Liberal victory and Laurier's succession as prime minister were not lost on the Quebec Bridge Company. Late that year Parent was invited to join the company's board as the representative of the city of Québec, which he did the following April.

At the same time, the company's efforts to secure government financial help intensified. Late in 1896 the board had applied to both the Québec provincial government and the Québec City Council for grants of $1 million or guarantees on $1.5 million in bonds to support the work. No money was forthcoming from the provincial government, but Premier Edmund J. Flynn was reported to be "very encouraging." "We can anticipate that the Company will receive substantial support from this direction," reported *La Semaine Commerciale*.[16] At City Hall a committee recommended a $500,000 subsidy. Although the council deferred taking action, it seemed clear that the Québec city government under Parent would support the project.

Early in 1897 the board reopened the company's subscription books for further stock subscriptions, and in May another deputation was organized to call on Prime Minister Laurier at Ottawa to press the case for Dominion support once again. While no specific financial help was forthcoming from the May 20 meeting, the prime minister all but promised that it would be, if we are to take at face value a report of the meeting included in the annual report presented by President Forsyth at the company's general annual meeting the following September.

"I consider the Quebec Bridge as a commercial necessity of the present moment," Laurier was quoted as telling the deputation. "Your worthy mayor reminds me that I have said one day in the city, of which he so ably manages the affairs, that when the Bridge Company would be reorganized so as to be able to come before us with a serious proposition the Government would be ready to listen to them and

The long effort to build a bridge at Québec finally began to move forward in April 1897, when Québec lawyer, businessman, and Liberal Party politician Simon-Napoléon Parent joined the board of the Quebec Bridge Company and then assumed its presidency the following September. Then mayor of Québec, a member of the Québec legislature, and a protégé of Canadian Prime Minister Sir Wilfrid Laurier, Parent had the political skills and connections to line up the government subsidies that would be needed to realize the bridge project. National Archives of Québec (Neg. P600, S5, PLN175).

to help them. Well, I repeat it, the Government is ready to give and will give a reasonable assistance to that important enterprise.

"You have been expecting this bridge for nearly fifty years, " Laurier continued. "Well, I can assure you that the supreme ambition of my life will be to realize your hopes, which have been so long deceived."[17]

The reorganization of the bridge company alluded to by the prime minister was not long in coming. Several days before the September 2 annual general meeting, Forsyth had submitted his resignation, clearing the way for Parent to be elected president at the board's annual election of officers following the annual general meeting.

Before accepting the presidency, Parent traveled to Montréal to meet with his long-time political ally, Prime Minister Laurier, to discuss the prospects for Dominion financial assistance. Sir Wilfrid told him, Parent reported to the board, that he wished to make the Quebec Bridge his personal affair, but that it would be impossible for him to promise that the bridge subsidy would be voted at the next session of Parliament.

"Mr. Laurier added," reported Parent, "that if the subsidy could not be voted next session the Company would have a letter from him, after having consulted his colleagues, which would guarantee the voting of a subsidy for the following session."[18]

All of this had been encouragement enough for the bridge company board to press ahead with the additional engineering and survey work that would be required for a call for tenders. The year before, the question of the best site for the bridge had been taken up once again, this time by Québec Premier and Minister of Public Works Flynn, with the result that the Chaudière site was again recommended as the best choice.

Flynn had assigned the task to C. E. Gauvin, a civil engineer and the superintendent of surveys in the Crown Lands Department. After reviewing all of the plans and sites, Gauvin had dismissed both the Île d'Orléans and Point-à-Pizeau sites as ones "which can have no chance of success in the selection which will eventually be made." Gauvin ruled out the Île d'Orléans site because of the very high cost of building and maintaining the two extremely long spans that would be required, the obstruction to navigation that the south channel span would create, and the need to enter the city by way of the St. Charles River drawbridge. The Point-à-Pizeau site, he said, was inferior to the Cap-Diamant site directly opposite Québec: "If an expenditure of twelve million and a half dollars is to be incurred, it would be as well for a few hundreds thousands of dollars more to build the bridge at Québec itself. The choice therefore remains between the site at Cape Diamand and that at the Chaudière.

"From a technical point of view, the Chaudière site is far superior to its Québec rival," he declared, for "the length of the bridge there would be only half that of a bridge before the city, and the foundations of the piers of the first would reach only a depth of forty feet below the highest waters, while the supports of the second would have to go down to 135 feet below the same level."[19]

Gauvin went on to dismiss the arguments against a bridge anywhere above Québec that had been made by Professor Bonnin in his 1890 report. The primary purpose of the bridge, he said, was to connect the railways on the north and south shores, not to provide a more convenient connection between Québec and Lévis. The latter purpose would not be well served in any case by the high level bridge that would be needed for navigational clearances, even if it were built at the Cap-Diamant site. He likewise rejected Bonnin's argument that a bridge near Cap-Rouge would somehow draw trade away from Québec, since "in any case at whatever spot the bridge may be built, Québec, the seaport, must be the terminus and the point of junction of the railways on both shores."[20]

In June 1897 Edward Hoare had reviewed with the board the surveys and plans he had developed several years earlier, and he was asked to verify his preliminary surveys of the shoreline. At the board's request, Hoare also called on Collingwood Schreiber, the chief engineer for railways and canals at Ottawa, to discuss the company's plans for the project and to establish the government's requirements for the review and approval of the bridge site and plans.

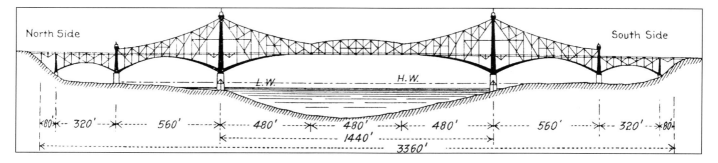

North Side   South Side

L.W. ——————— *H.W.*

|←80→|←-- 320' ---→|←------ 560' ------→|←--- 480' ---→|←-- 480' --→|←--- 480' ---→|←------ 560' ------→|←-- 320' --→|←80→|

|←-------------------------------------- 1440' --------------------------------------→|

|←--- 3360' ---→|

Boston civil engineer Edward S. Shaw offered still another plan for the Quebec Bridge in 1897. As depicted here in a drawing from the October 14, 1897, *Engineering News*, Shaw's plan called for a rather elegant cantilever structure with curved bottom chords. The bridge would have had a main channel span of 1,440 feet. Author's Collection.

The prospect of one of the greatest bridge projects of the time continued to draw some notable engineers to Québec, and there were soon still more design proposals to consider. In March 1897 Boston civil engineer Edward S. Shaw submitted a preliminary design for a cantilever bridge at the Chaudière site that had been commissioned by *La Semaine Commerciale*, a Québec business weekly which had reported extensively on the bridge project for several years and whose editor-in-chief, Ulric Barthe, also happened to be the bridge company's secretary. Shaw's well-developed plan proposed a cantilever with a central span of 1,440 feet and anchor arm spans of 560 feet that would have carried a double-track railway and two roadways for vehicles and pedestrians. Two steel main towers would have reached 360 feet above the high water level.[21] The bridge would have cost just under $3.1 million, Barthe reported to the board.[22]

Late in 1897 J. A. L. Waddell of Kansas City, Missouri, a bridge engineer of international stature, met with the board to present his plan for a bridge at the Chaudière site and to offer his services as consulting engineer. Waddell's plan called for a cantilever structure with a main span of 1,600 feet center to center between the main piers, and with cantilever towers 300 feet high. The bridge would be built with a single track, with provision for later expansion to a double-track structure and the addition of bracket supports for a roadway for electric cars or vehicles. The structure could be built, said Waddell, for a maximum cost of $2.9 million, bluff-to-bluff. In no position yet to contract with anyone, the bridge company declined the draft agreement offered by Waddell.[23]

Much more important to the future of the bridge, as it turned out, were several developments over the preceding summer. Edward Hoare had written about the project to David Reeves, an old acquaintance in the United States and president of the Phoenix Bridge Company at Phoenixville, Pennsylvania. In response, the Phoenix company had sent John Sterling Deans, its chief engineer, to see Hoare while Deans was attending the annual convention of the American Society of Civil Engineers held at Québec beginning on June 30.

Deans visited the Chaudière site with Hoare and proposed that the Phoenix company would prepare plans for the bridge free of charge to the Quebec Bridge Company, to be followed by a binding tender for construction of the bridge. Hoare accepted the offer and provided Deans with the necessary survey data concerning the site, as well as current prices for stone, timber, and other locally available construction materials.

Also present at the ASCE convention was New York–based consulting engineer Theodore Cooper, one of the leading bridge engineers of the late nineteenth century. Cooper learned about the bridge project at the meeting, and a few days later John Deans wrote to Hoare, advising that Cooper would be happy to give the Quebec Bridge Company the benefit of his experience. Although nothing immediate came of this suggestion, Cooper would be drawn into the project as its consulting engineer within the next few years.

The long-awaited Quebec Bridge now seemed to be moving rapidly toward reality. At an early July meeting of the board, the exact location of the bridge at the Chaudière site was resolved. Edward Hoare reported on his further study of the relative merits of sites east and west of the confluence of the Chaudière with the St. Lawrence. While the easternmost site would save the cost of a second bridge over the Chaudière, reported Hoare, the savings would be offset by the higher cost of foundations at the eastern site, where the river depth was much greater.[24]

Late in the year the Phoenix company completed a preliminary general plan for a cantilever bridge at the site that was based upon a clear span of 1,600 feet between pier centers and a clear height of 150 feet above extreme high water. This plan formed the basis of a January 1898 application by the bridge company to the railway committee of the privy council for approval of the plan and site for the Quebec Bridge. The government's approval came on May 16, 1898, with the requirement that detailed plans were subject to the approval of the chief engineer of the Department of Railways and Canals before work could commence, and to the approval of the governor in council.

Early in the year, Stearns Brothers, a Brooklyn, New York, firm, had begun drilling in the riverbed at the Chaudière site the test borings that would be required for design of the main piers. Because of the hardness of the rock and compacted boulder gravel encountered, the work took fully six months to complete, despite the use of diamond drills. At the beginning of July, Edward Hoare was authorized to begin preparing for both the substructure and superstructure of the bridge detailed specifications that would form the basis for a call for tenders, working with the bridge engineer of the Department of Railways and Canals. The specifications were completed and approved by chief engineer Schreiber before the end of August.

At the bridge company's annual general meeting on September 6, President Parent firmly laid the site question to rest. He cited the high costs of any of the alternatives to the Chaudière site. "The capital stock of this Company and its range of resources are too limited for such gigantic schemes to be entertained," he declared. "[The directors'] only choice was whether a bridge at Chaudière, or no bridge at all."[25]

Confident that government financial assistance would be forthcoming, the directors later the same day authorized publication of the general plans and specifications and issued a circular inviting tenders for the work. While the specifications were for a cantilever bridge, tenderers were allowed to propose a suspension bridge alternate, for which they would be required to furnish complete specifications.

Some forty-five firms in Canada, the United States, and Europe requested plans and specifications; and on March 1, 1899, the date for receiving tenders, the bridge company received a total of six tenders for the superstructure of the bridge and two tenders for the substructure work.

A Canadian firm, the Dominion Bridge Company of Montréal, submitted tenders for both a cantilever and a suspension bridge, while the remainder of the superstructure tenders were from American firms. The Phoenix Bridge Company also submitted tenders for both cantilever and suspension bridges. The Keystone Bridge Company of Pittsburgh submitted a tender for a cantilever bridge only, while the Union Bridge Company of New York submitted a tender for a suspension bridge. An additional tender for a cantilever bridge from the New Jersey Steel Company of Trenton arrived late and was rejected. Substructure proposals were received from a Canadian firm, William Davis & Sons of Cardinal, Ontario, and the Engineering Contract Company of New York.

Recognizing the unprecedented magnitude of the work it was about to begin, the bridge company board determined that it would appoint a consulting engineer to examine and report on the plans and tenders received. At the February 23, 1899, board meeting at which this decision was made, board members considered the names of six prominent engineers for the task and quickly agreed that they would ask Theodore Cooper if he would agree to act for them. The secretary wrote to Cooper the same day to offer him the post. Cooper quickly responded, accepting the assignment.

The bridge company's president, S. N. Parent; its secretary, Ulric Barthe; and Chief Engineer Edward Hoare met with Cooper at New York on March 23 to resolve the details of Cooper's appointment and to agree upon a fee. Cooper agreed to make the analysis of tenders for a maximum fee of $5,000 and also provided estimates of his charges for later inspection of the work, should that be required. All of the plans and tenders were then sent to Cooper for his evaluation.

Cooper's report on the plans and proposals was submitted late in June. He recommended dismissal of the suspension bridge proposals from the Dominion and Union bridge companies for reasons of the relatively high tenders or incompleteness of their proposals. The Phoenix Bridge Company suspension bridge proposal "has been worked out much more thoroughly than the other suspension bridge designs," Cooper reported. "The lines of the structure are very pleasing, giving a combined effect of grace and strength."[26]

Developed by Gustav Lindenthal, another of the leading American bridge engineers of the time, the Phoenix proposal was based upon an innovative design that would provide the necessary stiffness by trussing the suspension cables. This would have been achieved with stiffening trusses which incorporated the cables for their upper members, while the lower members would have been rigid chords of plates and angles. The vertical members also would have been rigid, while the diagonals would have been adjustable wire ropes. The design required the use of an as-yet-untried system of wire links for the cables, instead of continuous wire cables, together with pin connections. "That such links can be made is undoubted," said Cooper, "but their successful and economic manufacture has yet to be developed."[27] In any event, the Phoenix tender for its suspension bridge proposal was $600,000 higher than the company's cantilever bridge tender, and Cooper recommended its exclusion for that reason.

The Keystone Bridge Company and Dominion Bridge Company tenders for a cantilever bridge were based upon the same design. In fact, the two companies had agreed to a division of the work if either of them should obtain the contract. The plan proposed by the two companies was based upon anchor arms of 500 feet and cantilever arms of 500 feet, with a 600-foot suspended span at the center, giving a channel span of 1,600 feet between centers of the main piers and an overall span length of 2,600 feet. The trusses were to be spaced at 71 feet, center to center. The suspended span was to be 90 feet deep, with parallel top and bottom chords. The cantilever arms were to be 250 feet deep at the towers, with the top chords sloping each way on straight lines.

The Phoenix Bridge Company cantilever bridge proposal was similar in its overall dimensions, with a 67-foot center-to-center spacing of the main trusses. The suspended span was to have a curved top chord, rising from a depth of 84 feet at each end to 120 feet at the center. The cantilever arms were to be 295½ feet deep at the towers, with the top chords descending in each direction on curved lines. Adjusting for some lighterage costs, Cooper revised the total cost for the Phoenix tender to be $2,438,612.

After the Dominion and Keystone tenders were revised to correct a misunderstanding of the live load capacity required by the specifications, the revised Keystone tender of $2,402,500 was the lower of the two for the identical superstructure plans.

"Both the Keystone and the Phoenix plans of cantilever superstructure are in accordance with the specifications and are acceptable designs," reported Cooper. With various adjustments for higher costs for the piers and the additional customs duties for the greater weight of steel required for the Keystone plan, Cooper determined that the Phoenix proposal was the most favorable by more than $120,000.

"I hereby conclude and report," he wrote, "that the cantilever superstructure plan of the Phoenix Bridge Company is the 'best and cheapest' plan and proposal of those submitted to me for examination and report."

The unit prices offered by the two substructure bidders, said Cooper, "are fair competitive prices."

"As the plans for the piers and foundations furnished by the above bidders are only general in character and may, or rather I should say, will need modifications to adapt them to local conditions, which may affect the relative values of the two plans, I make no recommendation in favour of either party."[28]

In a lengthy supplementary report, Cooper set out his views on the probable need for substantial modification to the accepted proposal. "Any plan or proposal accepted by the Quebec Bridge Company," he wrote, "will undoubtedly need more or less modification, either in the line of bettering its general appearance or to adapt it to any new conditions which may be developed by a more extended study and examination of the river bottom and other circumstances." Cooper was particularly concerned about foundation conditions in the river and urged that additional borings be made and trial shafts sunk into the material on the river bottom. "Before proceeding with the channel piers, the character of the material of the river bottom upon which the stability of the piers will depend, should be determined with greater certainty than can be done with a few isolated borings," he wrote. "For any depths exceeding those to which it is proposed to sink these channel piers, the additional cost, risks, and uncertainties increase very rapidly. It is imperative, therefore that it be known beforehand that the material upon which the caissons are to rest and get their support is suitable for the loads to be imposed upon it by such an important structure."

Cooper anticipated that such further investigation of the foundation conditions might necessitate significant modification to the plans for the superstructure. "I would suggest therefore," he said, "that provision be made in the superstructure contract for any modifications that may be made by your engineers, either in changing the length of the spans, within reasonable limits, in modifying the carrying capacity of the structure or in increasing or decreasing the quantities of materials."[29]

Two months later, on August 22, the bridge company directors met and resolved to award contracts for the substructure work to the Davis firm and for the superstructure work to the Phoenix Bridge Company, "provided," wrote S. N. Parent to John Deans of the Phoenix company, "you accept in payment your share of the amount of $1,500,000 in subsidies or their equivalent, and the difference in bonds given in trust as collateral security."[30]

As it turned out, these conditions and the precarious finances of the Quebec Bridge Company meant that it would be several years more before work could actually begin, but at long last it appeared as if the dream of a bridge over the St. Lawrence at Québec was about to become a reality.

CHAPTER 3

THE ENGINEERS AND
THE BRIDGE BUILDERS

A youthful Theodore Cooper is shown in this photograph dating to some time around his 1858 graduation in civil engineering from Rensselaer Polytechnic Institute. Over the next forty years, the determined young engineer would rise to the front rank of American bridge engineers. Rensselaer Polytechnic Institute Archives.

W ITH THE BOARD'S DECISION OF AUGUST 22, 1899, TO AWARD SUBSTRUCTURE AND superstructure contracts, the Quebec Bridge Company had brought together the full range of engineering, fabrication, erection, and construction resources that it would need to execute one of the most demanding bridge projects ever undertaken.

As its own chief engineer, the bridge company had Edward Hoare, who had been involved with the work almost since the formation of the company in 1887, and who had conducted the surveys and studies that had led to the choice of the Chaudière site and the adoption of a cantilever truss as the preferred bridge form. Hoare was a civil engineer of long experience, most of it in railway location and construction. His engineering career had begun with marine work in an engineer's office in London, England, in 1866. Three years later Hoare emigrated to Canada, where he spent the next thirty years in railway construction work in Ontario and Québec.

For the chief engineer of such an immense undertaking, however, Hoare's bridge construction experience was limited, being confined to what he himself would describe as "the general run of bridges you have on railway work."[1] Before joining the Québec Bridge project, the longest bridges Hoare had ever built involved single-track spans of 200 to 300 feet on the Great Northern Railway. But if the bridge company's own chief engineer lacked significant experience in long-span bridge design and construction, its choice of a consulting engineer more than made up for it.

Then 60 years old, Theodore Cooper stood in the very top rank of American bridge engineers, having been, as his memoir in the *Transactions of the American Society of Civil Engineers* some years later put it, "for more than a quarter of a century, a foremost authority on bridge design and construction."[2] Born at Cooper's Plain, in Steuben County, New York, in January 1839, Cooper was one of nine children of physician John Cooper, Jr. His parents were among the earliest settlers of Steuben County, having moved there from Pennsylvania shortly after their marriage. Cooper graduated in civil engineering from Rensselaer Polytechnic Institute at Troy, New York, in 1858 and then worked as an assistant engineer in survey work on the Troy & Greenfield Railroad and the Hoosac Tunnel before entering the U.S. Navy as a third assistant engineer in the fall of 1861. He was ordered to duty on the gunboat *U.S.S. Chocura*, which joined the fleet at Hampton Roads early in 1862 and was present at the second appearance of the Confederate ironclad *Merrimac*. Cooper remained with the ship during actions in Virginia and in the blockade of the Texas coast until he was ordered to the U.S.

Naval Academy in 1865 both to assume duty as an instructor and to take charge of all new construction work at the academy. His naval career included two years in the South Pacific aboard the *U.S.S. Nyack* before he resigned in 1872 to take up engineering work.

Cooper's involvement in bridge design and construction began that year, when he was appointed as an inspector under Captain James Buchanan Eads in the construction of the St. Louis Bridge, engaged first at the plants of steel suppliers and fabricators and later as inspector of the erection of the bridge. This landmark structure pioneered the use of steel in major bridges and the use of the cantilevering method to erect the bridge's three long arch spans.

Cooper's engineering skill and judgment became evident as he wrestled with the difficult erection problems of this unprecedented structure. He displayed uncommon toughness of character and devotion to his duty, as well, as evidenced by an incident reported by C. M. Woodward in his notable history of that great bridge. In Cooper's log of the work at the bridge for December 2, 1873, Woodward found this cryptic entry:

> The inspector (present writer) tripped on an unbalanced plank, on outside of joint 30, rib C, Span III, at 11 a.m., and fell to the river below, a distance measured this afternoon and found to be 90 feet. Escaped uninjured, excepting a stiffness resulting from the shock.[3]

This was Theodore Cooper in old age. His long and distinguished career came to an end with the Quebec Bridge. Rensselaer Polytechnic Institute Archives.

In a fuller account of the incident he later gave Woodward, Cooper recalled plunging nearly to the bottom of the river, finally reaching the surface still clutching in his hand the lead pencil he had been using when he fell. "A boat from the East Abutment soon picked him up," wrote Woodward. "In an incredibly short time he changed his clothes and walked into the office of the company as though nothing had happened."[4]

Following his work on the St. Louis Bridge, Cooper became superintendent of the shops of the Delaware Bridge Company at Phillipsburg, New Jersey, and then was superintendent and assistant general manager of the Keystone Bridge Company at Pittsburgh. He also designed and built several major industrial plants before establishing his own consulting engineering office at New York in 1879. Cooper's consulting practice included design work for rapid transit projects at New York and Boston and the design of several important bridges in the eastern United States. In 1894 he was appointed by President Cleveland to a commission to recommend a safe and practicable span for a railroad bridge across the Hudson River at New York.

Theodore Cooper was perhaps best known as one of the leaders in the late-nineteenth-century development of improved standards and practices for the design and construction of bridges. In 1878 he developed an iron bridge specification for the Erie Railroad that was the most comprehensive yet used and was adopted by many other railroads. This led to publication in 1884 of his widely used *General Specifications for Iron Railroad Bridges and Viaducts,* which went through seven editions by 1906. Cooper also developed the almost universally used system, which bears his name and which is still in use today, of locomotive and train loading for bridge design. In 1879 he published an influential paper, *The Use of Steel for Bridges,* and his *American Railroad Bridges,* published by the American Society of Civil Engineers in 1889, was a widely recognized history of the development of bridge engineering to that time. Both papers were distinguished by the award of the society's Norman Medal.

Despite his prominence in bridge engineering, however, Cooper had never designed and built a truly major structure himself. He must have seen his appointment by the Quebec Bridge Company as an opportunity to cap his distinguished career as the consulting engineer for one of the greatest bridge projects of the time, the great cantilever bridge across the St. Lawrence River at Québec. "My chief interest in this work is to obtain a work," he wrote several years later, "which I feel will crown my professional career of over forty years."[5]

In its choice of the Phoenix Bridge Company to build the great bridge across the St. Lawrence, the Quebec Bridge Company had allied itself with one of the leading North American bridge design, fabrication, and erection firms of the late nineteenth century. The Phoenix bridge building company was a wholly owned subsidiary of the Phoenix Iron Company of Phoenixville, Pennsylvania, and a principal consumer of the parent company's iron and steel production. The iron company could trace its origins to the establishment of a nail works in what was then known as French Creek in 1790. Lewis Wernwag, a noted early bridge builder, invested in the firm and became its superintendent and general manager in 1813, expanded and improved the plant, and renamed it the Phoenix Iron Works. New investors came into the business several decades later, and by the 1840s the Reeves brothers had acquired a controlling interest and begun an era of Reeves family control that was to last for more than a hundred years.

Bridge building at Phoenixville began around 1868 with the formation of Kellogg, Clarke & Company, a partnership of Charles Kellogg and Thomas C. Clarke, both of whom had extensive experience in iron bridge design and construction. This firm lasted for only two years, from 1868 to 1870, when it was disbanded.

Clarke then joined with the Reeves family to establish Clarke, Reeves and Company, which soon developed into a major builder of bridges and other metal structures. One of the company's major assets was the patented Phoenix Column, invented by Samuel Reeves in 1862. This was a sectional circular column made up of flanged wrought-iron segments that could be riveted together in a wide range of sizes. It was an efficient and easily erected

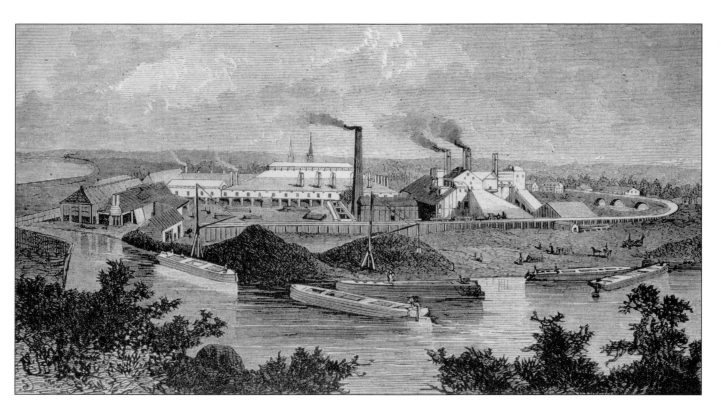

This was the Phoenix Iron Company works in 1873, as illustrated by an artist for the May 31, 1873, issue of *Scientific American*. In the foreground anthracite coal was being delivered to the iron works by the canal boats in the Schuylkill Canal. Author's Collection.

A notable early bridge project of Clarke, Reeves & Company, the predecessor firm to
the Phoenix Bridge Company, was the Erie Railroad's Kinzua Viaduct in northwestern
Pennsylvania. At the time of its completion in 1881 the 301-foot-high, 2,051-foot-long
structure ranked as the world's highest railway bridge. Library of Congress
(Neg. HAER-PA-7-27).

compression member that was widely employed in building construction, elevated railway
structures, and bridges. The Phoenix Column was used in the erection of what was the
most notable bridge constructed by Clarke, Reeves. This was the Erie Railroad's Kinzua
Viaduct in northwestern Pennsylvania, completed in 1882. With a length of 2,053 feet and
a height of 301 feet above Kinzua Creek, the structure ranked for a time as the highest
railway bridge in the world.

Thomas Clarke left the firm in 1884 to join with others in the formation of the Union
Bridge Company at New York. The Phoenixville firm was reorganized and emerged as the
Phoenix Bridge Company, now a wholly owned subsidiary of Phoenix Iron. While Clarke,
Reeves had concentrated largely on the fabrication and erection of standardized bridges,
the new firm was more interested in undertaking larger and more complex projects.

By the 1890s the firm had developed into one of the leading American bridge firms, with
a reputation for well-designed and well-built bridges, rapid erection, and low prices. Among

the notable bridges built by Phoenix during this period was a major crossing of the Ohio River for the Chesapeake & Ohio between Cincinnati and Covington, Kentucky. Built during 1888–1889, this structure included two simple truss spans of 476 feet and a simple truss central span with a record length of 545 feet. In 1890 Phoenix completed a crossing of the Colorado River near Needles, California, for the Atlantic & Pacific Railroad, a Santa Fe predecessor, which set a new record for cantilever bridges, with a main span of 660 feet. During 1891–1892 the company completed the Southern Pacific's Pecos Viaduct in Texas, a dramatic structure that was 2,180 feet long and soared 326 feet above the bed of the Pecos River. Made up largely of plate girder and truss spans, the structure incorporated a cantilevered main span at the center of the crossing. In 1895 Phoenix completed a new crossing of the Ohio River for the Big Four Railroad between Louisville and Jeffersonville, Indiana, which again established a record length for a simple truss span. The three main spans of the bridge were each 547 feet long, with trusses that were 80 feet deep. Still another major bridge was completed in 1896, when the company replaced the Chicago, Rock Island & Pacific's crossing of the Mississippi River between Rock Island, Illinois, and Davenport, Iowa, a 2,920-foot-long structure made up of seven fixed truss spans and a 365-foot swing span.[6]

Phoenix Bridge competed successfully against European companies in the international market. At one time in the 1890s, the firm had contracts in Russia, China, Japan, and Mexico, as well as its usual customers in the United States and Canada. Toward the end

Among the important bridge projects completed by the Phoenix Bridge Company during the 1890s was the Pecos River Viaduct, completed during 1891–1892 for the Southern Pacific. This spectacular structure was 2,180 feet long and stood 326 feet high above the riverbed. The cantilever truss at the center incorporated a clear span of 217 feet, 6 inches. This photograph dates to some time after 1910, when the viaduct was extensively rebuilt and strengthened. Southern Pacific Company.

This is a view of the Phoenix Iron Company's Shop 6, dating to about 1906. The long floor beam girders on the flatcars at center could well have been destined for a major structure such as the Quebec Bridge. Hagley Museum and Library (Neg. 71.MSS.916.3698).

The shops of the Phoenix Bridge Company were outfitted with the heavy shop equipment required for bridge fabrication. This view shows a spacer punch manufactured by the Thomas Spacing Machine Company of Pittsburgh. Hagley Museum and Library (Neg. 71.MSS.916.2750).

David Reeves, II, the third
generation of the Reeves
family to head the Phoenixville firm, had been president of both the Phoenix
Iron and Bridge companies
since 1878. He continued in
both positions until his
death in 1923. Historical
Society of the Phoenixville
Area.

William H. Reeves, a
younger brother of David
Reeves, II, served as general
superintendent of the
Phoenix Iron Company.
Historical Society of the
Phoenixville Area.

of the decade, the company ranked as one of the three largest bridge builders in the United States in terms of capacity, with a reported annual production capacity of 50,000 long tons.[7]

The key members of the management and engineering staff that Phoenix brought to the Quebec Bridge project were all exceptionally well-qualified men who were extensively experienced in bridge design, fabrication, and erection.

Both the iron and bridge companies were headed by a third generation of the Reeves family, David Reeves II, who had succeeded to the presidency at the age of 26 on the death of his father in 1878. The younger Reeves was a civil engineering graduate of Rensselaer Polytechnic Institute. During his presidency he had led the company's transition from the iron age into the steel era, and he had headed the company almost from the beginning of its major involvement in bridge building. His younger brother, William H. Reeves, also a Rensselaer graduate, served as general superintendent of both companies.

John Sterling Deans, the bridge company's chief engineer, was an experienced man who had spent his entire working life with Phoenix Bridge or the predecessor Clarke, Reeves firm. A native of Chester, Pennsylvania, Deans was born in 1858. He had received his professional education at the Philadelphia Polytechnic College, which he left before graduation at the age of 20 to take up a position with Clarke, Reeves at Phoenixville in 1879.

Deans was involved in the design of most of the major structures built by Phoenix Bridge over the next decade. He assisted in the design of the company's record-breaking Ohio River crossing at Cincinnati, was in charge of all work for the bridge in the Phoenix drafting room, and then served as resident engineer during erection of the structure during 1888–1889. Following completion of this work, Deans became the company's engineer of erection. He was advanced again in 1891 to principal assistant engineer and became chief engineer in 1893, following the resignation of Adolphus Bonzano, who had served the Phoenix Bridge Company and its predecessors in that capacity for twenty-five years.

The Phoenix Bridge Company's chief designing engineer was Peter L. Szlapka, an experienced civil engineer who had been with the firm for almost twenty years. Born in Poland in 1852, Szlapka had graduated from the Royal Polytechnic Institute at Hanover, Germany, before emigrating to the United States. He joined the Phoenixville firm as a draftsman in July 1880 and advanced steadily to the position of design engineer. Szlapka had been the designer for many of the most notable bridges built by the firm, including the Colorado River cantilever bridge near Needles, California; the Pecos Viaduct in Texas; and major crossings of the Susquehanna, Tennessee, and Missouri Rivers.

Though the Phoenix Bridge Company seemed exceptionally well suited to take on the enormous challenge represented by the Quebec Bridge, the firm's recent bridge-building history was not without some major mishaps. During construction of the record-breaking C&O bridge over the Ohio River at Cincinnati in 1888, for example, the company experienced a major failure. The main trusses for the span were being erected on temporary timber falsework in the river. As the truss erection was nearing completion on August 26, 1888, a large accumulation of driftwood carried down the river by floodwaters collapsed the falsework, dropping the nearly completed structure into the river. Fortunately, there were no injuries or loss of life.[8]

Much more serious in their consequences were two collapses during construction of the Big Four Railroad's Ohio River bridge at Louisville. Both occurred on December 15, 1893, during erection of the bridge's three record 553-foot main trusses. That morning a violent windstorm hit the structure, blowing an erection traveler off its tracks and wrecking the falsework under a partially completed truss, dropping it into the river with the loss of twenty-one lives. That night the winds toppled a second, nearly completed span off its piers and into the river. John Deans, the company's newly appointed chief engineer, blamed the collapse on a sudden cyclone. Others disputed that version of events and cited inadequate bolting and riveting of the partially completed structure. The following month a coroner's jury censured the bridge company for "negligence in failing to observe proper precautions in the construction of said work."[9]

Still another serious erection failure for Phoenix Bridge came in November 1898 near Cedar Grove, Virginia, when a Norfolk & Western bridge still under construction collapsed under the load of a train, leaving two men dead and a third badly injured. Falsework under the partially completed structure had been removed earlier in the day, and subsequent investigation indicated that a key joint in the bridge had not been adequately riveted or bolted.[10]

Whether accidents like these constituted just a run of bad luck or whether they reflected some basic flaw in the way the company managed its field erection is not clear. The company's standard approach to erection was to assemble every bridge at the plant to make sure that everything fit together properly before it was disassembled and shipped to the site for final erection. Erection plans and procedures were carefully worked out in advance for every bridge, and the field erection was carried out by a relatively small, experienced Phoenix Bridge crew that was typically augmented by a less skilled local labor force hired at the site of the work. This approach had generally served the company well over a period of nearly twenty years, and it would be the way it would approach the erection of the Quebec Bridge.

On November 17, 1905, the Phoenix erecting crew prepared to lift four bundles of tension eyebars into the anchor arm with the big traveler. The end of work for the 1905 season was only a week away, by which time six of ten panels for the south anchor arm would be completed. Hagley Museum and Library (Neg. 71.MSS.916.3882).

CHAPTER 4

THE GREAT BRIDGE
UNDERWAY

Anyone who had supposed that the Quebec Bridge Company's August 1899 decision to award contracts for substructure and superstructure work meant that construction would soon begin was in for disappointment. While the company may have otherwise been ready to get started, there was still the troubling problem of the financing that it would need for the great work that lay ahead. As of June 1899, the company had stock subscriptions of only $50,353, of which some $26,685 had already been spent for surveys and other expenses. In August Parliament finally voted a Dominion government subsidy of $1 million for the bridge, but this was still far short of what was needed.

This precarious financial situation lay behind the company's proposal to Phoenix Bridge that it accept a proportionate share of $1.5 million in subsidies or their equivalent, with the balance of the more than $2.4 million contract amount in bridge company bonds. This Phoenix was unwilling to do. Instead, the company offered to assist in placing the bridge company's securities with American financial institutions. This was done, but without success. "As I remember," John Deans later recalled, "the experts of the bankers reported at that time that they did not find a sufficient possible traffic in the near future to pay interest on the bonds. [They] all expressed their belief in the ultimate value of the property but the returns were too remote for bankers in this country."[1]

While the financial issues remained unresolved, other work went ahead. The most immediate was the further study of foundation conditions in the river that Theodore Cooper had recommended in his June 1899 report to the bridge company in which he evaluated the tenders. Under E. A. Hoare's supervision, further examination of the river bottom was conducted, and a half-dozen diamond-drill borings were taken to depths of as much as 86 feet in the river bottom. The results were forwarded to Cooper early in January 1900. After studying the new material, Cooper recommended significant changes in the placement of the main piers that would also require the first of several major changes in the design of the superstructure.

In a new report of May 1, 1900, to bridge company President S. N. Parent, Cooper recommended that the channel span of the bridge be increased from 1,600 feet to 1,800 feet. The reason for doing this, Cooper explained, was that it would both shorten the time required for construction of the piers and reduce the uncertainties and contingencies that would accompany their construction in the deep waters of the St. Lawrence. As located for a 1,600-foot channel span, said Cooper, the two main piers would require foundations from 90 to 95 feet below ordinary high water, and they would stand in water from 30 to 40 feet deep, subject to the full effects of ice in the river. "As the river bottom rises rapidly towards the shore on each side of the river," he said, "it is readily seen that the foundation conditions and also the ice effects are greatly improved by lengthening the channel span." The change to an 1,800-foot span, Cooper estimated, would save about $400,000 in the cost of the piers and other masonry work, while the increased cost of the superstructure for the longer span would be about $600,000.

"But modifications can be made in the plans," he asserted, "which, in my opinion, are desirable and justifiable, and which in no manner reduce the carrying capacity of the structure or render it incapable of fully performing all its duties satisfactorily, which would reduce the above increase in cost to about $450,000.

"From either point of view," Cooper concluded, "whether the increased cost of making the change in the span be $50,000 or $200,000, I consider the change justifiable for the following reasons:

"First. The construction of the larger and deeper piers of the 1,600-foot span will require at least one more year than those for the 1,800-foot span.

"Second. The contingencies of the construction of the deeper piers in the deeper water, where they might possibly be subject, in their incomplete condition, to the heavy ice floes of the main channel, would be far greater than for the piers further inshore.

"Third. The effect upon any future financing by reducing the time of construction and minimizing the real and imaginary contingencies."[2]

Cooper submitted his report to President Parent on May 1, 1900. Only four days later, the bridge company board unanimously adopted his recommendation for a change in the channel span length to 1,800 feet. This would exceed the main span length of the Firth of Forth Bridge by 90 feet, and it would make the Quebec Bridge the longest cantilever bridge in the world.

While the decision to adopt the longer span was clearly based on sound engineering reasons, the singular status it would give the Quebec Bridge was not lost on the bridge company board. "On account of the change of plans caused by the lengthening of the channel span from 1,600 to 1,800 feet, Québec will have the honor to possess the largest bridge span in the world, which will be the most marvelous feat of engineering which any country can show," reported President Parent at the bridge company's annual meeting on September 4, 1900. "Such a feature as this cannot but reflect great credit on Canada, more especially so on the province and city of Québec. In fact, it has already powerfully advertised our city abroad, and caused most favorable comments in the leading press of America and elsewhere."[3]

At the same May 5 meeting, the board formally appointed Cooper, whose work until then had been limited to advising on the tenders, as its consulting engineer. Under this new arrangement, Cooper took on the responsibility for shop inspection of steel fabrication and erection. Cooper had estimated that the cost of an assistant for shop inspection would be $15,000 to $20,000, while the charge for his own work would be $7,500 a year.

Even before Cooper had submitted his report, the Quebec Bridge Company had proceeded to negotiate contract terms with its prospective substructure and superstructure contractors. During April 1900 the details of a contract with substructure contractor William Davis and Sons were worked out, although the contract itself was not executed until June 19. On April 12 bridge company president S. N. Parent and directors Rodolphe Audette and Herbert Price met with Phoenix chief engineer John Deans at Theodore Cooper's office in New York to conclude an agreement for the award of a contract for the superstructure and steel anchorages to the Phoenix Bridge Company. The award was to be based upon the cash prices of Phoenix's tender of March 1899, subject to modifications that had been proposed by Deans in a letter of August 23, 1899, to S. N. Parent. Recognizing that the Quebec Bridge Company was financially unable to proceed immediately with the work, Deans had offered to adhere to the terms of the Phoenix tender, allowing the bridge company to order the work at any time in the near future, "say one or two years," provided that either party could request price revisions based upon the ruling price of metal at the time the work went ahead.[4] In the April 12 agreement, this time extension was set at three years from the date of the agreement, with the price of metal to be mutually agreed upon at the time each part of the structure was ordered. Phoenix also agreed to provide details of the metal anchorages by June 15, 1900, in order to permit a start to the substructure work.

Events began to move rapidly. Following the May 5 decision of the board to lengthen the main span to 1,800 feet, the two contractors were asked to modify their plans accordingly. The Phoenix Bridge Company promptly accepted the change in span length, and the contract with substructure contractor M. P. Davis was modified to reflect the changes. The following month, on June 15, Hoare, Cooper, and Deans met in New York to agree upon the price to be paid for the anchorage steel, and substructure contractor Davis began preparatory work before the summer was out. Although the bridge company still lacked the financial capacity to proceed with the superstructure, there was enough financing available from the Dominion, provincial, and Québec City subsidies to initiate substructure construction.

In preparation for the work, the contractor opened a granite quarry on a mountainside near Rivière-à-Pierre, some 45 miles west of Québec on the Batiscan River, and constructed a mile-long spur to link the quarry to the main line of the Quebec & Lake St. John Railway. Eight large derricks, each of 15-ton capacity, were installed to handle the stone at the quarry, in the cutting yard, and at the storage and loading yard. A counterbalanced 3-foot, 6-inch gauge railway installed on a 25 percent grade was used to move stone from the cutting yard down to the storage yard. Steam drills and black powder were used to quarry the stone, and as many as 100 stonecutters were employed at the site.

At Sillery, on the north shore of the river about 4,000 feet east of the bridge site, the contractor built a complete steam sawmill and planing mill to supply timber to the nearby launching ways, where the timber caissons for the bridge's two main piers would be constructed. Construction plants erected on both shores of the river included derricks for erection of the abutments, anchor piers, and main piers; compressed air plants; stone crushing plants and concrete mixing plants; storage sheds; and offices. Trestles laid with 3-foot, 6-inch gauge tracks for material transportation were constructed to link the plant facilities with a working platform around each of the main piers.

Cut stone from the Rivière-à-Pierre quarry was shipped to Québec in trainloads of twelve to fifteen cars, transferred to scows at Louise Basin, and then moved by tugs to the bridge site. Stone for the north main pier was unloaded at high tide to the working platform at the pier site, but the boulder-strewn north shore prevented the scows from unloading stone for the anchor pier and abutment at the bridge site. This material was unloaded at a temporary pier near the caisson launching ways and then transported to the bridge site by means of a double-track 3-foot, 6-inch railway line laid along the shore. Stone for the south shore work was unloaded at the main pier working platform and either used there or transported to the shore by rail cars.

At long last work on the bridge began on October 2, 1900, with a grand ceremony on a glorious autumn day. Hundreds of carriages and four steamships transported the crowd from downtown Québec to the bridge site. Presiding over the affair was S. N. Parent, president of the bridge company and mayor of Québec, who had just taken office as premier of Québec as well. Distinguished guests included Prime Minister Laurier, Dominion and provincial ministers, judges, legislators, and the bridge company directors. Speeches were made, and then Sir Wilfrid laid a granite corner stone for the north anchor pier with a silver trowel.[5]

Another major element of work was initiated late in the year, when the Quebec Bridge Company contracted with Phoenix to erect the 214-foot deck truss approach spans that were needed at either end of the bridge. The bridge company's precarious financial situation, however, still made it impossible to initiate work on the main span itself, and it would be more than two years before this part of the work could proceed.

Meanwhile, substructure contractor Davis was making rapid progress on the foundations for the bridge. Construction of the contractor's plant had been completed well before the end of 1900. By the end of the construction season, the base of the north anchor pier and the steel anchorage had been built up above the high water line. Rock excavation for the north and south abutments continued during the winter, and the contractor began construction of caisson No. 1 for the north main pier at the Sillery launching way.

Both main piers were to be built using the pneumatic caisson method, in which excavation for the piers would be carried out below water level from within what amounted to an upside-down box from which water was excluded by air pressure. At the same time, the pier was constructed on top of the caisson, the weight of the pier helping to drive the caisson into the river bottom.

The caissons for the Québec Bridge were in keeping with the scale of the structure. Each of them was 49 feet wide, 150 feet long, and 25 feet high and weighed 1,600 tons. The entire caisson was fabricated from Georgia yellow pine. All of the main timbers were 12 inches by 12 inches, while the struts between chambers of the caisson were 16 inches by 16 inches. The outside sheathing of the caisson was made up of two layers of crossed diagonal planking spiked to the sidewalls, while a single layer of planking was used to sheath the ceiling and walls of the working chamber and both sides of the dividing bulkheads. The working chamber was 6½ feet high and was divided into six compartments by transverse bulkheads that were 2½ feet thick. The sidewalls were beveled at the bottom to form a cutting edge 9 inches wide that was shod with a ¾-inch by 6-inch by 6-inch angle.

The six working chambers were reached through shafts built up of 8-foot cylindrical sections of wrought iron, 36 inches in diameter. These were bolted together with gaskets and outside flanges. Two were plain shafts used for materials only, while the other four were ladder shafts used for both materials and workmen. The shafts used by workmen were converted into air locks by inserting diaphragms containing doors between sections of the shaft. Special air locks at the tops of the material shafts allowed the passage of iron buckets 34 inches in diameter and 48 inches deep used for the removal of excavated material. The same locks and shafts were used to place concrete when the caisson was in place and the air chamber was to be sealed. Six blowout pipes 4 inches in diameter also were provided for the removal of mud, sand, and small stones by means of air pressure.

One of the first major events in the construction of the Quebec Bridge was the launching of Caisson No. 1 at Sillery on June 20, 1901. Built of Georgia yellow pine, the 1,600-ton timber structure was 49 feet wide, 150 feet long, and 25 feet high. It is shown here just before the sideways launching, aided by a liberal application of beef tallow to the launching ways. Drawing by Werner K. Sensbach from an illustration in the July 20, 1901, *Le Soleil* of Québec.

Both caissons were constructed on inclined timber launching ways at the Sillery site and launched sideways into the river with the aid of a liberal application of beef tallow, "thoroughly and freshly applied."[6] The caissons were then floated into place at the pier site, where a working platform of some 12,000 square feet had already been constructed on piling driven into the river bottom. Once the caissons were grounded in place on the river bottom, they were filled with concrete, except for the working chamber, which prevented them from floating free at high tide.

Once the caissons were filled with concrete, masons began placing the masonry piers on top of them, while gangs of workmen began work in the chambers excavating the riverbed to sink the caissons to their final position. The excavated material was a mixture of sand, gravel, and boulders that was removed by means of the bucket hoists, or by air pressure through the blowout pipes. Boulders too large to fit into the iron buckets were drilled and broken by dynamite. Some 3,000 pounds of dynamite were used for this purpose in sinking the south pier alone.

Caisson No. 1 was launched at 9:10 a.m. on June 20, 1901, and floated into position at the north pier site an hour and ten minutes later. Once the caisson was properly located and sufficiently loaded with concrete, the air pumps were started, and excavation was begun in the working chamber on an around-the-clock schedule. Two months later Chief Engineer Hoare reported to the board that the open crib above the caisson working chamber had been completely filled with concrete, and granite masonry forming the base of the pier had been laid to a height of 15 feet, while the excavation under the river had been completed to an average depth of 11 feet. The entire pier was complete before the end of the 1901 construction season.

The south pier was completed in similar fashion the following year. Caisson No. 2 was launched and moved into position on May 26, 1902. Sinking began on June 7, and the work was completed on October 17. The caisson had been sunk a total of 59 feet in just 131 days, an average rate of progress of 5.4 inches per day. On some days the crews had sunk the caisson by as much as 10 inches.

The number of men employed in the air chamber of the south caisson ranged from 250 to 300. Initially they were divided into three shifts of eight hours each. This continued until a depth of 50 feet was reached, at which time the work schedule was changed to four gangs, each working six hours. This was modified again when a depth of 65 feet was reached, when eight gangs were employed, each working only three hours, until the final depth of 89 feet was reached. Once the caisson had reached its final position, the working chamber was filled with concrete. Given the size of the chamber, this proved a major undertaking. When the chamber for the north pier was filled, for example, it took 144 hours of work over a seven-day period to place 1,500 cubic yards of concrete in the chamber. Record progress was made on the night of November 3, 1901, when 250 cubic yards of concrete were placed during a twelve-hour period.

The south pier had been carried to a greater depth than originally planned after some unsuitable material was encountered, making it the deeper of the two main piers. Because of this, the air pressures used in the working chamber reached a maximum of 36 pounds per square inch, but without developing any serious cases of caisson disease, or the "bends," among the caisson workers. For a time, there were fears about the safety of the caissons. Until some corrective measures were adopted, there were problems of excessive water leakage into the caissons. And on one occasion during an extreme high tide, some spikes were pulled out under water pressure, and a section of the 3-inch planks lining the air chamber roof forced downward, creating fears that the roof was giving way. On a visit to the site in August 1901, Theodore Cooper himself went down into the north caisson to make a personal examination and pronounced the caisson perfectly safe.

The tops of the completed piers stood about 26½ feet above the river's highest water level. The north pier rose 63 feet above its foundation, while the much deeper south pier stood 85 feet above its foundation. The piers were tapered at a batter of one inch per foot to dimensions of 30 feet by 133 feet at the top. Except for the top 19 feet of each pier, which was made of solid granite throughout, the piers were built of granite face work with a concrete backing, with facing stones that ranged from a 24-inch to a 48-inch rise and averaged about 80 cubic feet. Together, the two main piers contained about 35,000 cubic yards of masonry, resting on the concrete-filled caissons.

Work had proceeded simultaneously on the anchor piers and abutments on each shore. The north shore anchor pier and abutment were substantially complete at the end of the 1901 construction season, while those on the south shore followed a year later. The U-shaped abutments were about 80 feet wide, with 40-foot wing walls on each side, and were founded on solid rock. The rectangular anchor piers were 102 feet wide and 22 feet deep at the coping and stood 65 feet high from their foundation to the top of the coping. Designed to resist uplift forces from the cantilevered superstructure, the two piers together contained about 500 tons of steel anchorage material embedded in about 14,500 cubic yards of masonry.

Under the separate contract established with the Phoenix Bridge Company, work also proceeded on the two approach spans. Fabrication of the steel for the two spans was begun at Phoenixville in August 1901, and the material was delivered to Québec before the end of the year. Erection of the north approach span began in 1902 and was completed the following year, while the south approach span was complete by September 1903.

All was now in readiness for the superstructure of the bridge itself, but little progress had been made since 1900 in the effort to fully finance this work or to establish an actual contract for the work between the Quebec Bridge Company and Phoenix.

By the spring of 1903, however, there was an entirely new political issue beginning to emerge that would broaden the imperative for the completion of a crossing of the St. Lawrence at Québec and pave the way for a resolution of the financing problem. The Conservatives had built the Canadian Pacific, the transcontinental railway that had tied Canada together. Now the Liberals, who came to power in 1896, set out to build a second, and more northerly, transcontinental railroad of their own.

In a lengthy and impassioned speech to the Commons in July 1903, Prime Minister Laurier told the members that Canada would have a second transcontinental. There were several reasons for this ambitious venture, he told them. A second route to the Pacific would provide competition to the CPR, which had none in western Canada. For Québec and the Maritime Provinces, a more direct route to the west would assure the St. Lawrence waterway and the Atlantic ports of the Maritimes a greater share of the growing export traffic in timber and grain from the western provinces and territories, much of which was then moving through ports in the United States. A new line well to the north of the CPR also would open to colonization vast undeveloped areas of Ontario, Québec and New Brunswick.[7]

This new transcontinental route would be made up of two parts. The privately owned Grand Trunk Pacific, with government aid, would build west from Winnipeg to the Pacific Coast. The government itself would build the new National Transcontinental Railway, which would extend over a 1,844-mile northerly route that would link the Canadian ports in the Maritime Provinces with Winnipeg, cutting some 200 miles from the existing rail route between Winnipeg and Halifax. Beginning at Moncton, New Brunswick, the NTR would build a new line across New Brunswick to Québec, following a much more direct route than that of the Intercolonial Railway. From Québec the NTR would build west across the Canadian Shield to Winnipeg, where it would be linked with the Grand Trunk Pacific. Completion of the bridge at Québec would represent a vital element in the realization of this new transcontinental route.

Not everyone thought it was a good idea. A *Montréal Star* editorial declared that "we should not waste any money on that mad route, unknown, unsurveyed, and uninhabited, through the north country, over granite ranges from Winnipeg to Quebec."[8] Even Laurier's own minister of railways, Andrew Blair, a member of Parliament from St. John, New Brunswick, thought it such a bad idea that he resigned his ministerial post and retired from Parliament. Blair objected that the measure had been prepared without consultation with him, that it was ill considered, would put a heavy charge on the treasury, and would destroy the value of the Intercolonial Railway by paralleling it.

But build it they would, and it would have to have a bridge at Québec.

True to his earlier assurances of government support to the Québec Bridge project, and with the additional imperative of the bridge as a key link in the National Transcontinental scheme, Prime Minister Laurier marshaled the necessary support in Parliament for an additional financial measure by which the government would guarantee what the Montréal *Gazette* called "that political conceit, the Québec Bridge over the St. Lawrence River."[9]

In October 1903 the bridge company board approved a proposed agreement with the government that laid out the terms of this additional financial support which would permit the Quebec Bridge & Railway Company[10] to proceed with the remaining elements of the project. Under this agreement, the Dominion government would guarantee payment of the principal and interest on bonds to be issued by the bridge company and would hold a mortgage on the bridge. Before the month was out, the Laurier government had submitted a bill to Parliament that would grant the bridge company a national guarantee of its bonds, both capital and interest, to the extent of $6,678,200. The bill passed a few days later, and, all conditions having been satisfied, a final guarantee agreement was executed between the bridge company, the Canadian government, and the Royal Trust Company the following February 1.

Even as the National Transcontinental Railway plan and the new measure to guarantee the bridge company's bonds were making their way through the political process, the bridge company and Phoenix Bridge had finally moved to establish a firm contract for the design, fabrication, and erection of the main superstructure.

Reflecting both the terms proposed in John Deans' letter of August 23, 1899, and the agreement of April 12, 1900, between the two companies, a final contract had been entered into on June 19, 1903. The document reflected the changes in span length proposed by Cooper in 1900, providing for a bridge with a central span of 1,800 feet and side or anchor spans of 500 feet, and it established completion date of December 31, 1906, barring strikes, floods, or other causes beyond the control of the Phoenix Bridge Company. Most important for the Phoenix company, and in keeping with a change that Deans had advocated, the contract provided for payment on the basis of unit prices for steel and timber rather than the lump sum price for the complete bridge that had been the basis for the original proposal of March 1899. Consequently, the potential increase in steel quantities required by the change in span length was not a problem for Phoenix. If more steel were required, the Quebec Bridge & Railway Company would pay for it.

Even though both companies signed the contract, it was still made provisional by the Phoenix Bridge Company. In an accompanying letter, Phoenix President David Reeves stated an understanding that the agreement would not become operative until the proposed legislation providing the necessary bond guarantee measure had been authorized by Parliament and all necessary financial arrangements made. Since the work could not begin until this had been done, Reeves also refused to guarantee completion by the end of 1906, although "we will do our best to keep [the date]," he promised. Instead, Reeves offered a new completion date of December 31, 1908, after which the Phoenix company would pay damages of $5,000 per month if the structure were not complete.[11]

By late February 1904, S. N. Parent was able to inform Reeves that the necessary legislation had passed and that all required financial arrangements had been made. By mid-March the contract was operative, and the work of fabricating and erecting the bridge finally could begin.

Much had already been accomplished. The previous May, Cooper had drafted the revisions to the bridge company's original specifications that he had alluded to in the supplementary report of June 23, 1899, and his May 1, 1900, proposal that the span length be increased. These were changes that Cooper believed could reduce the cost of the structure without either reducing its carrying capacity or compromising its performance in any manner. The original specifications of 1898, which had been drafted by Edward Hoare, were little more than a modified version of general specifications for steel and iron bridges developed in 1896 by the Department of Railways and Canals. While appropriate for bridges of ordinary dimensions, these specifications were hardly adequate for a structure of such extraordinary scale as the Quebec Bridge.

Cooper's recommended changes included revisions to the loadings that were to be used for designing the structure to bring them more into conformance with his own prediction of the loadings that would actually be imposed upon the structure. The design wind pressures acting on the structure were reduced, while the specified train loadings were increased. Even so, the specified train loading was no greater than that normally used in Canadian practice, and somewhat less than other major long-span bridges of the day. Far more significant were the increases that Cooper proposed in the maximum unit stresses, which would allow about 21,000 pounds per square inch under ordinary loading conditions and 24,000 pounds per square inch in the structural steel under extreme loading conditions. These were unit stresses that were later characterized as being "in advance of current practice and . . . without precedence in the history of bridge engineering."[12]

Cooper's revised specifications quickly generated a major controversy with the Canadian government. This was concerned, however, not so much with the technical merits of the proposed changes, but rather with questions of engineering authority and responsibility. As provided by the 1900 subsidy act, which required the approval of any changes to the plans or specifications by the governor in council, Cooper's amended specifications were submitted by the Quebec Bridge Company to Collingwood Schreiber, chief engineer of Railways and Canals, for the necessary approval. These were then turned over to Robert C. Douglas, the department's bridge engineer, for his review.

Douglas' report recommended that many of Cooper's amendments be adopted, but he also criticized the high unit stresses proposed and Cooper's suggestion that train loadings could safely be increased in future. Douglas also proposed that the bridge company be required to submit new specifications, rather than just proposed amendments to the original 1898 specifications.

Despite his bridge engineer's reservations, Schreiber elected to support the changes proposed by Cooper in a letter to L. K. Jones, the secretary of Railways and Canals:

> Mr. Cooper is a bridge engineer of high standing in New York, and a man of repute and reliability. He has made a very careful study of the necessities of the superstructure, which, I may say, was especially imperative in view of the unusual magnitude of the span and of the general design of the work. His modifications may therefore reasonably be considered to be in the best interests of the work, and being engaged continuously upon the work during construction Mr. Cooper will be in the best position to note the requirements of the structure as the work progresses.[13]

Schreiber went on, however, to recommend that the department employ a competent bridge engineer to examine the detailed drawings and to approve or correct them as necessary, submitting them for the final acceptance of the chief engineer of Railways and Canals. An order-in-council based upon Schreiber's recommendations was approved on July 21, 1903; there was an immediate outcry from Theodore Cooper, the Quebec Bridge Company, and the Phoenix Bridge Company.

Informed by Schreiber of his plans to engage a consulting engineer who would have, in effect, final authority to approve plans for the bridge, Cooper immediately set forth his objections in a July 31 letter to Edward Hoare. "This puts me in the position of a subordinate," he wrote, "which I cannot accept."[14]

Informed by Cooper of the new development, John Deans, the Phoenix Bridge Company chief engineer, intervened with a series of letters, telegrams, and telephone calls to Hoare, protesting the new arrangement. "It would be disastrous to have proposed appointment finally made," he told Hoare in an August 3 telegram.[15] "We must insist upon having the whole matter stopped," he wrote to Cooper.[16]

In any event, Cooper carried the day. Early in August he went to Ottawa to take up the matter with Schreiber. Cooper himself was uncertain of the outcome after he had left Schreiber, but the result proved to be a new recommendation from Schreiber for a modification of the order-in-council that eliminated the plan for appointment of a consulting engineer by the Department of Railways and Canals. The new arrangement for approval of the plans, as set forth in a memorandum from a committee of the privy council, was this:

> The minister [Department of Railways and Canals] further represents that the chief engineer has this day reported, stating that, as the result of the personal interview had with the company's consulting engineer, he would advise that, provided the efficiency of the structure be fully maintained up to that defined in the original specifications attached to the company's contract, the new loadings proposed by their consulting engineer be accepted; all detail parts of the structure to be, however, as efficient for their particular function as the main members for theirs, the efficiency of all such details to be determined by the principles governing the best modern practice, and by the experience gained through actual test; all plans to be submitted to the chief engineer, and until his approval has been given not to be adopted for the work.[17]

While there was later disagreement over just how much authority this action gave to Cooper, his interpretation of the order-in-council seemed to be that it gave him a free hand, providing only that the efficiency of the structure was maintained up to the standard of the specifications attached to the subsidy contract of 1900. Cooper's satisfaction with the new arrangement was made clear in a letter to Edward Hoare following approval of the new order-in-council. "I think under fair and broad-minded interpretation, this will allow us to go on and get the best bridge we can, without putting metal where it will be more harm than good."[18]

While there remained a requirement to submit all plans for the approval of the chief engineer of Railways and Canals, it was treated as a perfunctory formality. When later modifications to the specifications appeared desirable, Cooper made them without reference to the government engineers, and there was no evidence that Schreiber ever questioned a decision made by Cooper or interfered in any way with the work.

The perfunctory nature of plan reviews by the Department of Railways and Canals is illustrated by a later comment from the department's bridge engineer, Robert Douglas, who conducted these reviews for Schreiber. "I was not guided by anything except Mr. Cooper's signature," said Douglas of his examination of the drawings; "practically, he was responsible for the plans."[19]

Clearly, Theodore Cooper now had full and undivided authority and responsibility for the fundamental technical decisions that would guide the design and construction of the Quebec Bridge.

While the Phoenix Bridge Company had established that the contract for the superstructure would not become operative until Parliament had approved the bond guarantee bill and the necessary financial arrangements were made, David Reeves had agreed that the company would proceed with all possible speed with the stress sheets and detailed drawings as soon as the revised specifications had been approved.

The Phoenix Bridge Company's preliminary plans for the bridge had gone through several stages of development from their earliest proposal of November 1897. The most recent, dating to April 1901, incorporated the longer central span adopted the year before. Some general study of the design details had been made by Charles Scheidl, one of the Phoenix design engineers, early in 1902, based upon the preliminary plans and stress sheets.

Following the receipt of Cooper's revised specifications in July 1903, work began in earnest on the details of the design. Guided by Cooper's revised specifications and other instructions from the consulting engineer, Peter Szlapka was responsible for all of the actual design work.

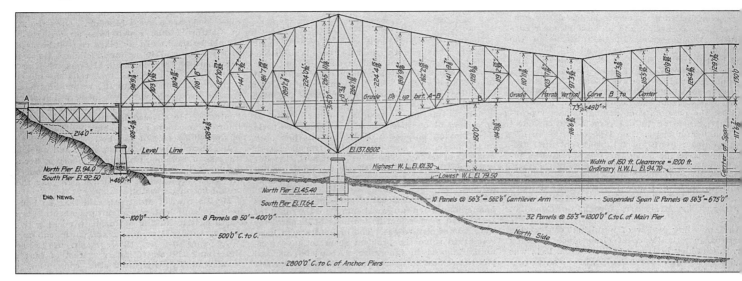

The prodigious dimensions of the Phoenix Bridge Company design for the Québec cantilever bridge are shown in this drawing from the September 14, 1905, issue of *Engineering News*. The main trusses increased in depth from approximately 97 feet at the end of the anchor and cantilever arms to 315 feet over the main piers. The 1,800-foot main span would give the structure the longest bridge span in the world. Author's Collection.

Once Szlapka had completed the general outline of the design, the work was turned over to Charles Scheidl, the engineer in charge of details. Scheidl supervised the Phoenix company's large staff of engineers and draftsmen, who completed the detailed shop drawings from which the structure would be fabricated. Details of floor beams and stringers, main shoes and pedestals, and connecting chords and their bracing had to be worked out. The packing, or arrangement, of the tension eyebars for the top chords had to be determined and the details of the anchorages developed. Next, details were developed for the anchor arm panel points and web intersections, followed by similar studies for the cantilever arms and the suspended span.

The bulk of the load carried by any bridge is the dead load of the structure itself, and the accurate determination of this load is a critical step in the design process. When the Phoenix design engineers had completed the details for the anchor arm, and those for the cantilever arms and suspended span were partially completed, the weights for all members and details of the bridge were calculated and final stress sheets computed for the anchor arms. The weights developed from this analysis indicated that the half of the suspended span carried by the cantilever and anchor arms on each side would weigh 2,421 tons, while each cantilever arm would weigh 6,603 tons and each anchor arm 6,659 tons. These dead load values were then used to determine the final design of the anchor arm, and later of the cantilever arms and suspended span as well.

The detailed work of stress analysis, design, and preparation of shop drawings for the fabrication of the bridge continued through 1904 and the first part of 1905. Cooper approved the stress sheets for the suspended span on March 29, 1904; for the anchor arms on June 30, 1904; and for the cantilever arms on May 25, 1905. The design and shop drawing work would continue into March 1907. Since the anchor arms would have to be erected first, the design effort was concentrated on this part of the work. The objective was to complete shop drawings for the anchor and cantilever arms no later than August 31, 1904, allowing the Phoenix shops eight months to fabricate material to permit a start to erection on May 1, 1905.

The structure that unfolded on the Phoenix Bridge Company drafting tables was a bridge of a scale unprecedented in North America. Each of the anchor arms spanned 500 feet, center to center of piers, while the 1,800-foot main span was made up of the two cantilever arms extending 562 feet, 6 inches outward from the main pier centerlines, supporting a 675-foot-long suspended center span. This main span provided a clear headway of 150 feet above the highest tide level over a width of 1,200 feet. The great trusses of the anchor and cantilever arms rose from a depth of almost 97 feet at the end to a height of 315 feet at the main piers and then descended to a depth of just over 97 feet at the outer end. The suspended center span rose from a depth of just over 97 feet at each end to 130 feet at the center. The anchor arm was subdivided by vertical members into ten frames, or panels, of 50 feet each, while the cantilever arms and the suspended span were similarly divided into 56-foot, 3-inch panels. The two trusses of the bridge were spaced 67 feet apart, center to center, allowing sufficient width between them to accommodate two railroad tracks, two trolley tracks, and two roadways, while sidewalks were to be carried outside the trusses on each side.

While typical cantilever bridge design practice was to employ straight top and bottom chords for the anchor and cantilever arms, for ease of fabrication and erection, those for the Quebec Bridge were curved. The top chords for both anchor and cantilever arms descended from the main posts to the end posts in a shallow curve, while the bottom chord members curved upward from the main pier supporting shoes in a parabolic curve to become parallel with the roadway toward the end of the span. According to Peter Szlapka, this curved lower chord was adopted for the sake of artistic appearance. Ornamental steel finials atop each of the main towers were another evident artistic touch.

The main structural members required for this enormous structure were massive ones. In keeping with normal North American practice, the bridge was designed as a pin-connected structure, with pin connections in the vertical posts and the top and bottom chords, while riveted joints were used at the intersections of diagonal compression members.

Each of the anchor and cantilever arm top chords, which were tension members, was made up of as many as twenty-eight steel eyebars. These were flat bars 15 inches wide and anywhere from $1^3/8$ inches to $2^1/4$ inches thick and as much as 76 feet in length, forged with enlarged ends which were drilled for the connecting pins. The most heavily loaded of these top chord sections had a total cross sectional area of 711 square inches.

The bottom chord members, which were the most heavily loaded compression members in the structure, were rectangular sections 54 inches deep and 68 inches wide, made up of four web sections of steel plate, each comprised of eight layers of steel plate as much as $^{15}/_{16}$ inch thick. Riveted diaphragms of steel angles and plate and diagonal lacing of steel angles joined the four webs together so they functioned as a unit. For the most heavily loaded sections adjacent to the main piers, these bottom chord members had a total cross-sectional area of 842 square inches of steel. The center posts over the main piers were 10 feet wide and 4 feet deep, similarly built up from steel plates and angles. The two posts at each pier were heavily braced, forming a huge transverse truss 67 feet wide and 315 feet high, each weighing 1,500 tons. The steel pins that held the principal members of the bridge together ranged anywhere from 9 inches in diameter to the 24-inch diameter pins in the supporting shoes at the base of the main posts. Some 12-inch pins in the top chord were as much as 10 feet long. The main floor beams, which carried the 67-foot-wide roadway and were located at each panel point of the trusses, were $10^1/2$ feet deep and weighed 30 tons each. The full weight of the bridge was carried on four massive wrought steel pedestal and shoe assemblies that supported the main posts of the trusses on their piers. Each of these assemblies stood almost 15 feet high and weighed just under 200 tons.

Long before the design and shop drawing work was complete, the Phoenix company had begun the work of fabricating the structure. This part of the work was actually carried out by the parent Phoenix Iron Company, Phoenix Bridge being only a design and erection firm. The first shopwork began in July 1904, and by the end of the year, eight panels of the anchor arm lower chords had been completed and were ready for shipment.

The structure would be the largest and heaviest ever fabricated at the Phoenixville plant, and the company invested over $200,000 in improvements to its facilities to handle the work. The eyebar plant was enlarged and improved, and buildings were altered and new overhead cranes installed to handle weights of as much as 100 tons. New machinery included a 64-inch double rotary planer for facing the ends of the large compression chords, a plate straightener for large, thick steel plates, hydraulic shears for heavy sections, larger boring mills, and a large vertical planer, while various alterations were made to other machinery.

The quantities and sizes of steel required for the structure exceeded the production capacity of the Phoenix Iron Company. Central Iron & Steel Company of Harrisburg, Pennsylvania, rolled more than 7,400 tons of eyebar blanks and some 13,620 tons of steel plate. Carnegie Steel Company at Pittsburgh supplied over 6,900 tons of steel plate in sizes that were too large to be made at either the Phoenix or Central plants. Bethlehem Steel Company manufactured almost 500 tons of the huge steel pins required for connections. The Phoenix plant itself rolled almost 8,300 tons of steel shapes for the Quebec Bridge and forged the eyebars from the blanks supplied by Central Iron and Steel.

Both the unprecedented size of the members being fabricated for the bridge and the unusually complex nature of some of the details made the work of fabrication uncommonly difficult for the shopmen at Phoenixville. The individual members had to be designed both so that the machines in the shop could make them and so they could be shipped by rail to the site. The joints in the lower chord panel points where sections of the curved chord were joined promised to be particularly difficult to fabricate, and the company constructed a full-sized wooden model of one of the anchor arm lower chord panel points, complete even to rivet heads, which was set up as a guide to the shop workers.

As the design and fabrication work proceeded, the manufacture of the big eyebars that would make up the principal tension members in the structure became a worrisome problem for Cooper. Typically, a sufficient number of eyebars were arranged in bundles to provide the required strength in a tension member. While the use of eyebars had become typical American practice, those required for the Quebec Bridge, of course, would have to be larger and heavier than anything done before. Early in June 1904, Phoenix Bridge submitted its plans for the top chords and diagonal tension members in the anchor arms, but Cooper refused to approve them. What was wrong, he told them, was that some bars were at an angle he considered unsatisfactory, not to mention some of them were as much as 2½ inches thick, even though he had laid down a requirement that no bar exceed two inches in thickness. "My experience had proved to my mind," he said later, "that when that thickness was exceeded satisfactory bars could not be obtained."[20] Peter Szlapka came to New York to protest, telling Cooper that he had had his best men on it for two months and saw no way it could be done to satisfy Cooper's requirements. Cooper himself set to work on the design, while Szlapka and his engineers continued to try to solve the problem. It was not until the end of July that the Phoenix engineers had come up with a design that Cooper was willing to approve.

A new problem arose the following January when Cooper's inspector at Phoenixville, E. L. Edwards, reported some unsatisfactory tests of some of the eyebars; the eye sections at each end were elongating under the loadings planned for the tension chords. The Phoenix Bridge Company seemed reluctant to solve the problem, and Cooper directed his inspector to refuse to accept any more eyebars until further notice. John Deans traveled to New York a few days later, and the two men worked out plans for a series of tests of eyebars with different head sizes and arrangements. These were completed during February, and a satisfactory modification to the eyebar design was adopted. At the same time, Cooper agreed to permit the use of nineteen eyebars that had been manufactured earlier, requiring that they be distributed more or less equally between the north and south spans.

Strangely, while requiring full-sized tests of these important tension members, Cooper had required no comparable testing of the principal compression members in the structure, even though he himself had advocated this measure for many years in his own widely used standard bridge specification. The reason was simple: "There is no machine or method existing by which any such tests could be made," he said later.[21]

In keeping with the Phoenix company's usual practice, the details of the erection scheme for the bridge had been carefully worked out at Phoenixville and the results incorporated in a book of field instructions. Copies were furnished to the erection foremen, who were expected to follow the instructions without any deviation that had not been approved by the company at Phoenixville. "In fact," commented erection inspector E. R. Kinloch, "you had only to follow instructions and the thing would get there itself if you followed the lines laid down."[22] There was one important variation from normal Phoenix Bridge Company practice, which was to assemble the complete structure at Phoenixville before it was shipped to assure that everything fit together properly. The Quebec Bridge was simply too big for this.

The planned erection sequence was to erect temporary timber and steel falsework to support the anchor arm during erection. Once this was complete and the anchor arm self-supporting, the falsework would be removed and the cantilever arm erected by cantilevering it outward, section by section, from the main pier. Phoenix then planned to erect half of the suspended span in a similar manner by cantilevering it outward from the end of the cantilever arm. Once the two halves of the suspended span had been joined at the center, temporary members used in the cantilevered erection would be removed to convert the span to a simple truss.

The structure was erected with a moving gantry crane, or "traveler," designed specifically for the Québec project with the aid of a model of the bridge. Built of steel, this enormous traveler was 54 feet long, 105 feet wide, and 220 feet high, with 70-foot top and bottom extensions. Fully rigged, the traveler weighed 1,120 tons. Instead of using the customary steam-powered hoisting equipment, the traveler was fitted with four special 125-hp electric hoisting engines and was designed to handle pieces weighing as much as 105 tons. Power was supplied from a hydroelectric plant at nearby Chaudière Falls. In another departure from normal practice, the traveler was designed to operate outside the main trusses of the bridge instead of inside, allowing the full structure and all bracing to be completed for each panel of the bridge before the traveler was moved forward to the next. Special steel falsework was used to support the traveler during erection of the anchor arms. Once erection reached the main pier, the traveler was carried on three lines of stringers supported by floor beams cantilevered outside the line of the trusses. After the erection work had been completed, the stringers were to be used to support the railroad tracks in the completed structure.

Typically, the erection work moved outward toward the center of the river. Sections of the bridge were brought up from the south bank storage yard at Chaudière on rail cars and then lifted into place by the hoists on the large gantry traveler. Some of these sections were as much as 105 feet long, and some weighed as much as 92 tons. The largest bundles of eyebars that had to be lifted into place in the top chord of the anchor or cantilever arms were 76 feet long and weighed 70 tons.

The bottom chord members of the anchor arm were supported at the panel points by steel camber blocking carried on the steel falsework. The erectors had to allow for the movement of the structure that would take place as the individual members were elongated or compressed under load as additional weight was added to the structure. The falsework had to be configured to conform to the initial configuration of the anchor arm as it was erected. As the load of the cantilever arm came on the structure and increased the stresses in the anchor arm members, the structure would gradually shift to its normal configuration. As this occurred the anchor arm would gradually lift free of the camber blocks on the falsework, which also could be lowered to assist in this movement. The falsework also was arranged so that jacks could be used to raise or lower the pin centers at the panel points to reach the exact fixed points required. The connections in these lower, compression chords required particularly careful attention, for exact alignment and full bearing across the joint between members was critical to their proper performance.

As the individual members were put into place in joints that were to be riveted, the connections were temporarily bolted up, with riveting crews to follow later. At the principal pin-connected joints, the huge steel pins a foot or more in diameter and as much as 10 feet long had to be driven into place. This was accomplished with a 4,000-pound swinging ram operated by a crew of six to eight men.

Preparatory work had begun at the bridge site on the south shore of the river on August 1, 1904, when materials began arriving for the falsework that would support the south anchor arm during erection. Construction of the falsework began in September, and almost

On September 4, 1904, framing for the falsework that would support the south anchor arm had just begun on the south shore of the St. Lawrence. This work was completed the following July, when erection of the anchor arm began. The traveler used for falsework erection is mounted on the approach span, which had been completed a year earlier under a separate contract with the Phoenix Bridge Company. National Photography Collection, National Archives of Canada (Neg. C9767).

half of it was in place by the beginning of December. Before the end of the 1904 season, erection of the traveler had begun, and the storage yard for bridge materials had been completed at Chaudière, about a mile from the bridge site. Bridge materials began arriving here from Phoenixville during the winter and were unloaded from a single track in the center of a 990-foot-long, 67-foot-wide crane runway and stored until needed at the bridge site. Two 55-ton electric cranes were used to unload and reload material.

Erection of the bridge itself could not commence until the Quebec Bridge & Railway Company had completed the rail connection to the bridge site. This was finally opened on July 9, 1905, and materials began moving to the site on rail cars. By July 22 the falsework had been completed and the traveler fully outfitted, and erection of the anchor arm commenced. The work went well, although there were a few problems that had to be worked out. The most serious mishap of the 1905 season occurred in April, even before erection had begun, when anchor arm bottom chord A9L—the second chord member inward from the main pier on the left, or Montréal, side of the bridge—was dropped and bent while being handled in the Chaudière storage yard. By July repairs had been completed based on drawings received from Phoenixville, and the chord was placed in the structure that fall. By the time work was stopped for the winter on November 24, six of ten south anchor arm panels were in place, and some 5,250 tons of steel had been erected.

The organization and staff put in place to manage this difficult project was somewhat unorthodox. The Quebec Bridge & Railway Company was represented by its chief engineer, Edward Hoare, who was responsible for general oversight and management of the project and for supervision and inspection of both the fabrication and erection work by

Erection of the bridge could not begin until rail access to the site was completed. A group of laborers at work on the rock cut for the approach to the bridge site on the south shore paused for a photograph on February 23, 1905. National Archives of Québec (Neg. P509,D4,P8).

Erection of the large traveler that would be used to erect the south anchor and cantilever arms of the bridge began late in 1904, and the 220-foot-high, 1,120-ton structure was completed and fully outfitted the following July. The completed traveler is shown here on August 8, 1905, two weeks after erection of the south anchor arm began. National Archives of Canada (Neg. PA108752).

A group of ironworkers posed with one of the bottom chord sections for the anchor arm as it was lifted off flatcars by the big traveler. It was August 12, 1905, and erection had been underway for only three weeks. Hagley Museum and Library (Neg. 71.MSS.916.3861).

After a little more than three months of erection work, the portal and first panel of the south anchor arm were in place at the time of this October 9, 1905, photograph. Visible behind and above the completed structure is the large traveler used for erection, which moved along tracked outriggers outside the lines of the two main trusses. National Archives of Canada (Neg. C18667).

60

Phoenix. Hoare was assisted at Québec by Ephraim R. Kinloch, who took up duties as inspector of workmanship and general erection in July 1905. Although not a trained engineer, Kinloch was an experienced bridge man, with nearly fifty years of experience in the erection of large bridges with a number of railroads and the American Bridge Company. Then employed by a Pittsburgh firm, Kinloch had favorably impressed Hoare by his work as the inspector for the two approach spans erected during 1902–1903. Hoare had kept in touch with Kinloch and persuaded him to take up the inspection post for the main span in 1905.

The Québec company hired four other inspectors to look over the manufacture of steel and shop fabrication in the United States. Theodore Cooper had wanted to employ trained and experienced engineers for this work, who could then take up inspection of the erection after the manufacturing work was complete. Hoare was uninterested in doing this, and Elsworth L. Edwards, who had some seventeen years of experience in materials testing, was appointed chief shop inspector at Phoenixville on Cooper's recommendation. Edwards was assisted at Phoenixville by Irvin W. Meeser, and by John N. Ostrom at the Carnegie rolling mill in Pittsburgh and Mr. Keenan at the Central Iron & Steel rolling mill at Harrisburg.

At Phoenixville, Chief Engineer John Deans had overall managerial responsibility for the work, while designing engineer Peter Szlapka and assistant engineer Charles Scheidl, and their designing and shop drawing staffs, produced the detailed drawings required for fabrication. Frank P. Norris, manager of the Phoenix Iron Company, oversaw the actual work of fabrication.

Superintendent of Erection A. B. Milliken, an experienced man who had been in his position for seventeen years, managed all of the Phoenix company's erection work. Several men had headed the field work at Québec in its early stages. E. J. Wickizer had been general foreman during the erection of falsework, which began in 1904, while Mr. Shoemaker was superintendent of erection during the first stages of the work in 1905. Once the work was in full swing, however, Phoenix sent its best man to become general foreman of erection for the largest bridge ever built by the company. This was 38-year-old Benjamin A. Yenser, who had worked in bridge erection all of his adult life, including some fifteen years with Phoenix. He was selected for the Québec job, said Chief Engineer Deans, "having shown unusual qualities as an erector, being extremely careful and conscientious, and having had large experience in the handling of men."[23] Four assistant foremen aided Yenser in managing the large workforce at the bridge site.

The Phoenix company usually brought relatively few erecting men of its own to a project, depending upon its carefully developed erection instructions and a cadre of skilled and experienced men to get the job done with men hired at the work site. Some of the erection crew had come up from the United States to work on the bridge, but most of them were local men. There were several men from Québec and the surrounding communities, but the largest number were an extraordinary group of men from the Caughnawaga Reservation, which lies across the river and about eight miles up the St. Lawrence from Montréal, just above the Lachine Rapids.

The Caughnawaga Indians are a rather small band, descended from Mohawks and other Iroquois tribes, who had been converted to Christianity by French Jesuit missionaries and settled above the rapids in the late seventeenth century. Most of them made their living

By the end of October, two full panels of the anchor arm were complete, and the big traveler had been moved forward to begin erecting the third panel. The heavy compressive members for the curved bottom chord were already in place all the way to the main pier. Hagley Museum and Library (Neg. 71.MSS.916.3879).

On May 7, 1906, just three weeks after erection work had begun for the season, the members of Québec Local 87 of the International Association of Bridge and Structural Iron Workers gathered at the south portal of the bridge for this photograph. Some of the men came from distant points in Canada and the United States, but most were from the Québec area or were Mohawk ironworkers from Caughnawaga, near Montréal. Historical Society of the Phoenixville Area.

in the fur trade or river rafting or farming until the railroad came to their community in 1886. The Canadian Pacific Railroad was building a new cantilever bridge across the St. Lawrence at Lachine, and the CP and Dominion Bridge Company, the builder, agreed to hire Caughnawagas to work on the project as part of a deal for the right to use reservation land for the south shore bridge abutment. Initially, the Indians worked as laborers, but it soon became apparent that they had no fear of heights and adapted quickly to the dangerous work of bridge erection. The company was soon training them to work as riveters, and the Caughnawaga had found a new vocation.[24] Bridgemen from the Caughnawaga band who had learned their trade on the Lachine bridge began traveling to bridge jobs far and wide, taking with them young men from the village as apprentices. The numbers of skilled Caughnawaga proliferated, and by the time the Quebec Bridge job came along, there were more than seventy skilled bridgemen on the reservation. About half of them headed north to work on the big project.

The Phoenix Bridge Company had its engineers on the project site, too. C. W. Hudson, an assistant engineer in Peter Szlapka's designing department who had designed the huge main traveler, was sent to Québec to oversee its erection, and he also served briefly as resident engineer of erection on the project until the post was taken up on a permanent basis by Arthur H. Birks in September 1904.

The resident engineer's job was an important one, for he would be the Phoenix company's senior engineer at the bridge site, responsible for providing technical oversight and assistance to the erection work. Although he was only 25 years old, Birks came to the assignment with an exceptional record of accomplishment. He was an honors graduate from Princeton University and had joined the company's engineering department in 1902 on the recommendation of Professor G. F. Swain after completing a graduate course and teaching in civil engineering at the Massachusetts Institute of Technology. After six months in the drafting department, Birks was transferred to the erection department, and over the next several years he worked on the erection of almost two dozen major bridges before moving to the biggest job of them all. "A statement of Mr. Birks' experience in no sense conveys a proper estimate of his ability, which was unusual for a man of his years," said Chief Engineer Deans later. "He was specially fitted by character and temperament for the work entrusted to him."[25]

A second Phoenix engineer at the site was Frank E. Cudworth, a young Dartmouth civil engineering graduate who was the resident engineer in charge of instrument work.

The relative position of consulting engineer Theodore Cooper in the formal project hierarchy seemed ambiguous. On paper, at least, he advised Quebec Bridge & Railway Company Chief Engineer Edward Hoare and Phoenix designing engineer Peter Szlapka, and he approved all drawings before they were sent through Hoare to the Department of Railways and Canals for final approval. In fact, Cooper became the dominant figure in all major decisions affecting the project. Once Cooper had obtained what he interpreted to be final authority to revise the specifications without further referral to the Department of Railways and Canals in 1903, the Phoenix Bridge Company looked to Cooper alone on these matters. Edward Hoare, inexperienced in a major work of the character of the Quebec Bridge, referred all major engineering decisions to Cooper and did not even bother to review the drawings as they came through his office on the way to the Department of Railways and Canals. While the department retained the authority for final review and approval of drawings, these reviews seem to have been perfunctory, and no design decision or detail was ever questioned. In fact, bridge members were often already being fabricated before drawings had even reached the government offices in Ottawa for approval. The only inspections of the work made by the Department of Railroads and Canals were for purposes of making the monthly progress estimates that were the basis for payment of the government subsidies to the bridge company.

Despite all of the responsibility that fell to him, Cooper was surprisingly ill compensated for his duties. When he had originally taken on the job in 1899, he had agreed to accept a fee not exceeding $5,000 for his review and analysis of the original tenders, with a further fee of $7,500 per year for his services during construction. This was later renegotiated by the Quebec Bridge Company to provide an annual payment of $4,000, from which Cooper paid all costs for his office staff. All told, over the eight years he was associated with the project, Cooper was paid a total of just $32,225.

While Cooper had visited Québec several times during the foundation work and had been to Phoenixville once or twice to examine the steel fabrication, ill health kept him away from the bridge site throughout the period of the erection work. In at least a half-hearted way, he had discussed withdrawing from the project with both S. N. Parent and John Deans somewhere around 1904. Both, he said later, objected vigorously, protesting that they could not find anyone else upon whom they could agree or in whom they could have the same confidence. "Realizing this difficulty," said Cooper, "and feeling also a pride and a desire to see this great work carried through successfully, I took no further action."[26]

The inability to see first hand what was happening at the Québec site placed Cooper at a serious disadvantage. Because of this, his primary link to the status of the work became a young engineer named Norman R. McClure. A 1904 civil engineering graduate from Princeton, McClure had acquired some railroad construction and bridge experience through employment, during summers and following graduation, with the Pennsylvania, Baltimore & Ohio, and Ontario & Western Railroads. Although McClure was actually on the payroll of the Quebec Bridge & Railway Company, he was appointed by Cooper as an inspecting engineer for the work on the recommendation of the Phoenix company. There was some friction with Edward Hoare over this appointment. Cooper wanted a qualified engineer on the project, while Hoare had already hired E. R. Kinloch as inspector of workmanship and general erection. Hoare soon agreed to the appointment, however, and McClure joined the project in April 1905. After several months at Phoenixville becoming familiar with the work and assisting in shop inspection, he moved to Québec at the end of August to take up his duties on the site.

Following the winter shut-down, erection work resumed at the bridge on April 16, 1906. On May 14, 1906, when this photograph was made, another two panels of the anchor arm had been completed, and the big traveler had been moved forward to begin the eighth of the anchor arm's ten panels. This view shows rather clearly how the large traveler moved along tracks mounted on outriggers outside the line of the main trusses. Hagley Museum and Library (Neg. 71.MSS.916.3891).

On May 21, 1906, the Phoenix Bridge crew prepared to lift into place a section of one of the center posts over the main pier. These sections, some of which weighed close to 100 tons, were among the heaviest pieces handled by the erection crew. Hagley Museum and Library (Neg. 71.MSS.916.3894).

Design and fabrication work continued through the winter of 1905–1906 while erection was shut down. Disturbing news came to Theodore Cooper early in 1906. Under pressure to get the design work done and the bridge under construction, the Phoenix design office had never recalculated the actual dead load weights of the bridge members as the detailed design and shop drawings were completed to compare them with the estimated weights developed late in 1903, upon which the entire design was based. On February 1 E. L. Edwards, the chief shop inspector at Phoenixville, submitted a report on material that was based upon actual shipping weights. For the first time, Cooper became aware that the bridge was going to be substantially heavier than the weights used for the design calculations. Edwards' report placed the actual weight of each anchor arm, including the center posts, at just over 9,000 tons, almost 2,400 tons more than that used for design purposes.

Cooper made an estimate of the increased strains that would result from this increased load, finding that they would be about 7 percent greater than originally calculated. Both Cooper and the Phoenix design staff then re-estimated the weight of the remainder of the structure, concluding that the entire superstructure would now weigh anywhere from 35,500 to 36,500 tons, as compared to the original estimate of less than 31,400 tons. When final weights were calculated a year later, this had grown to more than 38,800 tons, increasing the unit strains in the anchor arm by as much as an estimated 10 percent.

At this point the south anchor arm, center posts, and two panels of the cantilever arm had been fabricated, and six panels of the anchor arm were already in place. Despite the unprecedented allowable stresses that had been originally adopted for the design, Cooper reluctantly concluded that even these still higher strains were within the limits of safety. To have done otherwise would have required major changes or replacement of the work already completed. Aside from changes in the design of the suspended span, which had not yet been completed, nothing was done to allow for this increased loading, and the project continued to move ahead.

Work at the site began again on April 16, 1906, and the entire south anchor arm, less a few decorative details, was in place by June 27. Generally, the work went well throughout the 1906 season, but there were a few problems. In April a section of one of the center posts was damaged when a hoisting chain slipped, but it was satisfactorily repaired that summer. On June 2 Norman McClure reported to Cooper that the bearing surfaces at the top of the center post were uneven and would not provide a good bearing for the center post caps. For the only time during the course of the erection, Cooper wired Hoare, stopping the work until the problem was corrected. Repairs were made in accordance with Cooper's detailed instructions, and the work continued.[27]

Late in July McClure became concerned about irregularities in the webs of some of the anchor and cantilever arm chord members that had already been erected. In sighting from end to end, the webs appeared crooked and gave a wavy appearance. McClure reported deflections of as much as a half inch in 36 feet in several members to Cooper in September. Cooper replied that he didn't like the distortions but didn't see that anything could be done at that stage.

In August the Phoenix erection crew began the removal of the steel falsework under the south anchor arm. This was a task that required careful planning and execution, as the trusses were expected to lift off the falsework as additional weight was added in the cantilever arms and blocking was removed under the anchor arm trusses. Cooper instructed

With studied nonchalance, the ironworkers guided a bundle of eyebars for the anchor arm top chord into place at the top of the main post over the pier on June 20, 1906. Once the bars were in place, a huge steel pin would be driven through the pinholes at the top of the post and the heads of the eyebars to firmly link them in place. Within another week, the entire south anchor arm would be in place. Hagley Museum and Library (Neg. 71.MSS.916.3903).

McClure about how he wanted the removal handled, and there was a brief controversy when the Phoenix crew proceeded with the work under new instructions from Phoenixville without even advising McClure. A sharp letter from Edward Hoare to John Deans made it clear that the Quebec Bridge Company expected its erection engineer to be kept fully informed of any important proceedings on the project. In any event, the removal of the falsework was substantially completed by November 28, and the entire anchor arm truss had swung free of any temporary support.[28]

Work continued on the south cantilever arm, and this was substantially complete by the time work was shut down again for the winter season at the end of November. During the 1906 season about 10,500 tons of steel had been erected. Work had also started on the north shore about mid-July, and some of the falsework removed from the south shore anchor arm had been reassembled for erection of the north anchor arm by the end of the season.

In another view of steel delivery by water, the big traveler has begun the lift of a big floor beam into the span. At the date of this November 7, 1906, photograph, four panels of the south anchor arm had been completed. Work would be shut down for the winter season at the end of the month. Hagley Museum and Library (Neg. 71.MSS.916.3933).

Facing page:

(Top, left) Piece by piece, the great bridge came together above the St. Lawrence. A big floor beam was lifted into place in the south cantilever arm on July 18, 1906. Hagley Museum and Library (Neg. 71.MSS.916.3912).

(Top, right) By August 14, 1906, erection was nearly complete for the first panel of the south cantilever arm. The posts at the end of the panel were already in place, and only the last sections of the top chord eyebars remained to be installed. Hagley Museum and Library (Neg. 71.MSS.916.3918).

(Center) The first south cantilever arm panel was nearly complete on August 15, 1906, as the last bundle of tension eyebars was lifted into place in the top chord on the east side of the bridge. Hagley Museum and Library (Neg. 71.MSS.916.3920).

(Bottom) Some sections of the bridge came to the site by water. On September 22, 1906, two tugs maneuvered a barge with a main floor beam into position under the south cantilever arm. The big traveler would then be used to lift the beam into place in the bridge. National Archives of Canada (Neg. PA108762).

The great bridge at Québec looked like this at the beginning of the 1907 construction season. Both the anchor and cantilever arms had been fully erected. Some temporary supports remained under the anchor arm, while the big traveler was positioned to start the erection of the south half of the suspended center span, cantilevering it outward from the end of the 562-foot, 6-inch cantilever arm. This photograph was taken from the ice of the St. Lawrence on February 24, 1907, and it would be another two and a half months before erection would resume. Hagley Museum and Library (Neg. 71.MSS.916.3937).

CHAPTER 5

COUNTDOWN TO DISASTER

Y THE BEGINNING OF 1907, THE GREAT BRIDGE HAD BECOME A MASSIVE PRESENCE on the St. Lawrence above New Liverpool (now part of St-Romuald). The entire south end of the structure had been completed by the end of the 1906 construction season. The south anchor arm of the main structure extended 500 feet from the anchor pier to the main pier, balancing the completed cantilever arm, which projected another 562 feet, 6 inches out over the river from the centerline of the main pier. Above the main pier, at their deepest points, the structure's two enormous trusses were 315 feet deep. At the finials that topped the tower over the main pier, the structure's highest point, the bridge stood more than 400 feet above the river's high water level.

Under the Phoenix Bridge Company's work plan for the 1907 season, construction of the south half of the bridge would continue with the erection of the south end of the 675-foot suspended span. This would be accomplished by temporarily cantilevering the half span from the outer end of the cantilever arm, using temporary tension members to link the top chord of each cantilever arm truss with the top chord of the suspended span. Once the north half of the bridge had been completed in a similar manner some two years later, the two halves of the suspended span would be joined and the temporary top chord links removed, and the central span would then function in its permanent capacity as a suspended simple span.

Originally, it had been planned to erect the south half of the suspended truss with the large, 1,100-ton gantry traveler used for erection of the anchor and cantilever arms. Once erection had reached the midpoint of the bridge, the traveler was to be disassembled and reassembled on the north side of the river to erect the north half of the bridge in a similar manner. Under this plan, however, the bridge would not have been completed until probably some time in 1909. As early as 1903, the Dominion Government had unofficially indicated its desire that the bridge be completed in time for the 1908 Québec Tercentenary, when it could be formally opened by the Prince of Wales, the future George V, as a major event of the celebration. For this, and other reasons, Phoenix Bridge had revised its plans to accelerate the design, fabrication, and erection of the bridge.

One of the ways the work could be accelerated was to revise the erection plan. Instead of employing the large traveler to erect the south half of the suspended span as originally planned, it had been decided at the beginning of 1906 to build a second, smaller traveler of 250 tons that would move along the top chord members of the trusses to erect the suspended span. For entirely different reasons, Cooper had objected to the use of the large traveler for the erection of the suspended span, considering it unduly hazardous and unnecessary.

This change in the erection scheme would allow the large traveler to be taken down and reassembled on the opposite shore by the end of the 1907 season and to begin erection of the north half of the bridge at the beginning of the 1908 season. On the north shore, work had already begun the previous July on the construction of the scaffolding that would be required to erect the north anchor arm. Delivery of completed steel work would not be a problem, since the steel members for the north half of the bridge had already been fabricated at Phoenixville at the same time as the identical members for the south half.

Work for the 1907 season began in March with the preparation of a storage yard for materials on the north side of the river at Belair, near the junction of a Canadian Pacific line and the planned National Transcontinental Railway. Construction of scaffolding at the north end resumed about May 15 but proceeded at a leisurely pace, since the rail connection needed for steel deliveries had not yet been completed. Erection of the south end trusses resumed on May 1, with work during the first month confined largely to riveting of members already in place. The large traveler was used to install the connecting links between the cantilever arm and the suspended span, and the small traveler was assembled. Erection of the suspended span began on July 13, employing the small traveler; and work began to dismantle and remove the large traveler.

But even before the work reached this point, the engineers at the site first noticed that something was not quite right with the structure. There were problems with the huge lower chord members of the anchor arm. These, and all of the other problems that followed, concerned chord members that were loaded in compression.

The design, fabrication, and erection of these enormous compression members for the main chords of the bridge were among the most difficult tasks undertaken by the engineers. Compression members must be carefully designed to avoid buckling under load. Just how much load a compression member can safely carry is a function of both the amount of material and something that engineers call the slenderness ratio, which is a way of expressing the stiffness of a compression member. It can easily be shown, for example, that a compression member made up of a hollow metal pipe or tube can carry a greater load without buckling than can a solid metal bar or rod of identical length and cross-sectional area. This relative stiffness, which is determined by both the amount of material and its distance from the center of gravity of the section, is expressed as its radius of gyration; and the ratio of this value to the unsupported length of a compression member is its slenderness ratio.

Ready for lifting into the bridge on June 4, 1907, this was one of the two temporary top chord tension links that would permit the south half of the center span to function temporarily as a cantilever during erection. Once both halves of the center span had been erected in this manner, they would be joined at the center and the links removed, allowing it to function as a simple span. Hagley Museum and Library (Neg. 71.MSS.916.3943).

As bridge span lengths and loadings increased dramatically in the late nineteenth century, bridge engineers were hard-pressed to design the much larger compression members that were required. What was needed were sections that were both economical and easily erected. One answer was the use of a hollow circular member. This gave the best possible slenderness ratio by placing the maximum amount of material at the greatest distance from the center of gravity. As early as 1862, Samuel Reeves, a son of one of the founders of the Phoenix Iron Company, had patented the Phoenix Column, an innovative design that used rolled wrought iron segments riveted together through flanges to form a circular column that was highly resistant to buckling. British engineers John Fowler and Benjamin Baker took a somewhat similar approach on a much larger scale during the 1880s in their design of the landmark Firth of Forth Bridge in Scotland. The principal compression members for this enormous structure were made up of riveted steel, double-wall tubular sections 12 feet in diameter. Tubular sections, however, were difficult to fabricate and erect and any joints or connections exceedingly difficult to make. American engineers preferred to design and build rectangular sections built up from rolled plates and angles.

Regardless of what form was used for the compression members of a bridge, design, fabrication, and erection of any joints or splices required extreme care to assure that loads were applied axially and that a full, uniform bearing across the entire joint or splice was obtained. Any eccentricity in the application of load could create bending in the compression member and unequal stresses across the joint or splice. Once any buckling began, it tended to increase with the continued application of load.

Aside from their unprecedented size, the principal compression members designed for the Quebec Bridge were typical of American practice at the time. Each of the bottom chords was made up of four massive steel plate webs or ribs, each of these in turn made up of four rolled plates stitched together with rivets to form a single built-up plate almost 4 inches thick, each finished with angles at top and bottom. The four ribs were stiffened and bound together top and bottom by diagonal lacing made up of 4-inch by 3-inch angles weighing 8½ pounds per foot. Each of these bottom chord members was 4 feet, 6½ inches deep and 5 feet, 7½ inches wide overall and had a total cross-sectional area of 780 square inches. The length of each chord member varied from 50 feet at the shore end of the anchor arm to as much as 57 feet adjacent to the main pier, dependent upon its inclination in the curved line of the bottom chord. But as enormous as they were, each of the main chord compression members would have fit inside the huge tubular sections used for the corresponding chords of the Forth Bridge.

Compressive loads were transmitted from one segment of the bottom chord to the next by butt connections. While this was a common practice for making connections, it was one that required particular care so as to make each joint as rigid as possible and to achieve full bearing across the entire area of the butt connection. This would assure that the compressive loads remained axial and that a uniform stress distribution was obtained across the bearing area.

To assure this full bearing across the entire cross section of bottom chord members at splices, each end was milled to close tolerances after fabrication at the Phoenix plant. So large were the compression chords that the Phoenix company had to buy a new 64-inch double rotary planer that was capable of facing them. The most complex splices were those at the panel points, which required an angled connection because of the curved alignment of the bottom chord and also included a pin connection with the vertical posts of the trusses. These difficult splices were made in the fabricating shop, where, as previously mentioned, the bridge company had built a full-sized wooden model of one of the lower chord joints to help make sure the shopmen fully realized the mechanical accuracy that was required to assure that the members went together properly in the field.

A field splice made with splice plates was located about 10 feet from the panel point in each bottom chord member. At both shop and field splices, solid batten plates took the place of the diagonal latticework, and steel plate diaphragms were installed between the ribs on either side of all splices. All of the field connections were initially bolted and then riveted at a later date.

Because the chord members were expected to deflect slightly as they came under load, they were initially cambered in the erecting shop to offset this. As the structure was erected, then, it was expected that adjoining chord members would initially be in contact only at either the upper or lower edges and that the full bearing across the entire joint would be achieved only as the chord members "turned" or deflected slightly under load. Only temporary bolts or drift pins held the joints until this had occurred and they could be riveted. It was generally recognized that the chord splices were in a very delicate condition until this had been done and they were made as rigid as possible. "These splices when properly and fully riveted were the strongest part of the compression chord," said Cooper later; "when unriveted or improperly bolted they were in a condition of great hazard and uncertainty. As these splices in the anchor arm could not be riveted until the camber action had taken place and the joints had come in full and proper bearing, they were, if improperly stayed and bolted, very dangerous points and should have been most carefully watched and protected."[1]

While riveting of the joints had to be delayed until they had closed, there was later some criticism that the Phoenix company's progress in riveting the structure had fallen further behind than was necessary for this purpose. Actually, it had been originally planned to delay much of the riveting until erection of the entire south half of the bridge was complete and all joints were at their full stress. At a meeting in May 1907, Cooper and Peter Szlapka, the Phoenix designing engineer, had decided that riveting could be done at once at all joints where the connecting pieces had taken their full bearing. While only about 54,000 rivets had been driven during all of 1905 and 1906, by the end of July, more than 150,000 rivets were in place, with riveting of the anchor arm 90 percent complete and the cantilever arm 40 percent complete.

The first sign of trouble came in mid-June, when the erecting crew noted that some of the joints were not closing as expected. Those between lower chords A5L and A6L (the designations representing anchor arm members in the fifth or sixth panel on the left, or west, side of the structure) in the anchor arm remained open as much as $1/16$ inch on the lower side long after all other joints had closed. Norman McClure, the inspector of erection, reported the problem by letter to Cooper in New York on June 15. The workers were having difficulty in riveting the bottom chord splices of the south anchor arm, he reported, because the faced ends of the two abutting middle ribs were not matching. At their lower sides, these were out of line anywhere from $1/8$ to $1/4$ inch, with the offset decreasing to nothing near the mid-depth of the ribs. "This has occurred in four instances so far," he told Cooper, "and by using two 75-ton jacks we have been able to partly straighten out these splices, but not altogether. These were probably in this condition when erected, but owing to the pressure of the bottom cover plate, it was then impossible to detect them, and it was only when this plate was removed for riveting that the inequality was noticed." The problem splices, reported McClure, were those between chords A3R and A4R, A7R and A8R, and A8R and A9R in the east truss of the anchor arm, and between A8L and A9L in the west truss. "You will note that this occurs only on inside ribs," commented McClure, "which are provided with but a single thin splice plate each. I think that a heavy plate on each side of these ribs, bolted up tight when chords were erected, would have remedied this, i.e., drawn the ribs together till the 'faced ends matched.'"[2]

McClure was only the first to dismiss the bridge's problems as some pre-existing condition, rather than the effect of loading. In any event, Cooper seemed unconcerned. "Make as good work of it as you can," he replied on June 17. "It is not serious. It would be well to draw attention to as much care as possible in future work to get the best results in matching all the members before the full strains are brought upon them."[3]

Early in August new and more serious problems developed as erection of the suspended span proceeded, adding still more load to the completed sections of the span.

McClure wrote Cooper on August 6 to advise of a misalignment found in the inside ribs at the splice between chords 8L and 7L in the west truss of the south cantilever arm as the splice was being riveted. "Owing to the limited space between the two inside ribs," McClure advised, "it would be impossible to jack this splice back, and as the condition is not nearly as bad at the top of the splice, we have proposed putting a diaphragm between the two inside ribs to cover the first five rivets up from the bottom on each side of the splice. . . . This provision, together with the top and bottom cover plates, should be sufficient to hold this splice against the thrust due to its being out of line, which thrust when under its maximum compressive stress I estimate at not over 60,000 pounds."[4]

McClure enclosed with his letter a sketch of the proposed work to correct the problem. At the same time Arthur Birks, the Phoenix company's young resident engineer, forwarded a copy of the proposed corrective measure to his superiors at Phoenixville. This time Cooper was much more concerned. "Method proposed by Quebec for splicing joints at lower 7 and 8 chords is not satisfactory," he wired the Phoenix company on August 8. "How did bend occur in both chords?"[5]

Cooper posed the same question in a letter to McClure the following day, in which he also outlined an alternate method of correcting the misalignment. This would involve the use of fifteen to twenty 1-inch bolts, threaded for nuts at both ends and passing through the two bent webs that would be used to pull them into proper line. Spacers and through bolts might be required to hold them in line, he commented, and some means would have to be taken to stiffen the outer web against bending when the bolts were tightened.

The same day John Deans, the Phoenix chief engineer, wired Cooper that Peter Szlapka had been at the site and would be back the next day with full information about the chord joint, after which he would write fully about the matter. Cooper replied the same day, outlining to Deans the same corrective proposal he had sent to McClure. Cooper, too, seemed to attribute the problem to a pre-existing condition, rather than to any effects of the loads on the members. "It is a mystery to me," his reply to Deans concluded, "how both these webs happened to be bent at one point and why it was not discovered sooner."[6]

Szlapka did not return to Phoenixville on Friday, August 10, as Deans had expected, and it was the following Monday before he reached the office and Deans was able to reply to Cooper. It was a reassuring response, and he, too, was convinced that the misalignment was something that had happened before the chord had been erected into the span.

"All ribs of the chord 7-L have a complete and full bearing on ribs of 8-L," he wrote to Cooper. "The bend was no doubt put in the rib in the shop, before facing and was probably done when pulling the ribs in line to make them agree with spacing of these ribs and the clearance between ribs, called for on the drawing. The bend being on only one rib of one chord, there being a full bearing over the entire rib, all splice plates being readily put in position, we do not think it necessary to put in the diaphragm suggested by the erection department."[7]

Deans' confidence, as it turned out, could not have been based upon anything that Peter Szlapka saw at the bridge site. Szlapka later stated that he had not examined the splice in question during his visit and, further, that during three visits to the site, he had never looked at any of the chords. In any event, Theodore Cooper was far from satisfied with this response from Deans.

"The information regarding chord splice 7 and 8-L, is so different from the dimension sketch sent by Mr. McClure, I can take no action on this matter till the exact facts are presented," he wrote on August 13. "Please have your resident engineer and Mr. McClure re-examine this joint and send the exact condition of this rib, as to the amount of the bends and relation of the bearing surfaces to each other. I don't see how one rib being bent, only, as stated in your letter, there can be a complete and full bearing of these ribs. Neither can I understand how pulling the ribs into line at the shop could bend it out of line."[8]

McClure wrote to Cooper again on August 12, expressing doubt about the various theories concerning how the chord members could have been bent prior to erection. "One

The south end of the bridge looked like this on August 14, 1907. The 250-ton small traveler had been erected on the top chords of the suspended span and was ready to continue its erection, while the large traveler stood ready to be dismantled and shifted to the north shore. By this time the anchor arm had lifted off its temporary supports, and the latter had been removed. Although nothing looks amiss here, the engineers were already growing worried about some ominous bends in the lower chord members. Hagley Museum and Library (Neg. 71.MSS.916.3956).

thing I am reasonably sure of," he wrote, "and that is that the bend has occurred since the chord has been under stress, and was not present when the chords were placed."[9]

McClure went on to report to Cooper the settlement of a three-day strike by the erection workers. Those opposed to the settlement, he reported, were leaving; and the work force was greatly reduced on both sides of the river. His letter concluded with the disturbing news that the splice between chords 8L and 9L on the west truss of the south cantilever span was now in the same condition as that between chords 7L and 8L. In this case the bend was only 5/16 inch, while that between chords 7L and 8L was reported as being ¾ inch. "This is the same rib," reported McClure, "and the bend is in the same direction as that reported for the other splice."[10]

By this time McClure had concluded, correctly as it turned out, that the bends had occurred after the chord was placed under stress. But still no one was able to see that the unthinkable was happening. The Quebec Bridge was slowly beginning to collapse.

Cooper was not satisfied with any of the explanations for the bends and developed a new theory of his own. "None of the explanations for the bent chord stand the test of logic," he wrote to McClure on August 15. "I have evolved another theory, which is a possible if not the probable one. These chords have been hit by those suspended beams used during the erection, while they were being put in place or taken down. Examine if you cannot find evidence of the blow, and also make inquiries of the men in charge."[11]

On August 16 McClure reported to Cooper the results of his joint re-examination with Birks of the problem at the joint between chords 7L and 8L in the west truss of the cantilever arm. He and Birks were in agreement that the condition was as he had originally reported it to Cooper on August 6. Mr. Deans had simply taken a different meaning from Birks' original report to him. McClure also re-emphasized his belief that the bends had occurred after the members were erected into the bridge.

"Aside from the fact that it would be hardly probable that these two ribs of different chord sections should be bent the same way, exactly the same amount in the shops to dimensions ½-inch to ¾-inch less than called for," he wrote, "I am reasonably sure, as I said before, that this condition did not exist before the erection of these chords, as I have personally inspected every member yet erected in this bridge thus far, except the bottom chords of anchor arms, on the cars just before the erection, looking particularly for bends in ribs of compression members, and wherever discovered have taken measurements of the amounts and recorded them. If these ribs then had been this much out of line before erecting, it would be well nigh impossible to miss seeing them. Consequently the only way the bend could have occurred, it seems to me, is that reported in my letter of August 12."[12]

On August 15, 1907, E. R. Kinloch, the Quebec Bridge & Railway Company's inspector of erection, climbed to the dizzying height of more than 400 feet above the St. Lawrence to photograph progress on the erection. From the top of the large traveler, he recorded this view to the east showing the top chord eyebars and lateral bracing of the south cantilever span and the ornate finials that topped the main posts. National Archives of Canada (Neg. PA108745).

In a second photograph, facing to the west from atop the main posts, Kinloch recorded this view of the cantilever arm top chords and lateral bracing. Through the large traveler can be seen the small traveler, which by this time had taken over erection of the suspended span. National Archives of Canada (Neg. PA108746).

From a vantage point on the top of the large traveler, a photographer recorded this view of the small traveler in the process of erecting the south end of the suspended span on August 15, 1907. National Archives of Canada (Neg. PA108764).

Deans received a copy of the same report on the bends in the two chords and wrote to Cooper on August 20, acknowledging that both chords had one bent rib, and not just one as he had initially understood.

It was now two weeks since the problem with chords 7L and 8L in the cantilever arm had been discovered and more than a week since the similar problem in chords 8L and 9L had been discovered. Still, no corrective action had been initiated, nor had a course of action even been decided upon. Over the next week, Cooper and Deans exchanged letters. Cooper restated his theory that the members could have been bent by a blow during erection and his proposal for removing the bends by the use of long bolts. On August 26, having learned from McClure that he could find no evidence of the bent ribs having been struck, Cooper again wrote to Deans. "This only makes the mystery the deeper," he wrote, "for I do not see how otherwise the ribs could have been bent. When convenient I would like to discuss the best means of getting these ribs into safe condition to do their proper work."[13] Deans remained unconcerned about the problem. A day later he responded that he would have Szlapka call on Cooper at his first opportunity to discuss the situation.

Meanwhile, still more problems were developing at the bridge site. On August 20 E. R. Kinloch, the Quebec Bridge & Railway Company's inspector, discovered that chord 8R

in the cantilever arm was bent and that chords 9R and 10R also showed some distortion. Both problems were called to Birks' attention, but neither man felt they were important. B. A. Yenser, the erection foreman, was also informed of the conditions; but Norman McClure, Cooper's representative on the site, was ill and did not see the two problem areas until August 23. For several days Kinloch visited chord 8R and imagined that the bend was becoming greater, with all four ribs bent, but not in the same way.

On August 23 still another problem was found at the splice between chords 5R and 6R of the cantilever arm. One of the center ribs was found to be out of alignment by ½ inch at the bottom, the offset reducing to nothing at the top. At about 9 a.m. on Tuesday, August 27, the situation rapidly began moving toward crisis. A slight bend had been discovered several days earlier in chord A9L of the anchor arm and had been placed under observation. This was where some of the first misalignments had been noted in June. Inspecting the chord that morning, Kinloch found that the bend had greatly increased. Yenser and Birks were called over to look at it, and the three men spent close to half an hour examining the chord and several other lower chord members.

Yenser was particularly concerned, asserting that the bend had not been there before and that he would not put up any more iron until he found out what the problem was. "Birks kind of laughed at him," Kinloch said later, "and said that he had better wait until he found out, and that when he was condemning the chord he was condemning the whole bridge."[14] Kinloch, Birks, and McClure then measured the exact extent of the deflections. The results were ominous indeed. A rib of chord A9L that had been only ¾ inch out of line a little over a week before was now 2¼ inches out of line. All of the ribs in chords A9L and A9R were bent in the same direction, while the ribs of the adjacent chord A8R were bent in reverse curves.

The engineers, inspectors, and the erection foreman debated what to do about the problem. No one thought that disaster was at hand, but all except Birks believed the problem was serious. Despite the measurements, despite Kinloch's conviction that the bends had greatly increased, and despite the insistence of Mr. Clark, an inspector at the Chaudière

By August 23 the erection crew had completed the first three panels of the suspended span and was ready to move the little traveler forward to begin the next. Dismantling of the large traveler had begun but had not yet progressed very far. Hagley Museum and Library (Neg. 71.MSS.916.3958).

By the end of August 1907, substantial progress had been made for beginning erection of the north end of the structure during the 1908 construction season. Well over half of the erection scaffolding for the north anchor arm had been completed between the anchor and main piers when this view was taken on August 27. Hagley Museum and Library (Neg. 71.MSS.916.3959).

storage yard, that the chord had been absolutely straight when it left the yard, the Phoenix company's young resident engineer could not be convinced that the bends had recently developed. After all, engineers of great experience and wide reputation had designed the bridge, and he knew that the stresses in the members were still well below what they had been designed to withstand. Yenser and Kinloch suggested that McClure and Birks go to New York and Phoenixville for advice, but the two were reluctant, fearing their concerns would be laughed at. Yenser decided to stop any further erection until he could refer the matter to Phoenixville. Aside from that, no other action was taken until Edward Hoare could be consulted, and this did not happen until fully twelve hours after the problem had been discovered. To avoid reporting any particulars over the telephone, it had been decided that McClure would go to Hoare's home in Québec to inform him of the situation. Even then, reluctant to make any decision himself, Hoare merely approved the idea that McClure should go to New York with all possible information to seek the advice of Theodore Cooper.

While all of this was going on, great pains were taken to avoid alarming the workmen on the bridge. A riveting gang at work on the anchor arm had noticed the bends, and the erecting crew was already beginning to show some anxiety.

By the end of the day on August 27, McClure had reported the situation by letter to Cooper, advising him that erection would not proceed until a response had been received from him and Phoenixville. Birks had sent the same information to his superiors at Phoenixville. Wednesday, August 28, was a day of waiting and uncertainty at the bridge site as officials waited for some word from New York or Phoenixville. That morning Yenser had changed his mind and decided to continue erection work, and the men were uneasy and alarmed.

There is some evidence that Yenser himself had grave doubts about resuming the work. One workman, D. B. Haley, later commented that Yenser had moved the traveler out on the advice of Birks and against his own judgment and had sent one carload of steel stringers back to the storage yard. Haley also said he had heard Yenser tell Birks: "Why don't they let me take down that traveler and get that load off before we get more steel on?"[15]

In any event, before resuming work Yenser had first sought Hoare's approval. "I requested him to continue," wrote Hoare in a letter to Cooper that day, "as the moral effect of holding up the work would be very bad on all concerned and might also stop the work for this season on account of losing the men."[16] Hoare spent much of the day at the bridge site seeking some evidence of what had caused the bends. He discussed with others at the site some ideas of how the chords might be braced but decided to take no action until Cooper had been heard from. Hoare, too, seemed convinced that any defects in the chord had been there all along and outlined in his letter to Cooper his own theory concerning the bend in the chord. This, he suggested, might have been the result of its having been dropped in the storage yard in April 1905, when an angle at the north end splice was broken and several lacing bars twisted. Although these were all renewed and the ribs reported to be perfectly straight, damage could have been done when the middle of the chord deflected downward in falling. "Perhaps the stress in this chord has made previous defects more pronounced," he suggested to Cooper.[17]

The work force at the bridge was becoming increasingly uneasy as the engineers, inspectors, and foremen gathered to discuss the situation. Many had seen the obvious bends in the anchor arm lower chord, and those that hadn't had heard about them from their mates. That evening, after work had ended for the day, a number of the men went down to see for themselves. Among them were bridge workers D. B. Haley, president of the union local; George Cook, the union secretary; Tom Callahan; and Harry Briggs. "I found that it was bulging out on both sides," Haley later recalled. "All the webs and the chord. There were four webs and this chord, two outside ones and two center ones and they were all giving way. The two outside ones were going out."[18]

A few of the men became so uneasy about the situation that they laid off work the next day. One of them was John E. Splicer, who had

Made on August 28 by Frank E. Cudworth, the Phoenix Bridge Company's resident engineer in charge of instrument work, this may be the last photograph taken of the south end of the bridge before the terrible disaster late on the afternoon of August 29. The little traveler had been moved forward, ready to begin erection of the fourth panel of the suspended center span. Dismantling of the heavy large traveler had still made little progress. National Archives of Canada (Neg. PA29229).

been working on disassembly of the large traveler and who had talked with a group of the Caughnawaga bridge workers that evening about the troubling lower chord. "They said there was a place in that chord," Splicer said later, "I do not know whereabouts, where it was bent, and they were trying to jack it together, and they could not jack the plates together and riveted it up the way it was."[19]

That Wednesday afternoon, McClure had departed on a one o'clock train to meet with Cooper in New York the following morning. Birks reported further to his superiors at Phoenixville by letter, providing further observations about the nature of the bends, still maintaining his view that they had been there before erection. Work continued all that day and into Thursday, by which time the small traveler had been moved forward to begin the erection of the fourth sub-panel of the suspended truss. The completed structure now projected more than 730 feet out over the river from the centerline of the main pier.

On the morning of the 29th, Birks' report of the 27th was received at Phoenixville. Deans, Szlapka, and A. B. Milliken, the company's superintendent of erection, met to discuss the report and consider what to do. They finally decided it was safe to continue erection, and this was relayed to the site in telephone calls from Milliken to Yenser and Deans to Birks. Szlapka instructed Birks to inform Hoare that they had determined that the bends had been in the chords before they left Phoenixville. Deans also wired a reassuring message to Hoare: "The chords are in exact condition they left Phoenixville in and now have much less than maximum load."[20] Deans later maintained that this message did not refer to the chords measured on the 27th, but even if this were true, it is easy to see why Deans' message, together with the telephone call he had received earlier from Birks, had greatly relieved Hoare's concerns. "I felt quite comfortable that day about it," Hoare said later. "I knew it could not be long before the matter would be taken up."[21]

With these assurances in hand, the anxiety at the bridge site subsided as erection work continued. There was no evidence that any further measurements were made to check any movement of the suspect chords in the anchor arm.

Theodore Cooper, however, was not nearly as sanguine about the situation. When Cooper arrived at his office at 45 Broadway about 11 a.m. on the 29th, McClure was waiting for him. After a brief discussion of the situation, he wired Phoenixville: "Add no more load to bridge until after due consideration of facts. McClure will be over at five o'clock."[22]

Although they knew the small traveler had been moved out on the suspended span, neither Cooper nor McClure were aware that erection had resumed at the bridge site, and Cooper later explained that he felt the desired action would be obtained more promptly by telegraphing Phoenixville rather than the project site. McClure had promised to wire Kinloch at the site regarding Cooper's decision, but in the hurry to get to Phoenixville, he failed to do so.

Cooper's telegram reached Phoenixville at 1:15 p.m. but went unheeded in Deans' absence. Charles E. Connard, Deans' private secretary, later first denied any knowledge of the telegram but then admitted he had seen it. "It came late in the afternoon, and gave no warning to call the men off, so we held it for Mr. Deans," said Connard. "Comparatively little importance was attached to it."[23]

Deans returned to his office at about 3 p.m. and found the telegram waiting for him. Even then, Deans took no action other than to arrange for Szlapka and Milliken to meet with McClure when he arrived later in the afternoon. Following McClure's arrival at about 5:15 p.m., the men discussed the situation briefly before deciding to postpone any action until the following morning, when Birks' letter of August 28 was expected to arrive.

At almost exactly the same moment, as the erecting crew neared the end of its day's work at 5:30 p.m., the entire 19,000-ton south half of the Quebec Bridge fell without warning into the St. Lawrence with a thunderous roar that was heard as far away as downtown Québec, six miles downstream. Some of the survivors later reported that there had not been any loud sound initially; the first sign of the collapse had been a sinking of the bridge beneath them. The bridge fell almost vertically, at first slowly and then with a rush. The collapse was followed by the rise of a great cloud of dust and spray that obscured everything for a time.

Several witnesses distinctly remembered the sound of hundreds of rivet heads shearing off as the structure collapsed. John Montour, a Caughnawaga ironworker who had just been sent off the bridge early to buy food for his crew, could not see the collapse but heard it. "I could hear the sounds of the rivet heads shearing and popping like gun fire," he recalled many years later. "Then there was this tremor like an earthquake and a roar. Then this bad grinding sound and a thunder as the bridge fell into the water."[24]

Ulric Barthe, secretary of the bridge company, who had just left the structure with a party of visitors, described the sound of the collapse as "a great, prolonged and persistent thunderclap filling the air, followed by a sinister crackling similar to the patter of machine guns in battle. After the dreadful tumult of the collapse there followed what seemed, by contrast, a great silence, profound and mournful, as if all of nature was hushed and repulsed in horror."[25]

E. R. Kinloch, the Phoenix company's erection inspector, had just left the bridge and observed the fall from the centerline of the track, opposite his office. The portal posts of the bridge seemed to tremble and then sank down, as he put it, "as if they had been ice and were melting off at the bottom." The sight was too much for Kinloch to bear. "About that time," he later recalled, "I turned my back to it and did not look at it any more."[26]

The anchor arm broke near its center—one witness described its first movement as a rise near the point of the break—and then fell almost without movement to the right or

left. It was later determined that the collapse began with the buckling of the bent bottom chord member A9L, followed almost immediately, as the load transferred to the opposite member in the right truss, by a similar failure of chord member A9R. Both chords were found buckled into a sharply bent "S" shape in the wreckage.

As the bottom chords of the anchor arm gave way, no longer balancing the enormous lateral forces from the bottom chords of the cantilever arm, the bottom of the tower over the main pier was forced inward, while the top of the tower fell outward with the cantilever arm. Both the cantilever arm and the suspended span fell as a whole, the outer end of the cantilever arm swinging slightly to the east as it fell. The large erection traveler fell together with the cantilever arm.

The anchor arm lay exposed on the shore of the river in a great tangled heap of wreckage. "Nearly 15,000 tons of steel fell, and the principal members, which were the largest ever fabricated, are twisted, bent and broken so as to be hardly recognizable," reported *The Railroad Gazette*.[27] "Bending, crushing, buckling, twisting, shearing, and tearing are exemplified in the wildest variety of forms," commented *Engineering News*.[28]

Most of the wreckage of the cantilever arm and suspended span lay below water in the deep channel of the St. Lawrence. The largely intact eyebar tension members of the top chords of both anchor and cantilever spans were draped across the tangled wreckage of the anchor span, passed over the tops of the wrecked towers, whose ornamental finials protruded above the water about 100 feet outward of the main piers and then disappeared into the deep water.

"Bending, crushing, buckling, twisting, shearing, and tearing are exemplified in the wildest variety of forms,'" commented *Engineering News* of the scene of destruction after the collapse. This view of the wreckage was taken from the end of the south approach span the day after the disaster. Despite the severity of the collapse, the top chord eyebars survived almost intact, with only one broken bar. Smithsonian Institution.

Judging from the accounts of the survivors, it had taken no more than ten to fifteen seconds for the span to fall. Ingwall Hall, a steelworker who was standing on top of the small traveler at the outer end of the cantilever arm some 300 feet above the river, recalled a loud grinding noise and a trembling of the metal scaffolding of the traveler and then falling with the traveler towards the river so fast his eyes watered. The last thing Hall remembered was a tremendous bursting splash as the bridge hit the river until he found himself floating on the surface, minus two fingers.[29] Two other men, who had been working on the small traveler at the outer end of the cantilever arm and survived the fall, erecting gang members Charles Davis and D. B. Haley, remembered the steelwork of the bridge falling even faster than they did as the span fell.

"I was on he extreme end of it and the first thing I knew I caught myself going through the air," Haley later recalled. "I realized that the iron fell very much faster than I did and left me falling through the air. The next thing I remember I was deep in water. In a short time I came up—I swam up—some planks came up around me, I got on the planks and was rescued by a boat on the other side of the river twenty minutes or so afterwards, or as soon as they could get over."[30] J. J. Nance, who was running the electric hoisting engine on the small traveler, remembered only how fast the bridge fell as he went into the water, still holding the controller handle of his engine as he went to the bottom with it.[31]

Among the dead was the crew of a locomotive that was pushing two carloads of steel out to the traveler at the time of the collapse. As the bridge dropped, the train rolled to the end of the span and plunged into the river, carrying engineer John McNaughton and fireman Phileas Couture to their deaths.

On the anchor arm of the span, Delphis Lajeunesse was preparing to hoist a box of bolts up to his brother Eugene, who remarked that it was time to quit, when the bridge fell. Delphis rode the girder he was standing on 150 feet down to the shore of the river, where he watched Eugene crawl, injured but alive, from the wreckage.[32] One of the few men to get off the bridge before it fell was the timekeeper, Joseph Huot, who was on his way out onto the bridge when he heard the sound of a compressed air line pulling apart and the crack of the bridge collapsing. In the few seconds before the collapse was complete, Huot managed to turn and run some 75 feet to reach safety at the shore end of the anchor span, running uphill as the collapsing anchor arm began to tip toward the river.[33]

Percy Wilson, a laborer whose job was delivering rivets to the riveting crews, had just left the bridge when he heard a loud noise and turned to watch Huot run to safety as the bridge fell. "It took about five or six seconds," Wilson said later, "and then all I seen was floating timber on the river and a mass of steel was between the piers."[34]

A riveter named Alexander Beauvais, one of the few Caughnawaga bridgemen to survive the collapse, later told the Royal Commission investigating the collapse a particularly vivid story of his experience immediately preceding and during the fall of the bridge. Beauvais had been at work inside one of the bottom chords and gave evidence concerning two broken rivets he had found about half an hour before the collapse. "Can you account for these two particular rivets being broken? There were other rivets that may have been strained in the same way; why should they not have broken?" asked Henry Holgate, chairman of the Commission. "Of course, I did not test them," replied Beauvais. "If I had I would know just exactly what was broken and what was not, but while I was driving two or three other rivets, after that I found the first one broken off. He said, 'There is another one broken,' and I tested it with a drift pin and it was broken off straight. You could turn the one end and the other end would be still. It was impossible to pull it out because it was plugged in there. There were two rivets broken. I called Mr. Meredith, the rivet boss, and also to see that the ribs were bending in. He looked down there and told me that it was not any worse than the others. He did not think it serious."

"The ribs were bending in?" asked Prof. John Galbraith, one of the Commission members.

"Yes," replied Beauvais.

"Having got to the point where you saw these two or more rivets broken, do you recollect anything between that and the collapse of the bridge?" Holgate asked.

"I guess not," said Beauvais. "I was driving rivets, and I was about to shoot another rivet when the crash came down. . . . I was right inside the chord, and I had to come out underneath because I had to pry the plate off. . . . When this chord landed it did not land on the ground. It stood three or four feet in the air. I held on to the chord and never touched the ground."

"You were in what chord?" asked Holgate.

"No. 10, Montréal side," said Beauvais. "As soon as everything was still, I came out. It was easy to stay there because I was tight in there. I had one leg broken and my nose was broken."[35]

These men were among the very few survivors of the collapse. Of eighty-six men at work on the structure at the time, only eleven survived. Resident engineer Arthur Birks, who had just ridden out on the bridge on a carload of steel, went down with the bridge. Erection foreman Yenser fell to his death with the erection traveler. Assistant foremen John Worley and J. W. Aderholdt died with the bridge, too. W. W. Waitneight, the chief timekeeper, was the Phoenix Bridge Company's senior surviving supervisor, and it fell to him to organize the rescue effort, account for the men, and telephone the terrible news to Phoenixville.

Altogether, seventeen Americans died, while the fifty-eight Canadian victims included thirty-three of the Caughnawaga steel workers. The youngest victim was 14-year-old Stanley Wilson of nearby St-Romuald, who had been working on the bridge as a water boy for 10 cents an hour.

Moments after the bridge fell, workmen erecting scaffolding for the north end of the bridge took to the river in boats to rescue survivors. The steamer *Glenmont* had just passed the bridge when the collapse occurred, throwing water over the ship's bridge. The captain immediately lowered boats and began a search for survivors. There were few to be found.

John Montour, the young Caughnawaga ironworker who had been sent off the bridge to get food for his crew just before the collapse, was distraught. "When I had figured out what had happened, "he recalled later, "I didn't know what to do. I had to find out how many people from town were hurt, but they wouldn't let us near the site. Everybody in my crew died; including my mother's brother, my brother and cousin. It was bad. I knew I had to find another Indian. I finally met Joe Regis and we went to find a phone, to call town."[36]

Aside from a half-dozen men who somehow survived the plunge of the cantilever arm into the deep waters of the St. Lawrence, searchers in the river found only bodies. Most of the victims were carried to the bottom of the river with the wreckage. If the falling steel hadn't killed them, they were trapped in the wreckage and quickly drowned. By the following morning, only sixteen bodies had been recovered.

On the south bank of the river, where the anchor arm fell on the foreshore between the edge of the river and the steep wooded cliff, eight injured survivors were taken from the wreckage and rushed to the hospital at Lévis. Close to a dozen injured men, trapped in wreckage that had fallen on the tidal flats at the edge of the river, died particularly tortuous deaths. At about 6 p.m. the tide began to flood in the river, gradually rising some 13 feet and drowning the trapped men. There was nothing the rescuers gathered at the scene could do. There were no cutting torches or other heavy equipment available that was capable of freeing the men from the huge, twisted steel sections. From sunset until the moon finally rose about 10 p.m., the scene was lighted only by a few lanterns and bonfires that had been lit along the cliff. One of the first to arrive at the scene was Father A. E. McGuire, from the nearby parish of Sillery, who lowered himself down the cliff on a rope and waded out among the wreckage to give the doomed men the last rites.

News of the disaster traveled rapidly. Many of the men were from, or boarded at, the nearby towns of New Liverpool and St-Romuald, just down the south bank of the river, and by 7 p.m. a crowd of close to 300 distraught wives and children had completely blocked passage on the Garneau bridge, which crossed the Chaudière River where it joined the St.

Lawrence, just below the bridge site. Hundreds of other onlookers had soon been drawn to the scene.

New Liverpool and St-Romuald were hard hit by the disaster; eighteen of the victims came from the two towns. The Hardy family of New Liverpool lost 46-year-old Victor Hardy and his nephews Philip, Michael, and James. Michael and James were brothers.

But nowhere did news of the tragedy fall harder than it did on the little village of Caughnawaga, near Montréal. Only five of the thirty-eight men from the village on the bridge survived, and two of these were injured. The first news came in a telephone call to the Caughnawaga postmaster at about 6:30 that evening and soon had reached every corner of the village.

Early the next morning, about thirty men and women from the village left for Québec, returning the following morning with eight bodies, all that had been recovered. There was hardly a family in Caughnawaga that was untouched by the tragedy. Hardest hit of all was the family of Pierre D'Aillebout, which lost four sons, an uncle, a cousin, and a brother-in-law. Among the dead were three members of the Deer family, and two each from the Mitchell and Jocks families. Families of as many as seven or eight children were left destitute by the disaster. Altogether, twenty-four women were widowed and fifty-two children from the village were left fatherless by the disaster. Among the victims were most of the members of the village's lacrosse team.

News of the collapse reached Phoenixville by telephone that evening. When he was informed of the disaster, Peter Szlapka collapsed. Norman McClure telephoned the news to Cooper in New York at about 9 p.m. and stopped by to see him briefly the next day on his way back to Québec. He was asked later if the consulting engineer had expressed any opinion about the collapse. "He said: 'Well, it's that chord,'" McClure recalled. "I only saw him a few minutes; he was not feeling very good."[37]

There remained now the question of why and how the bridge had collapsed.

Just a few days before the disaster, members of the Caughnawaga lacrosse team, all iron-workers on the bridge, posed for this team photograph after a practice game, with the bridge as a backdrop. Eight of these fifteen men were killed in the accident, while one was injured. Kanien'kehaka Raotitiohkwa Cultural Center.

In this view of the collapse facing eastward from the south bank of the river can be seen the wreckage of the ornate south portal, which fell away from the approach span as the anchor arm broke near the center and fell. National Archives of Canada (Neg. PA 20612).

CHAPTER 6

AFTERMATH

THE FIRST FUNERALS WERE HELD ON MONDAY, SEPTEMBER 2. AT CAUGHNAWAGA THE crowd overflowed the little parish church, where Archbishop of Montréal Bruchesi presided over an emotional funeral service for the eight men whose bodies had been recovered. An Iroquois choir rendered liturgical chants in their native language, and the bodies were then carried in a procession to the churchyard cemetery, where the men were buried in a common grave. The crowd joined in chorus as two Iroquois sang a song of the dead for their men.

That same day, Sir Louis A. Jetté, lieutenant-governor of the province of Québec, and Québec Premier Lomer Gouin led a long funeral procession through the streets of New Liverpool and St-Romuald that bore the bodies of Victor, James, and Philip Hardy and 16-year-old Wilfrid Proulx, the only dead from the two villages that had yet been recovered. Following a funeral service at the parish church of St-Romuald, the bodies were carried to the parish cemetery, where they were buried in a common grave.

The body of Chester A. Meredith, the only American victim yet recovered from the wreckage, was sent home to Columbus, Ohio. Accompanied by his brother, the remains of the 26-year-old ironworker foreman were taken to his parents' home on Wesley Avenue after arrival in Columbus at noon Monday. The Tuesday afternoon funeral at the Fifth Avenue United Brethren Church was attended in a body by the local branch of the Bridge and Structural Iron Workers.

The search for bodies went on for several weeks. Two days after the collapse, Montréal jeweler John E. Birks, Arthur Birks' uncle, placed a notice in *Le Soleil* at Québec, offering a $300 reward for recovery of his nephew's body, and the Phoenix Bridge Company offered a $50 reward for each body recovered. Boatmen in large numbers took to the St. Lawrence to conduct the grim search.

A total of eighteen bodies had been recovered from the river or the wreckage of the bridge immediately following the accident. Gradually, the St. Lawrence gave up more. Five days after the collapse, the body of Honore Beaudry was recovered from the wreckage. On September 7, more than a week after the accident, three more bodies were found floating in the St. Lawrence opposite Île d'Orléans, some twelve miles below the bridge site. The next morning John Worley's body was found at St-Joseph, below Lévis. That afternoon, three more bodies were found in the river not far from the bridge, while a fourth turned up in Gilmours Cove, below Lévis. The next day the body of George Cook, a New York ironworker, was recovered opposite Sillery. On September 10 seven more bodies were pulled from the river near the bridge site, and an eighth was recovered near Cap-Blanc,

A view of the wreckage taken northward across the St. Lawrence shows the collapsed structure draped across the south main pier. Across the river can be seen the north main pier. In the foreground is the undamaged south approach span. National Archives of Canada (Neg. PA 20614).

below the bridge site. The next day two young boatmen out searching the river found the body of Arthur Birks at the same location. On September 12 three more bodies were found, one of them at a point opposite St-Laurent on Île d'Orléans, some twenty miles from the bridge site. One of them was that of American ironworker Joseph Ward, who had fallen from the bridge about a week before the accident, and for whose body a $200 reward had been offered.

By this time the river had yielded up the bodies of thirty-five victims. But some forty more would never be recovered, and their remains are likely still there today, entombed with the twisted steel wreckage of the bridge deep below the surface of the St. Lawrence.

As the additional bodies were recovered, they were sent home for burial. There were more funerals at the St-Romuald parish church. John Worley's body was sent home to Pennsylvania, and that of George Cook to New York. The bodies of four more Indian ironworkers made the journey home to Caughnawaga. Accompanied by a brother and sister, both of whom lived in Montréal, the body of Arthur Birks was returned home to Peoria, Illinois, where grieving parents buried their youngest son in Springdale Cemetery on September 14.

The first lawsuit was initiated on September 3, when Zephirin Lafrance filed suit against the Phoenix Bridge Company, asking $15,000 in the death of his 18-year-old son. By September 9 a total of eight legal actions had been filed by relatives of the victims, asking anywhere from $10,000 to $20,000 in damages.

Almost immediately after the accident, the various participants in design and construction of the bridge had begun to distance themselves as much as they could from any responsibility for the disaster. On the afternoon of August 28, as the men at the bridge site were attempting to determine what was wrong and what should be done about it, Edward Hoare had written to Theodore Cooper informing him, among other matters, that he had been approached by B. A. Yenser, who had asked if it would be all right to move the traveler forward and continue with the erection. "After ascertaining that the effects from moving the traveller ahead and proceeding with the next panel would be so insignificant I requested him to continue," wrote Hoare, "as the moral effect of holding up the work would be very bad on all concerned and might also stop the work for this season on account of losing the men."[1]

On September 2, after the collapse, Hoare wrote Cooper again to "correct a misstatement" in his letter of August 28, "which was written late and very hastily," and offered a revised version in which he maintained that he had not requested that the erection work be continued but had merely acquiesced to it. "As stated in my last letter, strictly speaking, I did not request the foreman to continue the work," wrote Hoare, "as he had already done so; at the same time we thought there was no immediate danger in adding so small a load."[2]

Press accounts of the disaster made much of Theodore Cooper's somewhat innocuous "add no more load to bridge till after due consideration of facts" telegram of August 29 to Deans at Phoenixville and its delayed delivery. "Bridge Warning Was Just Too Late," headlined the *New York Times*,[3] while a *Chicago Tribune* headline asked "Warned Too Late of Bridge Peril?"[4]

Comments to reporters by Cooper encouraged this kind of speculation. "Thursday morning my inspector came down to my office, and told me that things did not look well for the bridge," Cooper told a reporter for the *New York Times*. "He thought that it ought to be looked into. Immediately I wired the man in charge of the work there to get off the bridge at once and stay off it until it could be examined."[5]

In another interview Cooper carefully explained to a reporter for the *New York Times* that, as consulting engineer, he had no authority to order the men off the bridge. "I did not have that right; I am the consulting engineer only," Cooper was reported as saying. "And upon the report of my inspector I wired to the offices of the Phoenix Bridge Company, at Phoenixville, Penn., and warned them. I had no right to wire the men actually at work on the bridge."[6]

At Phoenixville, Phoenix Bridge Company General Superintendent William H. Reeves explained why no action had been taken in response to Cooper's telegram. The fact that the message was not explicit in advising the calling off of the men on the structure is assigned as the reason for the failure of other officials to act at once during the absence of Chief Engineer Deans, he told reporters. There was no suspicion of any immediate danger, he added.

"There was no negligence on the part of any one in the matter," said Reeves. "The message was not considered an urgent one at all. Had there been any thought of the lives of the men being in danger every effort would have been made to have the work stopped at once."[7]

Investigations of the accident were launched almost immediately. The day after the collapse, Prime Minister Laurier named three civil engineers, Henry Holgate, John G. G.

Another view of the collapse scene from the south shore shows the wreckage from a vantage point just west of the approach span. Despite the enormous force of the collapse of some 19,000 tons of steel, both the south anchor and main piers came through the disaster essentially undamaged. Smithsonian Institution.

This view of the wreckage from the south main pier facing southward shows how the structure fell almost vertically along its center-line. Buckled into a sharply bent "S" shape and buried deep under the wreckage in the foreground were the two anchor arm bottom chord sections, A9L and A9R, whose failure initiated the collapse. National Archives of Canada (Neg. C9766).

Kerry, and John Galbraith, to a commission of enquiry that would conduct a thorough investigation of the disaster; and by an order-in-council of August 31, the governor general empowered the three as a Royal Commission. Holgate and Kerry reached the bridge site on August 30, the day after the collapse, while John Galbraith arrived from Toronto to join them the following Wednesday. The men immediately began examining the wreckage of the bridge and supervising the marking and photographing of each member of the structure. By Saturday morning, August 31, the Québec coroner, Dr. G. W. Jolicoeur, had empanelled a coroner's jury, which that same day conducted inquests for fifteen victims of the collapse whose bodies had been recovered, and that afternoon visited the ruins of the bridge.

The principal engineers and builders for the project quickly gathered at Québec to view the wreckage and to help determine what had gone wrong. Matthew J. Butler, the deputy minister and chief engineer of the Department of Railways and Canals; Collingwood Schreiber, the former chief engineer; and masonry contractor M. P. Davis arrived from Ottawa. John Deans, Peter Szlapka, and A. B. Milliken left Phoenixville for Québec on Sunday. Theodore Cooper, too ill to make the trip, sent his assistant, Bernt Berger, from New York.

Tuesday, September 3, was a busy day. In the afternoon shareholders of the Quebec Bridge Company gathered for their annual meeting. An annual report prepared the previous week had been discarded and replaced by a hasty report prepared by Chief Engineer Hoare, outlining the particulars of the accident. The only bright spot in this otherwise depressing report was Hoare's advice that the bridge piers had come through the accident unscathed; the effects of the accident were confined to the steel work alone.

That morning Coroner Jolicoeur had opened a coroner's inquest into the circumstances of the accident. Surviving workmen, the engineers, and President Parent were questioned at length over the next nine days. At the end the inquest shed no light at all on the cause of the accident. The jury, after an hour's deliberation on September 12, reached this verdict in the death of Zephirin Lafrance:

"That the deceased died from wounds and nervous shock caused by the fall of the Quebec bridge, but we believe it our duty to declare that, taking into consideration the evidence heard during the inquest, all the necessary precautions were taken for the construction of the bridge without danger."[8] The verdict applied equally to all victims of the disaster.

Far more important to understanding what had happened was the work of the Royal Commission. The three engineers appointed by the governor general were well chosen for their task, and the thoroughness and objectivity of their inquiry and report stand even today as models of their kind.

Montréal civil engineer Henry Holgate, who was elected chairman of the commission, was an engineer of broad experience who was a member of both the Canadian Society of Civil Engineers and the American Society of Civil Engineers. A 44-year-old native of Milton, Ontario, Holgate had been apprenticed at the age of 15 to Colonel Fred W. Cumberland in the construction of the Northern Railway of Canada in Ontario. After some sixteen years in railway construction and bridge and structural design, Holgate moved to Montréal in 1894 and spent several years in construction and operation of electric railways. In 1901 he entered into an engineering partnership with Robert E. Ross largely devoted to the design and construction of hydro-electric plants. Just a year earlier, Holgate had been appointed by the Dominion government to investigate and report concerning a novel hydraulic lift lock being constructed on the Trent Canal at Peterborough, Ontario.

John George Gale Kerry of Campbellford, Ontario, was a 39-year-old civil engineer and educator and a member of the Canadian Society of Civil Engineers. A native of Montréal and an engineering graduate of McGill University, Kerry had worked in railroad surveying and engineering in Canada, the United States, and England before joining the applied science faculty at McGill in 1896, while continuing his engineering practice as a consultant to the Grand Trunk. Shortly before his appointment to the commission, Kerry had left Montréal to enter private engineering practice as a partner in the Toronto firm of Smith, Kerry & Chace.

John Galbraith was a prominent Toronto civil engineer and engineering educator. Born in Montréal in 1846, Galbraith had moved with his family to Ontario at an early age. In 1868 he graduated from the University of Toronto in mathematics and began an engineering career under George A. Stewart, then the chief engineer of the Midland Railway in Ontario. Over the next decade, Galbraith returned to the University of Toronto to complete a master's degree and then worked for a time on surveys for the Canadian Pacific main line before taking up his life's work in engineering education. In 1878 Galbraith was a forceful advocate for the reorganization of technical education in Ontario, and he was among the first faculty appointed to a new School of Practical Science at Toronto, serving as chairman of engineering. In 1889 he became principal of the school and was appointed dean in 1906, when the school was incorporated into the University of Toronto as its Faculty of Applied Sciences and Engineering. One of the leaders of his time in advancing Canadian engineering education, Galbraith was also one of the founders of the Canadian Society of Civil Engineers; and a few months after his appointment to the Quebec Bridge commission, he was elected the society's president.

In the language of the Royal Commission that appointed the three engineers, their task was simply to conduct an investigation into the cause of the collapse of the bridge and into "all matters incidental thereto."[9] But there was an even larger question to be answered as

(Above) News of the collapse drew the morbid and
the curious to the scene by
the thousands. This view
shows the crowd gathered at
the wreckage on the south
shore soon after the col-
lapse. National Archives of
Québec (Neg. P1000,S4
(GH870-71)).

(Right) An imaginative illus-
trator for *Scientific American*
perched the *U.S.S. Brooklyn*
atop the failed bottom chord
of the Quebec Bridge to
convey to readers of the
magazine's October 12, 1907,
issue the enormous load
carried by the member. At
bottom left is a perspective
view of the failed member,
while at bottom right its cross-
section is compared with
those of bottom chord members for the Firth of Forth
cantilever bridge and the
railroad arch bridge then
being planned for a crossing
of the East River at Hell Gate.
Author's collection.

well, and it was well stated in an editorial in *Scientific American*. "The tremendous significance of this disaster lies in the suspicion, which to-day is staring every engineer coldly in the face," said the journal, "that there is something wrong with our theories of bridge design, at least as applied to a structure of the size of the Quebec bridge."[10]

The commission undertook this daunting task with extraordinary energy and thoroughness. By the time their work was done, the three men had interviewed some forty-four witnesses, some of whom were recalled as many as ten times. They reviewed reports, plans, specifications, and the extensive correspondence among the several parties to the project. They studied the wreckage of the bridge carefully, and they visited the steel production and fabricating plants where the bridge members had been made. Special tests of model bridge members were conducted, and the noted bridge engineer C. C. Schneider was commissioned to conduct a thorough review of the design work for the bridge.

The commission began taking evidence at Québec on the afternoon of September 9 and continued for more than two weeks. Late in the month, the members traveled to Ottawa to take evidence there for two days and then returned to Québec for further examination of the wrecked structure and study of the plans and specifications. In deference to the ailing Cooper, the commission traveled to New York, convening there on October 14 to begin a week-long questioning of the consulting engineer. All three members then went on to spend a month taking further testimony and collecting information at the headquarters and plant of the Phoenix Iron and Phoenix Bridge companies at Philadelphia and Phoenixville, where they discussed the methods that had been used in laying out and building up the chords and examined the machines used in the fabrication work. During this period Kerry and Galbraith also visited the Harrisburg, Pennsylvania, works of the Central Steel and Iron Company, one of the steel suppliers for the Quebec Bridge, and several other steel and bridge works not connected to the project, to compare methods.

At the end of November, the commission returned to Québec for several more days of work there. Early in December one member of the commission returned to New York to take further testimony from Theodore Cooper. In January two of the members returned to Phoenixville for a week to witness a series of tests of model chord sections. Except for these trips, the three engineers worked almost without interruption until well into the next year, examining and discussing the evidence and preparing their report.

In their testimony to the commission, both Theodore Cooper and the principal witnesses for the Phoenix Bridge Company continued to emphasize the responsibility of the other for critical actions concerning the design and construction of the bridge. In his own testimony to the commission, Theodore Cooper was anything but circumspect in his comments about many of the other participants in the project. The Phoenix Bridge Company, Cooper maintained, had delayed for several years in beginning studies and plans for the project, leaving too little time for the study and preparation of the drawings. "I urged them at an early date to prepare their studies and plans as far as possible for the accepted 1,800 foot spans for which no plans had yet been prepared," Cooper testified, "stating that in an important work like this very cautious and very careful consideration would be required in each and every individual detail of the structure, and that this should be done before the rush of construction would come upon us. They gave this no attention, and practically made no steps towards preparing the plans until they had completed their financial arrangements and had executed their present contract."[11]

Numerous alterations were called for when the Phoenix Bridge Company's detailed plans did not fully come up to the requirements, Cooper testified; and he was often dissatisfied with the company's workmanship in fabrication. "In many directions the workmanship was perfectly satisfactory," he said, "but I had cause to make frequent complaints of the mechanical department, especially regarding the facing of the compression members and the boring of the pin holes."[12]

He found fault with the erection work, as well. Expressing his belief that chord 9 in the west anchor arm had been the point of initial failure, Cooper referred to the problems with the splice between chords 8L and 7L in the cantilever arm found early in August. ""I have spoken of their lack of caution in staying and protecting the splices of this lower chord," he said. "With the facts before us, seeing their lack of appreciation and consideration of the splices at 7 and 8 cantilever arm, there is grave suspicion in my mind that similar neglect and lack of appreciation may have prevailed before."[13]

The qualifications of the principal engineers on the site for the Quebec Bridge Company and Phoenix Bridge Company fell short, as well, according to Cooper. "For a man to be qualified, in my opinion, to have the supreme local control of the erection of a bridge as important as that under consideration," responded Cooper to a question from the commission, "I think he should have been a thoroughly technically educated and experienced bridge engineer. I regret to say that I do not think the chief engineer of the Quebec Bridge Company had these qualifications. In reference to the local control by the Phoenix Bridge Company, as stated before, I do not think they had the quality of engineer that the circumstances demanded.[14]

"I do think that it was perfectly possible by prompt and intelligent action to have stayed that chord and prevented the failure of the bridge," said Cooper. "The contracting company should have had on the structure an employee of sufficient intelligence to have appreciated the necessity for and to have given such an order," he continued. "At the same time, the responsible executive of the Quebec Bridge Company should not have hesitated in the absence of proper action by the contractor, to have given such an order."[15]

Only Norman McClure, whose hiring Cooper himself had recommended, met the consulting engineer's expectations. "Mr. McClure was the only person who had any preparation or qualifications for supervising the construction of that bridge," he told the commission.[16]

At the conclusion of testimony, which took more than a week, Cooper sounded a plaintive note in response to a final question regarding any recommendations he might make regarding the detailing of members such as the lower chord that had failed. "I shall decline to take any executive or responsible position in connection with the correction of the errors that we now recognize in this work," he concluded; "it must be referred to younger and abler men."[17]

After taking Cooper's testimony in New York, the commission members traveled to Phoenixville, where their work would include hearing testimony from the officers and engineers at the Phoenix Bridge Company. Disturbed by reports of Cooper's critical testimony, the bridge company was eager to counter his charges. "Within a week Mr. Cooper's allegations will be proven false," declared an unnamed Phoenix official to a local reporter.[18]

David Reeves, president of both the Phoenix bridge and iron companies, testified bluntly that Cooper had been responsible for the decisions that led to the disaster. When it became apparent that the dead load of the structure was in excess of the assumed weights used for design calculations, Reeves told the commission, "we called this matter to the attention of Mr. Cooper, but Mr. Cooper would not allow any increase whatever in these members, and decided they fully met the requirements.

"The cause of the failure cannot be found due to any departure from the specifications in design, material or workmanship, or lack of good judgment in the field," declared Reeves. "The profession is bound to look beyond that—in the employment of the unusually high stresses prescribed for compression members, beyond all precedent and, as it now appears, beyond the existing technical knowledge of their effect.

"Mr. Cooper made modifications to the unit-stresses to be employed upon the various members which very much increased them beyond any precedent, and by so doing placed the whole design in a field outside the benefit of experience," he continued. "Such high stresses had never before been used, and in using them he acted with the authority of the Quebec Bridge Co. and the Dominion of Canada vested in him. The fall of the bridge is to be laid directly to the change in unit-stresses as made by Mr. Cooper."[19]

John Deans and Peter Szlapka were considerably more respectful and circumspect in their discussion of Theodore Cooper's work in the design of the bridge but also managed to convey their view that the consulting engineer had been the final authority for any of the key decisions concerning the bridge. In a discussion with the commission regarding Cooper's authority over the erection work, for example, Deans remarked, ""Mr. Cooper, being in supreme authority, could have stopped or interfered with the erection through Mr. Hoare at any time that he saw fit."[20]

"I understood that Mr. Cooper had supreme authority in connection with the interpretation of the specifications, had authority to change them from time to time as he saw fit, and had authority to approve all of our general and detailed plans," Deans commented at another point in his testimony.[21]

In his testimony, Peter Szlapka disclaimed any responsibility for the unprecedented unit stresses that had been adopted for the design. Asked if he fully concurred in all the amendments made in the specification, Szlapka responded simply: "The amendments made in the specifications by Mr. Cooper were not subject to my approval."[22] Even so, Szlapka told the commissioners that he considered these increases in unit stresses to be within the limits of safety.

Cooper's comments and the conflicting testimony from the Phoenix Bridge Company principals caused a considerable stir in the press. "The sensational statements of Mr. Cooper, are contradicted by the equally sensational statements of the engineers of the Phoenix Bridge Company," headlined *Le Soleil* of Québec over a story about the testimony.[23]

While the commission's inquiry ranged across every facet of the planning, design, manufacture, and erection of the bridge, it was evident from the very beginning that the collapse had begun with the failure of bottom chord members A9L and A9R in the anchor arm, and the inquiry focused particular attention on the design and fabrication of these main compression members. The commission developed the view that these chords had failed by rupture of the diagonal latticing that held the parallel web plates in position, or by shearing of the lattice rivets, and strongly questioned the theory that had governed their design.

In response to questions from the commission, design engineer Peter Szlapka testified at length concerning his investigations and design calculations for these members, while a series of compression tests of model chord sections were made on the Phoenix Bridge Company's large testing machine in November and January. Initiated by Phoenix Bridge, the November tests were made under the supervision of Professor William H. Burr. The Phoenix testing machine not being capable of handling a full-sized section, the tests were made on a one-third-scale model of lower chord 9 in the anchor arm, which carefully replicated the details of the full-sized member. The testing began on November 22 and continued into the following day. When the test loading reached a level of 26,850 pounds per square inch, the chord section failed with what was described as "explosive violence" by the shearing of the latticing rivets. Failure of the latticing system was almost instantaneously followed by buckling of the four ribs of the chord section.

A second set of tests were conducted on January 28, 1908, to determine what the ultimate strength of the lower chord would have been if properly latticed. This time a test chord was prepared with a latticing system about twice the strength of that of the previous test. In these tests the latticing held firm, and the loading reached a stress of 37,000 pounds per square inch in the web sections before they failed as a result of buckling. Still other tests of lattice bars and rivets completed the testing work.

Parallel to the work of the Commission, the Dominion government's Department of Railways and Canals had commissioned C. C. Schneider to review the design and plans for the bridge and to report concerning their sufficiency, both as to conformity to the specifications that had been approved by the government and for the proposed reconstruction of the bridge.

Compression tests made on one-third scale model chord sections on the Phoenix Bridge Company's large testing machine confirmed the belief of the Royal Commission engineers investigating the collapse that inadequate design of these members had led to the failure. This is a view of one test section showing how the web sections buckled after failure of the inadequate diagonal latticing, which was intended to make the chord member function as a unit. Author's Collection.

Charles Conrad Schneider was an exceptionally good choice for this task, for he was both one of the country's pre-eminent bridge engineers and one of the most experienced of all in the design and construction of cantilever bridges. Born in Apolda, Saxony, in 1843, he had graduated from the Royal College of Technology at Chemnitz before emigrating to the United States at the age of 24. Over the next decade, he was engaged in a variety of bridge work with two bridge companies and the Erie Railroad, where he was one of the leaders in establishing improved practices for the design and bidding for bridges and for the inspection of their construction.

Schneider established his own engineering practice in the design of bridges and structures in 1878, and over the next several decades he was responsible for some of the most important bridges of the time. Soon after opening his own office, he became a consulting engineer to the Canadian Pacific for bridge design and continued to act for the company almost to the end of his life. Two of his most important bridges ranked among the earliest important cantilever structures in America. In 1883 he completed a major cantilever crossing of the Niagara River for the Michigan Central. The steel-and-wrought-iron structure stood 239 feet above water level and incorporated 200-foot anchor arms and a central clear span of 470 feet. One of his most important projects for the CP was the design of a 527-foot cantilever bridge over the Fraser River in British Columbia in 1887. This pioneer cantilever structure was replaced by a heavier span in 1910; but it was then re-erected on the CP's Esquimault & Nanaimo Railway on Vancouver Island, where it remains in service today.

Still other notable structures designed by Schneider included the Pennsylvania Railroad's second crossing of the Susquehanna at Rockville, Pennsylvania; the CPR's Lethbridge Viaduct in Alberta; and the interior steel framework that supports the Statue of Liberty. In 1886 he became chief engineer for the Pencoyd Iron Works at Philadelphia, which became a major designer and builder of bridges; and in 1900 he became vice president for engineering for the newly formed American Bridge Company. His professional papers won him the American Society of Civil Engineers' Rowland Prize and, twice, its Norman Medal. C. C. Schneider held several offices in the society and was its president in 1905.

Schneider began his work with an examination of the wreckage of the bridge, followed by a careful review of the plans. He computed the strains in the structure based upon the requirements of the specifications, comparing them with the figures developed by the Phoenix Bridge Company in designing the structure. The strains for both the floor system and bracing were found to be in conformance with the specifications, but those for the trusses were not. While live load strains agreed with those of the designers, Schneider found those for dead load to be substantially greater for most members. This was because he used the actual weight of the structure, while the original design had been based upon estimated weights, which had proved substantially lower.

Schneider's calculations indicated that the actual unit strains in most members of the trusses exceeded the limit of the specifications. In some upper chords of the cantilever arms, the allowable strains were exceeded by 10 to 18 percent, while those in most of the lower chords exceeded the specification limits by as much as 24 percent. For both the upper and lower chords of the anchor arms, the unit strains exceeded the limits of the specifications by anywhere from 11 to 20 percent. Those in the chords of the suspended span ranged from 7.5 to 18 percent above those allowed by the specifications. In some cases Schneider found web members in which unit strains exceeded the specifications by as much as 21 percent, and in one case by 57 percent.

In addition to inadequately sized truss members, Schneider found a number of deficiencies in the design of the bridge's details, particularly in those for compression members, where connections—such as the latticing—were insufficient to make the parts composing them act as a unit. This was particularly true of the lower chord members where the collapse had originated.

"The most pronounced defect in this respect," wrote Schneider, "exists in the lower chord members of the cantilever and anchor arms. These members consist of four separate ribs, not particularly well developed as compression members, and their connections to each other are not of sufficient strength to make them act as a unit."[24]

Even without the deficiencies of the truss members, Schneider concluded, the Phoenix design was not a suitable one. He found particular fault, for example, with the butt-jointed lower chord members of the bridge. They were neither continuous nor pin-connected, he noted, and it was impossible to make the whole section bear uniformly under the various conditions of loading. The curving, or polygonal, lower chords of the cantilever and anchor arms—adopted for esthetic reasons—created difficulties in both fabrication and proper fitting. These, he said, "make them not only more costly than chords forming a straight line, but also less safe."[25]

Schneider's report to Railways and Canals of January 1908 concluded that the trusses, as designed, did not conform to the requirements of the approved specifications and were inadequate to carry the traffic or loads specified. The latticing of many of the compression members, he said, was not in proportion to the sections of the members which they connected. Moreover, he concluded, the trusses of the bridge, even if they had been designed in accordance with the approved specifications, would not be of sufficient strength in all their parts to safely sustain the loads provided for in the specifications.

Schneider's report also laid to rest any thought of completing the bridge based upon either the original plans or some modification of them. It was impracticable, he said, to use the fabricated material now on hand in the reconstruction of the bridge. "The present design is not well adapted to a structure of the magnitude of the Quebec Bridge and should, therefore, be discarded and a different design adopted for the new bridge, retaining only the length of the spans in order to use the present piers."[26]

The commission had largely completed its work by the end of January 1908. John Galbraith had agreed to write the report, a task that took his undivided attention for a period of more than six weeks. The published report itself was an exceptionally thorough document of two volumes totaling nearly a thousand pages, in addition to numerous drawings and other material. The report included nineteen separate appendices discussing various elements of the investigation and incorporated both the reports of the various chord tests conducted at Phoenixville and C. C. Schneider's analysis of the design.

In its summary of findings, the commission clearly determined that the cause of the collapse had been the failure of the lower chords in the anchor arm near the main pier, and that the failure of these chords was due to their defective design. In carefully chosen words, the commission clearly placed the responsibility for this defective design on Peter Szlapka and Theodore Cooper. The design of the chords that failed, the findings noted, was made by Szlapka and had been examined and approved by Cooper. "The failure cannot be attributed directly to any cause other than errors in judgment on the part of these two engineers. These errors of judgment cannot be attributed either to lack of common professional knowledge, to neglect of duty, or a desire to economize. The ability of the two engineers was tried in one of the most difficult professional problems of the day and proved to be insufficient for the task."[27]

In other findings the commission determined the specifications for the work to be neither satisfactory nor sufficient, "the unit stresses in particular being higher than any established by past practice." The assumption of too low a value for the dead load, and the failure to have later revised this assumption, the findings said, was a grave error. "This error was of sufficient magnitude to have required the condemnation of the bridge," they reported, "even if the details of the lower chords had been of sufficient strength, because, if the bridge had been completed as designed, the actual stresses would have been considerably greater than those permitted by the specifications. This erroneous assumption was made by Mr. Szlapka and accepted by Mr. Cooper, and tended to hasten the disaster."[28]

While the errors that led to the collapse were clearly those of Szlapka and Cooper, the failure of others also contributed to the terrible loss of life. "The loss of life on August 29, 1907," the commission concluded, "might have been prevented by the exercise of better judgment on the part of those in responsible charge of the work for the Quebec Bridge & Railway Company and for the Phoenix Bridge Company."[29]

The commission's report was greeted with great interest in the engineering and construction communities, and its text was reproduced in full in *Engineering News* and other engineering and railway journals. The thoroughness and judicial nature of the report were widely praised. *Engineering News* called it "the most notable investigation of an engineering disaster that the present generation, at least, has seen."[30]

The repercussions of the Quebec Bridge disaster and the Royal Commission report that followed it continued for years among the people and the communities that, in some way, had been concerned with the work.

For an aging and ailing Theodore Cooper, the stinging professional condemnation of the commission findings brought an ignoble end to what had been a distinguished career. "Perhaps the most poignant feature standing out in the story of this catastrophe," wrote David B. Steinman, himself one of a later generation of distinguished bridge engineers, "is the tragedy of a human career wrecked at its climax."[31] Cooper withdrew from the practice of engineering to live out his years in a lonely retirement at New York. He died there on August 24, 1919, at the age of 80 after a four-week bout with pneumonia. Just two days previously, the Prince of Wales had presided at the formal dedication of the great cantilever bridge at Québec that Cooper had wanted as his greatest achievement, but of course it had been designed and built by others.

Edward Hoare returned to the kind of engineering work for which his long experience best fitted him, working for the National Transcontinental Railway Commission in the location and construction of Canada's new transcontinental railway.

For another decade John Sterling Deans continued to serve as chief engineer of the Phoenix Bridge Company, where his responsibilities included the construction of the Manhattan Bridge, then the heaviest suspension span ever built. He was named a vice president of the bridge company in 1915 and vice president and consulting engineer in 1917. After two years of failing health, he died at his home in Phoenixville on December 16, 1918, at the age of 60.

Peter Szlapka reacted angrily to the findings of the Royal Commission. While in his November 1907 testimony to the commission he had declined to criticize any of Theodore Cooper's design decisions, Szlapka had a different story to tell a few months later, following release of the report. In a March 11 interview, he told reporters he had criticized the very chord section that failed, callings its weakness to Cooper's attention. But Cooper, he said, had overruled the objection.[32] Szlapka continued in his designing engineer position with the bridge company for some time and then resigned to take up a position as a structural steel engineer in the construction of subways at Philadelphia. He retired from that position around 1933 and lived out his long life in the home he had built for his family in Phoenixville. He died in a Norristown hospital on January 27, 1943, just a few days short of his 91st birthday.

The Phoenix Bridge Company itself was strong enough to survive the blow to its fortunes and reputation caused by the disaster. Insurance covered the company's direct financial losses, and the company had a strong backlog of orders, including the contract it had landed in 1906 for the superstructure of the Manhattan Bridge over the East River at New York. This was a major suspension bridge with a clear span of 1,470 feet, and its successful completion in 1910 was a triumph for the Phoenix firm.

Yet there is little question that the Québec disaster had left its mark on the Phoenix Bridge Company. Many years later Clyde MacCornack, who succeeded John Deans as the company's chief engineer and later became its president, recalled that David and William Reeves lost their interest in great projects like the Quebec or Manhattan bridges after the disaster. "After the Quebec failure," he said, "the Reeves became afraid of everything. . . . [They] didn't want to handle any big jobs."[33]

Beset by competition from the giant American Bridge Company formed by J. P. Morgan in 1900, the new popularity of reinforced concrete as a bridge-building material, and a declining market for railroad structures, the Phoenix Bridge Company lost the commanding position it had held at the turn of the century. Even so, the company continued in business until 1962. During the fifty-five years that followed the disaster at Québec, the Phoenix Bridge Company built many notable bridges, but never again did it take on a project of the heroic scale of the Quebec Bridge.

Within the engineering community at large, the disaster brought a realization that engineers did not know as much as they thought they did about the design and behavior of extremely large and heavily loaded compression members. The large-scale testing, experimentation, and study that followed the disaster all helped to develop a more scientific basis for the analysis and design of large compression members and their connections that significantly advanced the art of design for a new generation of major bridges that followed.

In the little communities along the south bank of the St. Lawrence opposite Québec and at Caughnawaga, above Montréal, from which so many of the lost bridge workers had come, the lives of their survivors were forever changed. Life was harsh in the industrial economy of the early 20th century, and there was little social support available to the widows and fatherless children of the bridge workers. Records of the Phoenix Bridge Company indicate that the claims of most of the widows of the workmen from the Québec area were settled for anywhere from $1,000 to $1,225, with the largest amount—$1,800—going to the widow and seven children of Harry French. Claims of the parents of the young single men were typically settled for $450 to $500. The parents of 14-year-old Stanley Wilson, who had worked as a water boy at 10 cents an hour, got $450. The mother of Joseph Boucher, who was in bad health and unable to work, was paid $1,000 for the death of her son, who had been her sole support. Injured workmen got anywhere from $200 to $675, except for Charles Davis, so badly injured he could never work again as a bridge worker, who received $1,885, including his lawyer's costs.

Inside the St-Romuald church, one can still see a commemorative plaque that lists the 76 victims of the disaster, while at the cemetery, a finial from the doomed bridge still stands as a well-tended memorial and marker for the common grave of the bridge workers.

At Caughnawaga there was hardly a family untouched by the disaster. Surviving records of the Department of Indian Affairs indicate that lawyers squabbled for several years over the claims of the 24 women widowed by the accident, most of whom finally received settlements of about $1,000. Almost all of the Caughnawaga men belonged to the ironworkers union, which promptly paid each widow a $100 death benefit. Most of the married men had been prudent about taking out insurance, and the widows received insurance settlements totaling more than $17,000. Indian agent James A. Macrae was appointed guardian for the fifty-six minor children left fatherless by the disaster and in September 1908 accepted

Families of bridge workers
from St-Romuald lost in the
disaster used one of the steel
finials from the wrecked
structure as a marker over
their common grave in the
parish cemetery. Well
tended, it still stands there
today as a reminder of one
of the greatest construction
disasters in history.
William D. Middleton.

$100,000 in payment for their claims. A disaster fund set up by sympathizers that took in close to $8,000 made monthly payments of as much as $25 to families in need.

According to Caughnawaga folklore, the women of the community came together in council in the wake of the disaster and decided that never again should so many of their men work on a single project, a practice that remains in place to this day. About a mile and a half apart on the main road through Caughnawaga, one at each end of the village, the community erected two great iron crosses as a memorial to their dead. They remain there today as a reminder of what is still known in the village as simply "the disaster."

Whatever its impact on the Caughnawaga community, the disaster did not deter the men from pursuing the skilled trade of ironworking. Successive generations of the Caughnawaga and other Mohawks have followed the construction industry wherever it has taken them in North America and sometimes even abroad. Caughnawaga ironworkers helped erect the Empire State Building and many other great skyscrapers in New York, Boston,

Detroit, and other urban centers, as well as such major bridges as the San Francisco–Oakland Bay Bridge. As many as 400 to 600 men from present-day Kahnawake still proudly work as skilled ironworkers.[34]

For Virginia-born writer and beginning novelist Willa Cather, the story of the Quebec Bridge collapse provided a framework for the climactic scene in her first novel, *Alexander's Bridge*, published in 1912. In Cather's version, chief engineer Bartley Alexander died with his bridge, having rushed out on the span to warn the workmen off as the compression chords began to show signs of impending failure.[35]

What were the lessons from that terrible afternoon of August 29, 1907?

On one level, one might simply accept it as one of those periodic reminders that technological advance comes at a price. We regularly learn anew that past experience does not always provide us a clear path as we venture into new and untried regions. Consequently, bridges collapse, fireproof buildings burn, airplanes fall from the sky, and spacecraft explode.

But there were much more specific lessons in the failure of the Quebec Bridge, and they were ones that engineers and builders could apply to the demanding tasks of designing and building great structures. At the heart of the disaster, of course, were the grievous errors of Szlapka and Cooper in designing the structure, among them Cooper's adoption of unprecedented design stresses; Szlapka's underestimation of the dead load of the structure and failure later to recheck the weight, compounded by Cooper's decision to allow even higher stresses when the error became apparent; and the assumption that past design practices could be safely applied to a structure of unprecedented size without benefit of careful testing.

The best of engineers can make mistakes or suffer lapses in judgment, and good engineering practice is founded upon careful independent checking and review by knowledgeable peers. This was notably absent in the design of the Quebec Bridge, and it had much to do with Theodore Cooper, who seems to have been self-confident to the point of arrogance. In his testimony to the Royal Commission, Peter Szlapka recalled an incident when he had disagreed with a change in his general plan proposed by Cooper. Not willing to criticize Copper's proposal directly, Szlapka had commented that it might be criticized by the profession. To this, Cooper was said to have replied, "There is nobody competent to criticize us."[36]

That same arrogance seems to be reflected in Cooper's stubborn resistance to the appointment of a bridge engineer to review the completed plans for the Department of Railways and Canals ("this puts me in the position of a subordinate, which I cannot accept").[37] The department's chief engineer demurred, and Cooper lost the opportunity for review of his work by a professional peer who might have challenged the fateful design decisions.

Among the lessons to be drawn from the disaster, wrote the distinguished bridge engineer J. A. L. Waddell some years later, was this: "In every important bridge project the completed plans should be checked in detail throughout by some capable bridge engineer who is entirely disconnected from either the consulting engineer or the contractor."[38]

While design failures clearly set the Quebec Bridge on the path to failure, there were grievous errors of leadership and management as well; and if they did not cause the collapse, they surely contributed to the magnitude of the disaster. These were well articulated by the Royal Commission report. The unclear division of authority and responsibility among the Quebec Bridge & Railway Company, the Phoenix Bridge Company, and the consulting engineer created an uncertain situation at the bridge site that was compounded by the inadequate experience of several of the key technical staff.

Theodore Cooper was probably correct in many of his criticisms of the principal onsite staff of the Quebec Bridge Company and the Phoenix Bridge Company. Edward Hoare was by all accounts a competent and experienced railway location and construction engineer, well qualified in ordinary bridge work, but he was clearly not the experienced engineer of major bridges that should have been in charge of the project. Hoare deferred to Cooper in virtually every major technical issue or action. He forwarded the plans that came from Phoenix and Cooper to Ottawa without any substantive review of his own. His surveillance of the project seems largely to have been observations of what he could see from the track level, relying on Kinloch and McClure for more detailed examination of the work.

Arthur Birks, the senior engineer at the site for the Phoenix Bridge Company, was evidently a highly capable and promising engineer, yet he, too, lacked the substantial experience in the erection of major bridges that his responsibilities called for. Lacking that experience and the judgment that comes with it, and unwilling to believe that the work of such eminent engineers as Szlapka and Cooper could be faulty, he was unable to realize what was happening to the bridge or to take decisive action when the moment of crisis came.

Even Norman McClure, who enjoyed Cooper's confidence and who, more than either Hoare or Birks, realized that they were confronted with serious problems in the critical days just before the collapse, was relatively inexperienced and seems consequently to have been reluctant to strongly assert his views or to press for decisive action.

Theodore Cooper, an acknowledged leader in bridge engineering and far more experienced than any of them, overshadowed all of these men. All of them instinctively turned to Cooper for direction and decision, and in large measure he became the *de facto* chief engineer of the Quebec Bridge. It was a role he was, in many ways, ill equipped to fill. Poorly paid for his consulting duties, he could not afford the staff he needed to assist him. In ill health, he never once visited the bridge site after erection of the structure had commenced, and he was forced to rely upon letters, sketches, and photographs to understand the problems and questions that were presented to him for decision. Separated from the site of the work by almost 600 miles and subject to the vagaries of wire and postal communication of the time, Cooper was ill situated to provide the prompt and decisive action that the crisis of late August demanded. Why Theodore Cooper accepted this responsibility without, so far as is known, ever having demanded changes to the situation from the Quebec Bridge & Railway Company will always remain one of the mysteries of the tragedy. In any event, because of it was lost the opportunity to have averted, if not the collapse itself, at least the terrible loss of life that accompanied it.

"It was clear that on that day the greatest bridge in the world was being built without there being a single man within reach who by experience, knowledge and ability was competent to deal with the crisis," wrote the authors of the Royal Commission report.[39]

"Real authority lay at New York, 600 miles away," commented *Engineering News*, "with an engineer *who had never seen the structure for which he was actually carrying the entire engineering responsibility.*"[40]

Surely another lesson of the disaster was that the building of great engineering works such as this requires the presence of engineers with sufficient knowledge and experience, and the clear authority to act, who can respond decisively and effectively to whatever emergencies may arise.

There was yet another lesson to be drawn from the disaster in the view of the editors of *Engineering News*, laid out in a long and thoughtful editorial. "We now know," they wrote, "that the great bridge did give ample warning of the distress it was experiencing; and these warnings were seen and their significance was realized by the practical men on the ground."[41]

These practical men, unschooled in engineering, seemed to have had a much better understanding of the crisis they were facing. B. A. Yenser and E. R. Kinloch, both seasoned bridge erectors, knew that something was seriously wrong with the suspect compression chords. Horace Clark, the foreman of the bridge material storage yard, knew that chord A9L had been straight when it left the yard to be placed in the bridge. Yet Arthur Birks, who had not even been there at the time, persisted in his conviction that the troubling bend was something that had always been there and was, therefore, not that serious a problem.

"But all these positive facts and the intuitive perceptions of the men of largest practical experience," wrote the *News*, "were over-ridden and silenced by the very men who should have had the best knowledge, the men trained in the scientific analysis of structures and entrusted with responsible charge of the work.

"We all of us, juniors and seniors alike, need to know more, —to test our theories constantly in the light of new knowledge, to welcome such knowledge when it comes, well attested, from any source. Yes, surely, the great lesson of this greatest disaster is the lesson of humility."[42]

BOOK TWO

THE SECOND BRIDGE

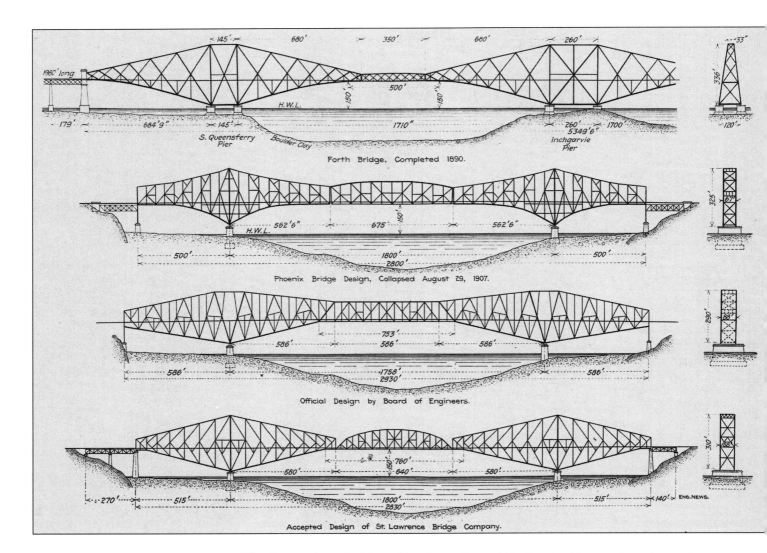

This drawing from the November 16, 1911, issue of *Engineering News* made an interesting comparison of the Firth of Forth bridge with three cantilever designs for the bridge at Québec. Shown at the top is one of the main spans of the Forth Bridge. Below are shown the Phoenix Bridge Company design which collapsed in 1907, the board of engineers design developed largely by Henri Vautelet, and the St. Lawrence Bridge Company design adopted for the bridge. Author's Collection.

CHAPTER 7

STARTING OVER

D ESPITE THE TERRIBLE DISASTER THAT HAD BROUGHT THE FIRST ATTEMPT TO AN
end, there was never any doubt that the effort to bridge the St. Lawrence at
Québec would continue. Construction of the National Transcontinental Railway had
begun in September 1905, and a crossing at Québec would be an essential link in this new,
all-Canadian route from the Prairie Provinces to the ice-free Atlantic ports.

Even in the days immediately following the collapse of the first bridge, there were confident assurances that the project would proceed. "It is the duty of all not to lose courage,"
wrote Prime Minister and National Transcontinental proponent Laurier in a telegram of
sympathy to Mayor Garneau of Québec, "We must immediately apply ourselves to the
reparation of loss and push the project with energy."[1]

"The great Quebec bridge project will be pushed to completion as speedily as possible,"
said a September 1 press report from Québec, "and the Phoenix Bridge Company will do
the work, notwithstanding the collapse on Thursday." The report was received with relief
in Phoenixville, where there were fears that the collapse of the bridge might lead to the
failure of the community's principal employer.[2]

There was much interest in continuing the project based upon the original design, with
such modification as the results of the Royal Commission inquiry might recommend.
While the entire south half of the bridge had been lost, the identical fabricated parts for
the north half were stored, ready for erection, at Phoenixville or at the Phoenix company's
Belair yard, several miles from the bridge site, and the masonry piers for the structure had
come through the accident unscathed.

C. C. Schneider's analysis of the design that accompanied the commission report would
seem to have ended any idea of continuing with the original plan. While Schneider had
found the original floor system and bracing of sufficient strength to carry safely the traffic
for which they were intended, the trusses, he said, did not conform to the specification
requirements and were inadequate to carry the traffic or loads specified. Even if they had
been in conformity with the specifications, he reported, they would not be of sufficient
strength in all their parts to sustain the loads provided for in the specifications safely.
Schneider's report had concluded:

> The present design is not well adapted to a structure of the magnitude of the Quebec
> Bridge and should, therefore, be discarded and a different design adopted for the new
> bridge, retaining only the length of the spans in order to use the present piers.[3]

Anxious to continue the project, the Phoenix Bridge Company negotiated a time extension for completion of the bridge with the Quebec Bridge & Railway Company in April 1908. Despite Schneider's recommendations, the company also initiated an effort to develop improved specifications and plans for the bridge that would permit re-use of the piers and at least some of the already fabricated material from the original design. The new specifications were based upon advances in materials and the practices of bridge building since the preparation of the original specifications in 1899, the company's hard-won experience on the first bridge, the work of the Royal Commission, and extensive testing. Utilizing testing machines of the U.S. Arsenal at Watertown, New York; the William Sellers & Company at Philadelphia; and its own testing machine at Phoenixville, the largest compression testing machine in the world, the company tested various grades of materials, model columns, eyebars, and riveted joints and latticing.

The company's proposed new specifications, completed in July 1908, increased many of the design live loads for the structure while reducing the allowable unit stresses. The combination of heavier loadings and lower stresses would have necessitated such increased dimensions and weight for the principal truss members that the use of medium carbon steel was considered impracticable. Instead, the new specifications called for the use of newly developed nickel steel, for which much higher unit stresses could be allowed, making it possible to keep the dimensions of the main truss members within those of the original design.

Meanwhile, however, the Dominion government had decided to exercise a 1903 legislative provision that permitted the government to take over the bridge undertaking upon giving one month's notice to the bridge company. By an order-in-council of August 17, 1908, the government formally initiated the takeover, to take effect on December 1, 1908. A few months later, the Quebec Bridge & Railway Company was assigned and transferred to the government, and the shareholders were paid off for a total consideration of just over $265,000. Phoenix Bridge, which had claims against the Québec company totaling almost $300,000, finally accepted $100,000 from the government in 1910 for a release from all claims. All material and property on the bridge site went to the Phoenix company.

At the same time it initiated the takeover, the government appointed a board of engineers that would act under the Department of Railways and Canals to oversee the reconstruction of the bridge. Taking heed of the organizational and management problems that had contributed to the August 1907 disaster, the government wanted to assure clear and unambiguous engineering authority over the work. "It is intended," said the appointing order-in-council, "that the entire responsibility for the design and for the reconstruction of the work shall rest with the Board alone."[4]

The board was made up of three distinguished engineers, one each from Canada, the United States, and England. The Canadian member, and the chairman and chief engineer of the board, was Henri Etienne Vautelet, a Montréal consulting engineer and a member of the Canadian Society of Civil Engineers. Born at Sedan, France, in 1856, Vautelet had been educated at the College St. Barbe in Paris and the School of Mines. He had been a long-time bridge engineer with the Canadian Pacific Railway and served as the railroad's assistant chief engineer from 1886 to 1902, at which time he left the company to begin his private engineering practice.

Maurice Fitzmaurice, the British member of the board, was a civil engineer of extraordinary experience in the construction of long-span bridges and other large-scale engineering works in Britain and abroad. Born in County Kerry, Ireland, in 1861, he had studied at Trinity College, Dublin, where he earned a bachelor's degree and, much later, a master's of engineering. For two years he was articled to Sir Benjamin Baker and then for several years worked under Baker and Sir John Fowler in the construction of the great Firth of Forth cantilever bridge. A subsequent assignment took him to America, where he was engaged in the construction of a ship railway on the peninsula between Nova Scotia and New Brunswick. Back in England, Fitzmaurice superintended the replacement of cast iron railway bridges with steel structures and was a resident engineer in the construction of the

Blackwall Tunnel under the Thames for the London County Council. In 1898 he was appointed chief resident engineer for the Egyptian government and placed in charge of construction of the Aswan Dam on the Nile, returning to England three years later to take up the post of chief engineer for the London County Council, where he was involved in a wide range of major works and was later knighted for his achievements.

The third member of the board was the well-known American bridge engineer Ralph Modjeski. Born in Bochnia, Poland, near Krakow, in 1861, Modjeski had emigrated to the United States in 1876 with his mother, the noted actress Helena Modjeski.[5] After touring with his mother as stage manager of her troupe for several years, Modjeski entered l'École des Ponts et Chausées at Paris in 1881, graduating at the top of his class in civil engineering in 1885 to begin a brilliant career in bridge engineering in the United States.

After two years as an inspector in the shops of the Union Bridge Company at Athens, Pennsylvania, Modjeski had joined the noted bridge engineer George S. Morison to work on a crossing of the Missouri River at Omaha, Nebraska, and the major cantilever bridge on the Mississippi at Memphis designed by Morison and Alfred Noble. Modjeski gained still further experience with long-span bridges after establishing his own consulting practice in 1893. In 1895 he designed a reconstruction of the Rock Island's crossing of the Mississippi at Rock Island, Illinois; and he collaborated with Alfred Noble in the design and construction of an enormous 2,800-foot, five-span cantilever crossing of the Mississippi at Thebes, Illinois, completed in 1904.

The board began its work at Ottawa on August 31, 1908, and soon afterward established offices at Québec and Montréal and began assembling an engineering staff to develop plans and carry out the testing and investigation work that would be needed to complete a new design.

As the government had moved to take over the project, S. N. Parent had urged consideration of the approach proposed by the Phoenix Bridge Company. This was reflected in a requirement of the appointing order that the board determine if the original plans, modified as necessary, could be adopted, permitting the use of the original piers and some of the material already on hand. As the board began its work, then, a first order of business was a study of the plans and specifications for the original bridge. Rather quickly, the three engineers came to an agreement that no part of the old material could be used in the reconstruction and that radical changes from the original specifications would be required for a structure that would be in conformity with modern engineering practice. Moreover, the dimensions and weight of the new structure, they said, would make it impossible to use the masonry piers of the original bridge.

Further borings of the river bottom in the vicinity of the original piers were carried well into the bedrock. The borings at the north pier established that it would be infeasible to increase the size of the original pier for the new bridge. Instead, the engineers decided to build a new, larger pier 57 feet south of the old pier. On the south shore, however, they decided it would be feasible to enlarge the old pier by sinking two new caissons along the south and west sides of the original masonry pier. The result of these changes at the two main piers reduced the planned main span length of the bridge to 1,758 feet.

Before taking up the details of the design for the new superstructure, the board conducted a careful review of the specification requirements and initiated an exceptionally thorough and comprehensive series of tests of materials, connections, and both tension and compression members. The specifications for the structure went through several revisions as the design evolved. The final version required that the bridge be designed for a live loading of two Cooper's Class E60 locomotives, with a following train load of 5,000 pounds per foot on each of two tracks, as well as heavy snow and wind loadings. Allowable unit stresses for carbon steel members were set at levels well below those that had been used for the ill-fated original bridge, with a maximum allowable tensile stress of 20,000 pounds per square inch in eyebars and a maximum compressive stress of 14,000 pounds per square inch. Extensive use was planned of the newly developed and much stronger nickel steel, for which 40 percent higher unit stresses were allowed.

Ralph Modjeski was the American member of the government board of engineers appointed to oversee the reconstruction of the failed Quebec Bridge. Experienced in the design and construction of several long-span crossings of the Mississippi and Missouri Rivers, Modjeski was the only member of the board to serve throughout the decade-long period that would be required to complete the project. Smithsonian Institution.

The testing program conducted by the board of engineers began in 1910 and continued through 1914 as required by various stages of the design and erection program.

Professor A. N. Talbott of the University of Illinois was engaged to conduct more than a hundred tests in university laboratories to determine the strength of nickel steel riveted joints in tension, and in alternate tension and compression, utilizing test pieces manufactured by the Pennsylvania Steel Company. Early in 1910 the board contracted with the Phoenix Bridge Company to test a total of sixty large, full-sized nickel steel eyebars. Another series of eyebar tests were carried out on the Phoenix testing machine in September 1912, when six eyebars were tested to determine the effects of elongated pinholes on their strength or action, while still another series of eyebar tests were made to determine the effects of lateral loads on the bars. Still other tests conducted at the Phoenix plant in 1912 compared the efficiency of steel plate tension members with that of eyebars.

The board also contracted with Phoenix to conduct a series of tests of model compression members. Sixteen nickel steel models based upon the board's design for the bridge were tested in 1910, followed by another sixteen tests of carbon steel models in 1912. In 1913 tests were conducted for another twelve nickel and carbon steel members based upon the adopted St. Lawrence Bridge Company design. In 1914 the St. Lawrence company also had tests made on the hangars that would be used for raising the suspended span into position in the bridge, first on models at McGill University and then on full-sized sections at the American Bridge Company plant at Ambridge, Pennsylvania.

The changes in the location of the two main piers adopted by the board had reduced the planned main span length to 1,758 feet, with side spans of 586 feet. A review of navigational requirements confirmed that the 150-foot clearance above extreme high water established for the original bridge was adequate. Based upon these overall dimensions, the board began to consider alternate designs for the superstructure. While the engineers favored cantilever construction from the beginning, two suspension bridge designs were also worked out and considered. Finding no material advantage for a suspension design in either weight or cost, and some disadvantages for a bridge carrying such concentrated loads, the board decided in favor of a more rigid cantilever structure.

Once the cantilever form was adopted for the new design, there was a wide range of alternatives to consider. Reflecting the difficult problems experienced in fabricating and erecting the curved chords of the original bridge, the board quickly agreed that the top and bottom chords of the trusses should be straight. Sloped and converging trusses, similar to those of the Forth Bridge in Scotland, as well as vertical but converging trusses, were considered, but the board finally settled upon vertical and parallel trusses that would be more widely spaced than those of the original span, which had a spacing of 66 feet, center-to-center of the trusses.

The board next developed a number of trial designs for a cantilever bridge but ended in disagreement concerning the web system that would be adopted. Board members Fitzmaurice and Modjeski, as well as consultants Paul Wolfel, chief engineer of the McClintic-Marshall Construction Company, and Phelps Johnson, the president of Dominion Bridge, favored some kind of double-intersection design, while the chairman and chief engineer, Vautelet, favored a design with a single-intersection Warren truss web system with subdivided panels. Despite the lack of agreement, Vautelet and the board's engineering staff completed working drawings for the design that he preferred, and the board finally agreed that tenders would be called based upon this "Board of Engineers Design," while the bridge companies competing for the contract would also be allowed to tender based upon original designs of their own. Preliminary specifications and plans were made available to the bridge companies at the beginning of January 1910, while complete specifications and plans were issued with a call for tenders in June. Proposals were received on October 1, 1910.

In June, Maurice Fitzmaurice resigned from the board, to be replaced by Charles MacDonald, a well-known American bridge engineer and a former president of the American Society of Civil Engineers. Born at Gananoque, Ontario, in 1837, MacDonald had moved to the United States at an early age to enter Rensselaer Polytechnic Institute, where he received a civil engineering degree in 1857. Over the next twenty-five years, MacDonald was engaged in a variety of railroad engineering and bridge work. In 1884 he organized and became president of the Union Bridge Company, which designed and built the major cantilever bridge across the Hudson River at Poughkeepsie, New York, and the notable Hawkesbury River bridge in Australia, as well as several major crossings of the Missouri and Mississippi Rivers. Already retired from active engineering work, the 73-year-old MacDonald agreed to serve on the board of engineers only so long as required to complete the evaluation of tenders and until a contract was awarded.

Four companies submitted tenders for the bridge. Considering the magnitude of the work, and in the interest of making the project a Canadian enterprise, the two leading Canadian bridge companies, the Dominion Bridge Company of Lachine, Québec, and the Canadian Bridge Company of Walkerville, Ontario, had joined forces as equal partners to form the St. Lawrence Bridge Company to tender on the Québec project. Tenders were also received from American, British, and German firms, including the Pennsylvania Steel Company of Steelton, Pennsylvania; the British Empire Bridge Company of Montréal and England; and the Maschinenfabrik Augsburg-Nurnberg of Gustavsburg, Germany. In addition to tenders on several alternates of the board design, three of the firms also submitted one or more tenders for alternate designs of their own, giving the board of engineers nearly a half dozen basic designs to choose from, with several times that number of alternatives in erection method and details of the design.

All but one of the proposals were based upon either the board design for a cantilever structure or the tendering bridge company's own cantilever design. The Pennsylvania Steel Company also offered an innovative suspension bridge design by bridge engineer Gustav Lindenthal that was an improved and updated version of his suspension design put forth by the Phoenix Bridge Company for the original Quebec Bridge competition in 1899. The earlier Lindenthal design had been based upon a system of trussed suspension cables, with the cables made up of a system of wire links instead of continuous wire cables. Lindenthal's new design employed intersecting suspension chains of nickel steel eyebars tied together with a system of web diagonals and carried on steel towers 430 feet high.[6]

The four firms offered a variety of erection alternatives for a cantilever bridge. Pennsylvania Steel, the British Empire company, and Maschinenfabrik Augsburg-Nurnberg all proposed to erect the anchor and cantilever arms concurrently, beginning at the main piers and working in both directions. Some type of temporary additional pier or support on the shore side of the main pier was planned to provide the additional support needed during erection, while a temporary erection tower would be employed to erect the trusses over and immediately adjacent to the main pier. Once this section of the trusses was in place, top chord travelers would move outward in both directions, cantilevering the anchor and cantilever spans as they went.

The St. Lawrence Bridge Company offered several erection options for the anchor and cantilever arms, ranging from concurrent erection of the two sections from a temporary high tower, similar to the method planned by the other three firms, to a more conventional

All but one of the tenders submitted for the bridge late in 1910 were for cantilever bridge proposals based upon either the board of engineers design or alternate designs developed by the competing firms. The one exception, shown here in a drawing from the November 23, 1911, *Engineering News*, was an innovative suspension bridge design developed for the Pennsylvania Steel Company by the noted bridge engineer Gustav Lindenthal. Instead of the usual wire suspension cables, the Lindenthal design incorporated intersecting suspension chains of nickel steel eyebars tied together with diagonal web members built up from steel plates. Author's Collection.

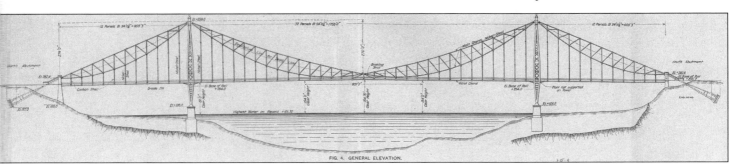

FIG. 4. GENERAL ELEVATION.

approach much like that used by the Phoenix Bridge Company for the original bridge. This would involve complete erection of the anchor arm first on temporary steel scaffolding, followed by erection of the cantilever arm by cantilevering it outward, using either an internal traveler or a top chord traveler for the erection.

The four firms proposed an equal variety of methods for the difficult work of erecting the bridge's suspended center span. All four offered proposals similar to the erection method employed by the Phoenix Bridge Company for the original span. This would involve erecting the center span by cantilevering it outward from the outer end of each cantilever arm until the two sections met and were joined at the center. The four firms also offered an alternate procedure under which the center span would be erected at another location and then floated into place on scows. One variation of this procedure involved lifting the center span into place in the bridge by the use of jacks, a process that would take several days, while another provided for the erection of the center span on high scaffolding towers so that it could be floated into place at the proper elevation for making the connection to the two cantilever arms. The British Empire Bridge Company proposed still another plan, which would have employed a temporary center span made up of two lightweight trusses. These would be floated into place and suspended between the ends of the two cantilever arms to form a staging on which the permanent center span could then be erected.

Although they were not accompanied by tenders, several other notable designs for the bridge were put forward that are worthy of mention. Easily the most innovative was a proposal by a Russian engineer, Professor G. G. Krivoshien of Petrograd, for a bridge with a combined suspension and arch main span, with anchor arms designed as rigid trusses. New York civil engineer Charles Worthington offered plans for a steel arch bridge of unprecedented dimensions that would have been unequalled in span length by any arch bridge before or since. Worthington's plan called for a main span of 1,800 feet, face-to-face of the main piers, made up of four segmented arch ribs that would be formed of steel box sections 9 feet wide, and ranging from a depth of 42 feet at the skewbacks to 21 feet at the crown. Each voussoir segment was to be about 9 feet long, and they would be erected by suspending them from cables above each rib, one by one. Once all were in position, and transverse bracing in place, the voussoirs would be lowered into their final position, one bearing against the other.[7]

Two other proposed plans were for cantilever structures not unlike those proposed by the four competing firms. A design by Claude A. P. Turner, a noted Minneapolis bridge and structural engineer, employed converging trusses that were more widely spaced over the main pier than at the ends of the anchor and cantilever arms.[8] Paul Wolfel also developed a cantilever design for a planned tender by McClintic-Marshall, which later decided not to compete.

The board of engineers devoted almost a month to study and review of the competing proposals and once again found itself in disagreement. Chairman Vautelet continued to favor his design — the board design — while Modjeski and Macdonald both favored any one of three alternate plans developed by the St. Lawrence Bridge Company. Unable to agree, the three men submitted a report to Minister of Railways and Canals George P. Graham at the end of October 1910, advising that one variation of the board design and the scheme of erection proposed by any of the four bridge companies, as well as any of the three St. Lawrence Bridge Company alternatives, would result in a satisfactory structure. The minister, however, insisted upon a specific recommendation.

Still unable to agree, Modjeski and MacDonald submitted a majority report, recommending the tender of the St. Lawrence Bridge Company for its Design B, while Vautelet submitted a minority report disagreeing with the other two engineers and favoring the acceptance of a tender based upon his design. In the face of this lack of unanimity on such an important question, Graham then appointed two additional engineers to confer with the board and submit a joint report. Both were well fitted for the assignment: Mathew J. Butler, a Canadian, was an experienced civil engineer and the former deputy minister and chief engineer for the Depart-

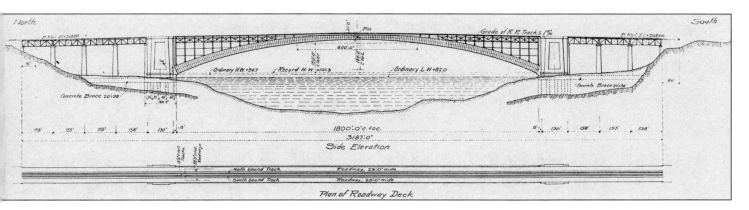

ment of Railway and Canals, while Henry W. Hodge was a distinguished New York consulting engineer of wide experience in bridge design and construction.

After a careful review of the tenders, the two men confirmed the majority report by Modjeski and MacDonald; and in mid-February, all four jointly recommended the acceptance of the St. Lawrence Bridge Company's tender based upon its Design B to Minister Graham, an action which was followed almost immediately by Vautelet's resignation from the board.

The four engineers gave these reasons for their choice:

> The type of design offers greater safety to life and property during erection, as well as economy and rapidity of construction.
> The design contains the minimum number of secondary members and requires few, if any, temporary members during erection.
> The system of triangulation, by dividing the web stresses, reduces the members to more practical sections and simplifies the details of connections.
> The design economizes material, as shown by the calculated weights of the two designs.
> The general appearance of the structure is, in our opinion, improved.[9]

Even before a contract award could be made for the superstructure, there were two major changes in the plans for the bridge. While the recommended Design B had included two railroad tracks, two roadways, and two sidewalks on the bridge, the government decided, in view of the large extra cost involved, to eliminate the planned roadways, a variation reflected by the St. Lawrence Bridge Company's Design X. At about the same time, some serious problems encountered in the construction of the new piers, which had begun the previous year, had led to reconsideration of the board's plans for the siting of the main piers. Late in March the board decided to abandon its original plan for the piers and instead elected to build two entirely new piers, each 65 feet south of the existing piers, thus restoring the main span of the bridge to its original 1,800-foot length. The St. Lawrence company agreed to accept this change to the design, and an $8.65 million contract for the superstructure was awarded to the firm on April 4, 1911.

The magnitude of the loss of life and the financial losses of the 1907 disaster with the previous bridge much in mind, the Dominion government laid the fullest possible responsibility on the successful contractor. One clause of the contract provided as follows:

> The Contractor must satisfy himself as to the sufficiency and suitability of the design, plans and specifications upon which the bridge is to be built, as the Contractor will be required to guarantee the satisfactory erection and completion of the bridge, and it is to be expressly understood that he undertakes the entire responsibility not only for the materials and construction of the bridge, but also for the design, calculations, plans and specifications, and for the sufficiency of the bridge for the loads therein

Another innovative design for the bridge was developed by New York civil engineer Charles Worthington, who proposed the massive steel voussoir arch structure shown in this drawing from the May 19, 1910, issue of *Engineering News*. Worthington's plan called for an arch with a clear span of 1,800 feet, which would have been longer than any railroad arch bridge built even to this day. Author's Collection.

specified. And the enforcement of any part, or all parts, of the specifications shall not in any way relieve the Contractor from such responsibility.[10]

Each of the firms competing for the project had been required to place a security deposit of $500,000 with the Minister of Railways and Canals; and upon signature of the contract, the St. Lawrence Bridge Company was obliged to increase this deposit to $1,297,500, representing 15 percent of the estimated cost of the work. In addition, the two parent companies, Dominion Bridge and Canadian Bridge, were required to sign the contract and to become joint and several guarantors of the work.

The bridge that was now about to begin rising over the St. Lawrence at Québec would be a formidable structure. Reflecting the lessons learned from the collapse of the previous bridge and significant progress in the materials and practice of bridge design in the intervening years, it would also be a very different structure from that of the design it replaced.

The work of design and the preparation of plans for the bridge were carried out by the St. Lawrence Bridge Company, while the board of engineers supervised and checked the work to ensure that it conformed in every respect to the specifications. Mindful of both the unprecedented nature of the structure it was building and of the failings that had led to the 1907 disaster, the board of engineers went to extraordinary lengths to ensure that every step taken in the design and construction would be the correct one.

"It was evident, therefore," wrote the board in its final report, "that the programme to be followed in working out the new design must eliminate every element of chance or doubt in every stage of the work. No assumptions could be made until traced back and found to agree with actual facts. No empirical formulae could be employed unless verified by actual experiment or having the sanction of universal practice. No ordinary or extraordinary type of design for members could be accepted as satisfactory without thorough study or actual full-size tests, nor could any calculation be assumed as correct until checked and re-checked by methods and repetition that would render assurance doubly certain. Consequently, entirely independent studies and calculations were undertaken by the Board's engineers.

"When the results of the two independent series of investigations were finally compared and when points of disagreement were discovered," continued the board's report, "these points were still further investigated until an actual agreement in every respect was arrived at. The result of such a comprehensive and harmonious method of collaboration was to create a feeling of extreme confidence in the minds of both the contractors and the Board, and an assurance that under such conditions no error of any appreciable amount could possibly occur."[11]

Both organizations came to their formidable task with well-qualified staffs of engineers, calculators, and draftsmen.

By this time the membership of the government's board of engineers had substantially changed. Upon award of the superstructure contract in April 1911, Charles MacDonald, who had acted as chairman since Henri Vautelet's resignation in February, had retired from the board as planned, leaving Ralph Modjeski as its only remaining member. By an order-in-council early the following month, Charles N. Monsarrat was appointed chairman and chief engineer. The 40-year-old Monsarrat was an experienced bridge engineer who would prove exceptionally well suited to the task. A native of Montréal, he had joined the Canadian Pacific engineering staff at the age of 19, rising steadily through the ranks to become the CP's engineer of bridges in 1902. Among the notable bridges

In May 1911 Charles N. Monsarrat joined the board of engineers as chairman and chief engineer, guiding the project through its successful completion. He came to the Quebec Bridge with broad experience in bridge design and construction with Canadian Pacific. Author's Collection.

Shortly after Monsarrat joined the board of engineers as chairman and chief engineer, the eminent American bridge engineer Charles C. Schneider was appointed to the board as its third member, replacing retiring Charles MacDonald. Several years later, after fabrication had begun, board members (from left to right) Modjeski, Monsarrat, and Schneider demonstrated the size of the 45-inch half pin hole at the faced end of an anchor arm bottom chord member in a photograph taken at the St. Lawrence Bridge Company's Rockfield (Québec) plant. Smithsonian Institution (Neg. 98-2566).

designed and built under his supervision were the CP's Fraser River cantilever bridge in British Columbia; the immense Belly River Viaduct at Lethbridge, Alberta; the high-level crossing of the North Saskatchewan River at Edmonton, Alberta; and the replacement of the railway's crossing of the St. Lawrence at Lachine, Québec. Another distinguished bridge engineer was added to the board a few weeks later, when C. C. Schneider, who had reviewed the design and plans for the original bridge for the Canadian government, was named as the third member, replacing MacDonald.

leading the St. Lawrence Bridge Company as president was Phelps Johnson, who brought more than forty years of bridge engineering experience to the Quebec Bridge project. It was Johnson who developed the "K" truss design used for the bridge. Author's Collection.

The St. Lawrence Bridge Company drew upon the resources of both its parent companies to assemble an experienced design, fabrication, and erection team. Phelps Johnson, the president of Dominion Bridge, also headed the newly formed St. Lawrence company. Born in the United States in 1849, Johnson was a largely self-taught civil engineer of long and varied experience in bridge design and construction. Educated in schools at Springfield, Massachusetts, he had then gone on to work as an office boy for a local engineering firm, where his ability earned him rapid advancement. Before he was 21, Johnson had become chief engineer for another Springfield firm, leaving the city in 1870 to take up a similar post for the Wrought Iron Bridge Company of Canton, Ohio. He went to Canada in 1882 to join the Toronto Bridge Company, which later became Dominion Bridge, where he had served as both chief engineer and manager before assuming the presidency of the company.

Francis C. McMath, president of the Canadian Bridge Company and also a civil engineer of wide experience in bridge work, was a consulting engineer to the St. Lawrence company. Born at St. Louis and educated there at Washington University, McMath had spent thirteen years with the Detroit Bridge Company, the last five as its chief engineer, before joining with others to form the Canadian Bridge Company in 1900.

George H. Duggan was the chief engineer for the St. Lawrence Bridge Company and the principal designer for the Quebec Bridge. Duggan was also chief engineer for Dominion Bridge, which he had first joined in 1886 after beginning his distinguished engineering career in the construction of the Canadian Pacific through the Rocky Mountains. Author's Collection.

George F. Porter, a Canadian Bridge man, was the engineer of construction for the Quebec Bridge. Author's Collection.

The chief engineer for the St. Lawrence Bridge Company and the principal designer of the Quebec Bridge was George H. Duggan, a widely experienced bridge engineer who was also the chief engineer for Dominion Bridge. Duggan, a Toronto native, had been educated at Upper Canada College at Toronto, with postgraduate study at the School of Practical Science at the University of Toronto. Before joining Dominion Bridge in 1886, Duggan had worked in the Canadian Pacific's engineering department in the construction of the railroad's Rocky Mountain Division.

George F. Porter, who was chief draftsman for the Canadian Bridge Company, was the engineer of construction for the St. Lawrence company.

In preparing to tender for the bridge in 1910, the engineers had carefully considered the features of the board design. It was, said Duggan later, "a bridge in which, if built, every confidence could be placed that it would perform the work for which it was designed. It was, however, manifest that many of the members would be much too large to manufacture with any existing equipment, and that the manufacture must be carried out with a degree of accuracy hitherto unattained to assure that the parts would go together in the structure and perform their intended functions properly."[12]

Because of these problems, as well as some erection difficulties that were inherent in the board design prepared by Henri Vautelet, the firm had developed the alternative design that was ultimately accepted for the bridge. This new design emerged from studies by Phelps Johnson that had suggested the adoption of what became known as the "K" truss, in which each panel of the truss was subdivided by two diagonal members that met at the midpoint of a vertical web member at each panel point to form the letter "K." This design, which was employed for both the anchor and cantilever arm trusses, had the advantages of dividing the shear loading on each panel between two diagonal web members instead of carrying it in only one; it eliminated the need for any temporary members during erection; and it greatly simplified the erection procedures over those that would have been required for the board design.[13] The suspended center span truss was designed with a modified Pratt truss web system.

The board's March 1911 decision to change the location of the main piers had restored the main span of the bridge to the 1,800-foot length that would make it the longest cantilever span ever built. With this increase in the main span, the length of the anchor arms became 515 feet and that of the cantilever arms 580 feet, while the suspended center span was 640 feet long. Including approaches, the overall length of the steel structure was 3,239 feet. The main trusses were spaced at 88 feet, center-to-center. At their deepest point over the main piers, the main trusses were 310 feet deep, center-to-center of top and bottom pins; and they

H. P. Borden, assistant engineer to Chief Engineer Monsarrat, later was appointed the third member of the board of engineers, following the death of Charles C. Schneider. Author's Collection.

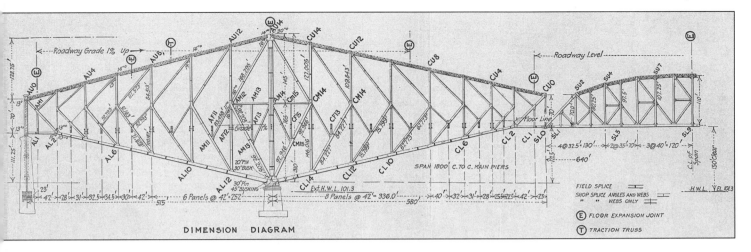

DIMENSION DIAGRAM

were 70 feet deep at the outer ends of the anchor and cantilever arms. The suspended span increased from a depth of 70 feet at each end to 110 feet at the center.

While the overall cantilever form of the new design was similar to that of the original Phoenix Bridge Company bridge, it was a much more solid and rigid structure. The use of eyebar tension members was confined to the top chords of the anchor and cantilever arms of the bridge. All other tension members in both the cantilever and anchor arms were riveted built-up members. This was both for reasons of their greater rigidity over that of eyebars and for appearance considerations. "As the eye-bars which would be used for such members were so entirely out of proportion to the very large compression members in their vicinity," wrote H. P. Borden, assistant to the chief engineer, "the use of the built-up tension members was justified from an esthetic point of view."[14]

The large bottom chord members in both anchor and cantilever arms were riveted built-up members that were designed as straight sections between the main pier and the end of each arm. While the ends of each section were to be planed to obtain good end-to-end bearing at splices, these connections were also designed with a fully riveted splice that could transmit the full load on the member. Compression members in the web area of the main trusses were similarly designed riveted, built-up members.

No steel sections less than a half-inch in thickness were allowed to be used in any of the main members, while a minimum thickness of $3/8$ inch was allowed for the steel used in such details as lattice bars and tie plates in the sway bracing. Rivets used for the built-up members and splices for both compression and tension members ranged from $7/8$ inch to $1 1/8$ inch in diameter. The longest rivets used in the structure were those in the bottom chord field splice adjacent to the main pier shoe, which had a "grip" of almost 10 inches.

The floor system for the bridge was carried on main floor beams, two at each panel point and one at the mid-panel point. These were built-up plate girder sections 10 feet deep and spanning 88 feet between the main truss centerlines and weighing anywhere from 50 to 60 tons. These floor beams in turn supported each of the two tracks on a pair of plate girder main stringers with a sub floor system of floor beams and stringers.

Extensive use of nickel steel, which permitted higher unit stresses, was made wherever its use would reduce the weight of the structure. Even so, the combination of the generally higher design live loadings with the more conservative allowable stresses adopted for the new design, compared with those employed for the first bridge, led to a much heavier structure than that designed by the Phoenix Bridge Company. While the total weight of the steel superstructure for the original bridge had been 38,500 tons, that for the new design came to 66,480 tons. Aside from even the greater capacity and safety inherent in this massive result of their conservative design approach, the engineers saw another virtue in the solidity of the structure. "I consider it perfectly legitimate to build a more expensive

Principal dimensions of the adopted design developed by the St. Lawrence Bridge Company are shown in this drawing from the April 30, 1914, issue of *Engineering News*. The use of eyebars was limited to the top chord tension members and the vertical links that tied the ends of the anchor arms to the anchor piers. The bottom compression chords, and both tension and compression web members, were built up from steel plates and angles, with either two or four webs tied together by diaphragms and lacing bar webs to act as a unit. Author's Collection.

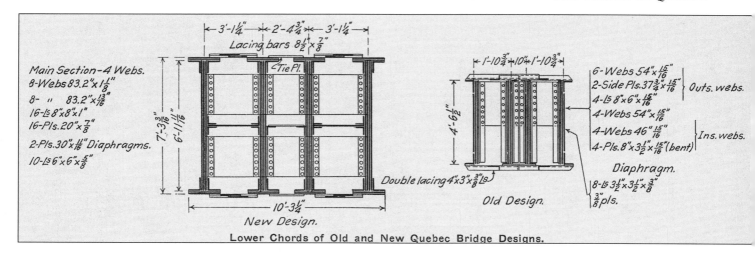

Main Section–4 Webs.
8-Webs 83.2"x1⅛"
8- " 83.2"x¹³⁄₁₆"
16-Ls 8"x8"x1"
16-Pls.20"x⅞"
2-Pls.30"x¹¹⁄₁₆" Diaphragms.
10-Ls 6"x6"x⅝"

Lacing bars 8½"x⅞"

Tie Pl.

Double lacing 4"x3"x⅜"Ls

New Design.

Old Design.

6-Webs 54"x¹⁵⁄₁₆"
2-Side Pls.37¾"x¹⁵⁄₁₆" } Outs. webs.
4-Ls 8"x6"x¹⁵⁄₁₆"
4-Webs 54"x¹⁵⁄₁₆"
4-Webs 46"¹⁵⁄₁₆" } Ins. webs.
4-Pls.8"x3½"x¹⁵⁄₁₆" (bent)

Diaphragm.
8-Ls 3½"x3½"x⅜"
⅜"pls.

Lower Chords of Old and New Quebec Bridge Designs.

The heavier loading standards and the more conservative design stresses adopted for the second Quebec Bridge are evident from these comparative cross sections from the September 26, 1913, issue of *Railway Age Gazette,* showing the bottom chord members for the new and old designs. The largest chord members for the new bridge (left) had a total steel cross sectional area of 1,902 square inches, while the corresponding section for the old design had only 842 square inches. Library of Congress.

structure than economy of the work itself would call for," said Ralph Modjeski, "if the more expensive structure will afford sufficient advertisement and publicity to compensate for the additional expenditure."[15]

Work on the design as it was finally adopted began in the fall of 1911 and continued through 1917. By the time the bridge was complete, the engineers had produced nearly 800 large plans to guide the fabrication and erection of the enormous structure, and they estimated that probably twice this number of preliminary drawings had been completed before the final plans were approved.

But well before the engineers had begun work on the final superstructure design, construction work had begun at Québec for the second attempt to bridge the St. Lawrence.

CHAPTER 8

UNDERWAY AGAIN

LONG BEFORE THE DESIGN WORK WAS COMPLETED OR A CONTRACT AWARDED FOR the superstructure of the new bridge, construction was underway once again at the Chaudière site. A first order of business was the removal of the wreckage of the collapsed span on the south shore of the river. This would prove to be no easy task.

In order to clear the site and to remove any obstacle to the building of the new piers, it was necessary to remove all of the wreckage between the old anchor and main piers and everything above low water level beyond the main pier. This represented some 9,000 tons of wreckage that lay in a tangled heap 70 to 80 feet wide, 500 feet long, and anywhere from 10 to 40 feet high between the anchor and main piers, and extending another 50 feet north of the main pier.

"The magnitude and difficulties of the job cannot be appreciated unless one has personally visited the wreck and seen this enormous tangle of huge steel members piled high and in utter confusion, yet with no loose ends," wrote H. P. Borden, assistant engineer for the board of engineers. "Every ton of metal moved, whether eyebar, chord or post, must first be cut loose from its neighbor or subdivided into many pieces before it can be handled. The various members are twisted and bent almost beyond recognition, yet they are still firmly bound one to the other."[1] A contract was awarded to a Québec firm, Charles Koenig and Company, in December 1909, and the tedious and difficult task of breaking the structure apart, cutting every member into manageable pieces, and removing the wreckage began the following month.

The required work was without precedent. Some of the large chord sections, weighing anywhere from 50 to 75 tons, had to be cut into as many as six or eight sections to permit handling with the 10-ton derricks used for the removal. The contractor experimented for several months with various grades and strengths of dynamite before finding the one that worked best for the task. Dynamite was used to break the wrecked eyebars at the head and to break apart the large panel points and other intersections in the trusses. Charges of as much as 80 pounds of dynamite were required to break apart the massive 80-ton shoes that supported the structure on the main pier. Once the members had been blasted apart, oxy-acetylene torches were used to cut the members into pieces of manageable size for removal. The work took more than two years; and by the time the task was completed at the end of August 1912, the contractor had used more than 20 tons of dynamite and some 90,000 cubic feet of oxygen.[2]

Simultaneous with the removal work, preparations for the substructure construction began on the north shore. In December 1909 work began at the north shore bluff on the

The first order of business for the builders of the new Quebec Bridge was the removal of the wreckage and piers from the collapsed span. Here, laborers worked to remove the north main pier on June 17, 1910. The granite facing stone was being salvaged for use in the piers of the new bridge. National Archives of Canada (Neg. PA 108799).

construction of supporting facilities, while at Sillery Cove, about three miles downstream from the bridge site, facilities were started for the construction of the caissons that would be needed to build the new main piers. A shed 200 feet long, 70 feet wide, and 40 feet high was built over the crib foundations where the timber caissons were to be built, allowing the work to proceed under all weather conditions. A double-track, narrow gauge railroad connected the shed with a storage yard and a saw and planing mill.

Tenders for construction of the new piers and removal of the old ones had been called late in October 1909, and the contract was awarded on January 10, 1910, to the M. P. and J. T. Davis firm, the same contractor that had built the piers for the original bridge; and the work began almost immediately. Aside from portions of the north and south abutments and the foundations of the original south main pier, none of the original substructure was to be used, and the Davis firm's contract required the removal of the remainder of the original piers to a level below that of the ground or river bottom.

Removal of the wreckage on the south shore would delay a start to substructure work there until 1911, and the contractor's first order of business was the construction of the caisson that would be required to build the foundation for the new north pier. One of the largest caissons ever built, this was an enormous timber structure 180 feet long and 55 feet wide. Construction of the caisson began at the Sillery Cove site on March 31 with the laying of a 30-inch by 30-inch cutting edge of Douglas fir. Below the 7-foot roof level of the working chamber, the caisson was framed of two layers of 12-inch by 12-inch timbers, finished on the outside with two layers of 3-inch planking. The roof of the working chamber was constructed of two courses of 12-inch by 12-inch timbers separated by two layers of 3-inch diagonal planking. Along its center line, the roof was supported by a longitudinal bulkhead made up of two thicknesses of 12-inch by 12-inch timbers. Eight cross bulkheads were framed into this longitudinal bulkhead, dividing the working chamber into eighteen sections. Manholes in the bulkheads allowed workmen to move freely between the chambers. Above the level of the working chamber, the walls of the caisson were stayed by three longitudinal and 17 transverse structures of 12-inch by 12-inch timbers which formed open wells, each about 9 feet by 10 feet. At the time it was launched, the caisson had been built up to a height of 22 feet, 9 inches, with another 9 feet to be added before sinking operations began at the bridge site. The walls would then be further built up as the sinking progressed.

The caisson was provided with six airlocks for material handling and another four ladder airlocks for workmen. Water for loosening and removing sand and gravel was brought into the caisson through two 7-inch water lines, while a 12-inch line brought compressed air into the working chamber. The working chamber was wired for electric lights and fitted with a telephone communication system.

Construction of a launching way for the 1,600-ton caisson began early in June. The caisson was supported on six oak cradles, each 60 feet long and shaped like an inverted trough, arranged to slide down launching ways built of yellow pine timbers and supported by concrete pedestals. The cradles and launching ways were planed smooth and treated with a hot application of tallow and plumbago to reduce friction. A 70-ton screw jack was placed behind each cradle to start the caisson moving when the time came for launching, while four 350-ton capacity hydraulic jacks were placed under the cutting edge at the upper side to lift and push the caisson. The sideways launching at high tide on July 7 was completed with deceptive ease. Just twenty-five seconds after the jacks had started it moving, the huge structure was floating safely in the river, ready to be towed to a nearby mooring for completion.[3]

Meanwhile work had continued on the north shore at the bridge site to prepare for sinking the caisson. A level area had been filled in at the base of the 150-foot cliff for a compressed air and boiler plant. A large concrete mixing plant, stone crushers, and a stone bin were also built at the foot of the cliff. A coal chute was built to the top of the cliff to supply the boiler

On July 7, 1910, a crowd had gathered on the bluff overlooking Sillery Cove to watch the sideways launching of the 1,600-ton caisson for construction of the north main pier for the new Quebec Bridge. The launching ways were greased with hot tallow and plumbago, hydraulic jacks started the huge caisson moving, and it was safely in the water in only twenty-five seconds. National Archives of Canada (Neg. PA 108800).

This interior view of the timber caisson shows it on July 22, 1910, when work was nearly complete. On August 1, the structure was towed to the bridge site to begin work on the north main pier. National Archives of Canada (Neg. PA 108801).

plant, while double tracks laid on top of the chute accommodated counterbalanced cars that transferred cement from railroad cars at the top of the cliff to the mixing plant. There was a stairway for workmen; and an inclined elevator fitted with tracks was installed for material handling by narrow gauge cars, which operated on both the upper and lower level.

Two trestles built on piles or cribs connected these facilities on the north shore with the main pier location, where a platform was erected that would enclose the caisson. This was fitted with three stiff-legged derricks and the necessary mechanical equipment for tending the caisson and handling the excavation buckets. The platform also accommodated contractor office and storage spaces; a dressing room, hot showers, and a coffee house for the sandhogs; and a doctor's office with a hospital air lock for the treatment of any men suffering from the "bends," or caisson disease.

While the caisson was still under construction, the contractor had begun dredging at the site of the north main pier. During May and June, about 7,000 cubic yards of sand and boulders, many of them weighing 3 to 4 tons, had been dredged from the site before the dredge broke down. By the end of July, the walls of the caisson had been built up to a height of 39 feet; and it was ready to move to the bridge site. On August 1 three tugs, two towing and one steering, took charge of the 2,000-ton structure and successfully towed it into position at the north pier site.

Concreting of the caisson to sink it into place on the river bottom began on August 15, and almost immediately the contractor began encountering unforeseen problems. Water began leaking through the roof or deck of the caisson, most of it entering along the line of the center bulkhead and at the juncture of the roof and the walls. A single pump was unable to keep the caisson clear of water, and a second was installed; but still the water was kept down only with difficulty, and there was usually one or two feet of water on the roof.

Despite the leakage problems, placement of concrete on the roof of the caisson continued, adding to its weight and causing it to sink lower in the water. During unusually low

tides from August 19 to 27, the caisson grounded for the first time at the northwest corner, where the planned dredging had not been completed, leaving a high area. On August 26 the contractor began running the air compressors at low tides to pump air into the working chamber in an attempt to lift the caisson and prevent the grounding. Even with two compressors running at full capacity, it proved impossible to lower the water level in the chamber by more than a foot below the roof level. Still another pump was added, but the problems continued. Shifting water on the deck made it impossible to keep the caisson level, and at times only one or two of the pumps could be used effectively. Concreting was stopped, but by this time 7 feet of concrete had been placed on the roof, and the caisson had sunk to a draft of about 23 feet, with one corner at times anywhere from 2 to 5 feet higher than the diagonally opposite corner.

Next, sandhogs entered the caisson and swam through the bulkhead openings to reach the northwest corner. A section of the temporary false bottom on the caisson was removed, and some material was excavated from beneath the caisson cutting edge. It soon became apparent, however, that insufficient material could be removed in this manner to permit the caisson to be landed on a level bed. It was then decided to fill the excavated area under the cutting edge with broken stone to bring it up to the level of the highest corner. This work began on August 28; but before it could be completed, new problems were encountered.

"On the night of August 30th," wrote the board of engineers in its final report, "the pump at the west end of the caisson broke down, and there was trouble starting the pump at the east end. Trouble was also experienced in obtaining sufficient steam to keep the compressors running at the required speed. As a consequence, the caisson began to sink until the 5-in. holes through which the mooring cables entered were submerged. At low tide on the

A view of the top of one of the two caissons at the north main pier site on September 20, 1911, shows the compressed air pumping equipment in use to maintain pressure inside the caisson. To the right can be seen one of the airlocks used for removing excavated material from the caisson. National Archives of Canada (Neg. PA 108803).

morning of August 31st the caisson grounded at both ends, causing a sag at the center of 15 in. Seams on the roof of the caisson opened up, and air could not be retained in the working chamber. The caisson lifted with the next flood tide, but grounded again at low tide, increasing the deflection at the center to 21 in."[4]

More seams opened in the roof, and the water kept gaining on the pumps. At times the water level inside the caisson was as much as 5 feet higher than the river, and by noon on September 1, the deflection at the center of the caisson had increased to about 2½ feet. Large holes were then drilled through the walls of the caisson to allow water to drain off at low tide. Check valves prevented water from entering the caisson at high tide. Next, two more pumps were brought to the caisson, making a total of five. On September 2 workmen began passing large quantities of sawdust through the air locks, which helped somewhat in stopping the leaks. Finally, the effort was given up. "At this point a consultation was held between the contractors and the Board of Engineers," wrote the engineers in their final report, "and it was decided that it would be useless to attempt to sink the caisson under existing conditions."[5] Plans were made to remove the caisson from the site and place it in a dry dock for repairs. This, too, would prove a difficult task.

There was now about eight feet of concrete, weighing some 4,600 tons, in place on the roof over the working chamber, and the caisson was drawing about 28 feet of water. In order to float the caisson, the concrete would have to be removed, a task that was accomplished with steam drills and dynamite. A timber platform was then constructed on top of the walls. This accommodated about 150 tons of granite blocks, which were used to trim the caisson as it was towed to the dry dock, and provided space for three steam boilers and five pumps that were installed to keep the caisson free of water during the move. Three tugs moved the caisson to Lévis on October 19. By the following morning, the caisson was listing so badly that it could not be placed in the dry dock. A second attempt on the following day was successful, and the damaged caisson was safely docked. The 1910 construction season was now at an end, and virtually nothing had been accomplished at the site of either of the two main piers.

In the light of the difficulties encountered in trying to sink the north pier caisson, the board of engineers reconsidered its plans for the substructure. The sinking of such a large caisson through the boulder subsoil of the north shore had proved much more difficult than anticipated, while the original plan to sink two long, narrow caissons to enlarge the original south main pier now seemed much more risky as well. Thus, it was at this point, in March 1911, that the engineers decided to abandon their original plan and instead to build two entirely new main piers, each of them 65 feet south of the original piers. This change restored the main span of the bridge to the same 1,800-foot length used for the original bridge. Under this new plan, two smaller caissons would be employed to build the north main pier, while the larger caisson originally built for the north pier would be repaired and used to build the south pier, where a sandy bottom offered much better conditions for sinking the large structure.

Some repair work for the large caisson had been started in November 1910, but winter weather brought the work to a halt before it could be completed. The repairs and extensive reinforcement of the caisson continued the following spring, and by late May the rebuilt structure was ready to be towed back to the bridge site. The move was completed without difficulty on the high tide of the morning of May 28, and the caisson was secured to cribs and guide timbers and settled on the bottom at the pier site. Sinking of the caisson would not begin until the following spring.

Work had begun at Sillery the previous fall on the construction of the two caissons for the planned enlargement of the original south pier. With the change in plans for substructure construction, this work was halted and the partially completed caissons taken apart and their material used in the construction of the two new caissons for the north shore pier. These were each 60 feet wide and 80 feet long and, except for their smaller size, similar in their construction details to the original caisson. The first of the two caissons was launched on May 29, 1911, and was ready for towing to the bridge site by early June. The tow was completed on the morning high tide of June 10, and by 7:20 a.m. the caisson was successfully moored in position over the west half of the north main pier site, which had previously been filled with sand to provide a level bed.

By June 21 the walls of the caisson had been built up to a height of 46 feet, and the first concrete was placed on the deck to begin the sinking operation. On June 24, after 400 cubic yards of concrete had been placed, the caisson grounded for the first time in 19 feet of water. Concreting continued around the clock; and by June 29, with a load of almost 4,000 tons of concrete in place, the cutting edge of the caisson had sunk to a depth of about 3 feet in the sand bed. Air was then forced into the working chamber, and five sandhogs entered the chamber to begin leveling high spots under the cutting edge. Excavation within the working chamber began on July 2. Blowpipes were used to remove the sand beneath the cutting edge, much of it being used to fill the east half of the excavation to form a bed for the second caisson.

Once again the boulder-strewn subsoil of the riverbed presented the contractors and engineers with some difficult problems. At the northwest corner of the site, where the ground was higher, a number of compressed air blowouts indicated that the cutting edge of the caisson had probably been damaged. An examination on July 8 found that the cutting edge at the northwest corner had landed on a large piece of granite—probably left from the building of the original north pier—and was badly damaged. Two similarly damaged areas were found on the south side of the caisson, where the cutting edge had encountered boulders 4 to 5 feet in diameter. Repairs were made to the damaged cutting edge and caisson walls, and the engineers devised a new procedure for sinking the caisson that would reduce the weight on the cutting edge.

A blocking system of nine massive timber towers was built up under the working chamber bulkheads to support the caisson while the ground under the cutting edge was excavated to a depth of about 2 feet. Additional concrete was then added to the caisson only as needed to add the weight necessary for sinking, which was regulated by washing away sand under the blocking. This allowed the caisson to settle anywhere from 1 to 2 feet until it came to rest on a new set of blocking. Numerous boulders, several of them 30 cubic yards or more in size, were encountered under the cutting edge. Some were pulled into the working chamber by a wire rope attached to a derrick on the platform above the caisson and then broken up by small blasting charges to be removed in pieces. Some, too large to be moved or lifted out through the material shafts, were drilled and blasted apart in place. The blasted material and small boulders were removed through the caisson's material shafts in half-yard buckets, while smaller material was blown out through the caisson's 4-inch blowpipes.

The second caisson for the east side of the north main pier was completed and towed into position alongside the first caisson on July 11, and sinking began nine days later. Air was forced into the working chamber, and the first sandhogs began work within it on July 27. Excavation began several days later, and the men soon ran into problems similar to those encountered in the adjacent caisson. The same blocking system used to sink the west caisson was then adopted, and the sinking was completed without further difficulty.

Sinking of the first caisson continued until October 8, when it had been sunk a total distance of 41.6 feet into the riverbed, while sinking of the second caisson continued until October 21, when it had been sunk a total of 38.3 feet. Both caissons were now at a depth about 20 feet above the bedrock in the riverbed. While the original intent had been to carry the pier to bedrock, it was now thought that the compact material of the riverbed, largely made up of boulders, would provide a satisfactory foundation, saving the considerable time and expense that would be required to reach bedrock. Tests of the bearing capacity of the soil confirmed that it could easily carry the loads of the bridge without any settlement, and the sinking was stopped.

Any loose material in the caisson working chambers was now removed, and trenches were dug under the cutting edges. These trenches were then filled with concrete to completely embed the cutting edge, and the entire working chamber and the material and man shafts were filled with concrete. Loose material was removed from the 10-foot space between the two caissons, and the area was dredged to a depth of 38 feet below high water. Timber gates were installed at each end and the entire space filled with concrete, enclosing six steel girders, each 6 feet deep, which had been installed between the two caissons. Work then began on laying up the masonry face of the pier inside timber cribwork, which would remain in place until the masonry extended above the high water level. The first granite face stone was laid on October 30, and a little more than 1,000 cubic yards of granite had been laid in the two lower courses before work ended for the season in November. The work site was then laid up for the winter, while the compressed air, steam, and electric plants used to support the sinking of the caissons were taken down, transferred to the south shore, and re-erected to support the sinking of the caisson for the south main pier during the 1912 construction season. Other substructure work completed during 1911 included the removal of the south main pier and north anchor piers for the old bridge. Granite face stones from both piers were stored, ready to be re-cut for use in the new piers.

The principal task facing the Davis firm for the 1912 construction season was that of successfully sinking the large caisson for the south main pier. Fully repaired after the unsuccessful attempt to use it for the north main pier, the caisson had been grounded on the south pier site, ready for sinking, since May 28, 1911. By the beginning of the 1912 season, all was in readiness to begin the sinking. The compressed air, steam, and electric plants from the north shore had been set up and additional air compressors and boilers installed. A concrete mixing plant and other support facilities similar to those used on the north shore were also put in place.

Work began late in April with a thorough cleaning of the caisson and recaulking of seams wherever required. Because of both the great size of the caisson and the severe wrenching it had received in the attempt to sink it for the north pier, the engineers had devised a reinforcing system of steel bars that would be encased in the concrete placed on top of the deck. This was made up of ten 2-inch-square longitudinal steel rods that were run through the east and west walls of the caisson and fitted with nuts and washers at each end and turnbuckles at the center to permit them to be tightened. These were placed about a foot above the deck, with another layer of twenty-eight 2-inch-square bars placed on top and at right angles to them. When the concrete reached a depth of 4 feet above the top of these rods, another layer of eight 2-inch square longitudinal bars was added.

The sinking method adopted for the caisson was somewhat similar to that developed the previous year for the north pier caissons. In addition to a system of fifty-four sets of blocking under the working chamber bulkheads, the caisson was supported during sinking by twenty-five timber posts under the roof and a system of thirty-eight ingenious sand jacks. Each jack consisted of a sand-filled steel cylinder 3 feet long with an internal diameter of 31 inches, resting on timber blocking. On each side near the bottom, three-inch holes allowed a two-inch pipe to extend across the cylinder. This was split at the center and opened to allow sand to escape from the cylinder. The piston was made of a fir block 2 feet, 6 inches square and 5 feet long, with the lower 4 feet rounded to a diameter of 29 inches, allowing it to fit into the cylinder with about an inch of clearance. This piston was attached rigidly to the roof of the chamber throughout the sinking operation.

When the caisson was ready for a drop, two men were positioned at each jack. One held a burlap sack at the outlet from the 2-inch pipe at the base of the cylinder, while the other controlled a water jet used to wash the sand out of the cylinder. In order to avoid straining the caisson by uneven settling, a system of light signals was devised to assure that each jack was lowered at the same rate. At the first flash of the light signal, the water jet was turned into each cylinder. As the sand and water ran out through the 2-inch pipe, the water passed through the burlap bag, while the sand remained. As soon as the bag was filled with sand, the lights were flashed a second time, signaling the men to turn off the water jets. Each cylinder contained about sixteen bags of sand, and the operation was repeated with new bags until each drop of 18 inches to 2 feet had been completed.

After each drop was completed, half of the sand jacks were left in place to support the caisson while the other nineteen were repositioned and filled with sand for the next drop. The first step in this operation was to attach the empty cylinders to the pistons by means of hooks, allowing the timber blocking under the cylinders to be removed, leaving both piston and cylinder hanging from the roof. The ground beneath each jack was then excavated sufficiently for the next stage of lowering, the blocking was replaced, and the cylinders were unhooked and lowered to rest on the blocking. The cylinders were then filled with sand in readiness for the next lowering operation. The load was then transferred to these jacks and the other nineteen were similarly repositioned and refilled with sand.

Excavation under the cutting edge of the caisson began on May 1, while concreting on the deck of the caisson began on June 1, with some 20 feet of concrete being placed over the next two weeks, adding enough weight to begin the sinking. From then on, concrete was added only when more weight was required for the sinking operation. Compressed air was forced into the working chamber for the first time on June 15. Sandhogs entered the chamber the next day, and the work proceeded continuously around the clock, except on Sundays, from then until October. Initially the work was carried on in three shifts of eight hours each, with about 110 men in each shift. The length of shifts was gradually reduced as the caisson sank lower, requiring increasing air pressures. On August 31 the work schedule was changed to four shifts of six hours, with about eighty men in each. This was changed again on September 10, with six shifts of four hours each, with about fifty men per shift, and again on September 20 to eight shifts of three hours each. The maximum air pressure at this time was 34½ pounds per square inch, well over double normal atmospheric pressure. On September 29 a schedule of two hours' work in each twenty-four was introduced, divided into two periods of one hour each, four hours apart. In October, as the caisson neared its final depth more than 100 feet below the extreme high water level of the river, the maximum air pressure in the working chamber reached 41 pounds per square inch, almost three times atmospheric pressure.

Steady progress was made in sinking the caisson with the sand jack procedure. The average rate of progress from beginning to end of the sinking was 9 inches per day. During July the caisson was sunk a total of 17.55 feet, increasing to 22.2 feet during August. The greatest rate of progress came in September, when the caisson was sunk 31.5 feet to bring it within less than 8 feet of its final depth. While good progress had been made, the sinking was not completed without some major problems.

"As the sinking progressed, old air leaks in the caisson opened up and new ones appeared," wrote the board of engineers in its final report. "At times all the compressors had to run at their maximum capacity. Much air leaked out through the concrete all along the inner side of the wall timbers and many schemes were devised to stop this loss of air. The leaks could not be stopped by depositing concrete over them, because the air under pressure made small holes in the green concrete, honeycombing it for a foot in width along the inner face of the wall."[6] Finally, a board was fitted between the concrete and the wall, the joints were made tight with burlap, and pipes were fitted every 20 feet to allow the air to escape. Once the concrete had set, the pipes were capped. This worked, although some loss of air continued.

A much greater problem developed near the center of the south wall at about 10:30 a.m. on July 20, when a fire was discovered in the oakum caulking between layers of timber sheathing. Pouring water against the wall from either side had no effect, and as the fire gained rapidly, all but a few men were ordered out of the working chamber, and preparations were made to flood the caisson. A number of 1-inch holes were then drilled into the caisson wall from the outside, and water was forced in under 100 pounds pressure. By 2:30 p.m. the fire appeared to be out, but the water streams were left on for another two hours until 4:30 p.m., when the full shift returned to the working chamber. Except for a slight increase in air leakage, the caisson appeared to have come through the fire undamaged. On August 15 a second fire, this time in the working chamber, was started by a short circuit in the electrical wiring. This one was put out

This was the status of substructure construction on the south shore of the river on August 2, 1913. Material storage and a compressed air and boiler plant were located in the level area in the foreground. Trestles connected the shore facilities with a platform that enclosed the south main pier caisson. This was fitted with stiff-legged derricks and other equipment needed to tend the caisson and handle the excavation buckets. The building on the near side of the caisson location housed contractor offices and storage; a dressing room, hot showers, and a coffee house for the sandhogs; and a doctor's office with a hospital air lock. Although hidden by the work building, the south main pier was nearly complete by this date. Across the river can be seen the substantially complete north main pier and anchor pier. National Archives of Canada (Neg. C 9768).

without significant damage in about twenty minutes, but the entire wiring system was replaced as a precaution.

Air leakage from the caisson continued to be a problem, and late in August a new method of stopping it was tried. Holes were drilled into the timber sheathing where the leaks were occurring, and dry cement was forced into the holes through pipes. In September still another procedure was tried. A special gun was rigged up to inject liquid tar into the spaces between timbers under 80 pounds of pressure. Small hand guns were then used to pump a neat cement grout behind the tar. Altogether about 1,000 holes were drilled and 400 bags of cement were used. It seemed to work, and there was a great improvement in the air tightness of the caisson.

Still more trouble came on August 20. When air pressure was reduced to accelerate the sinking operation, the cutting edge on the south side of the caisson was pushed inward by the outside pressure. An attempt to force it back into position failed. Caulking in the wall where the damage occurred was loosened and partly pulled out, allowing a large volume of air leakage from the chamber. There was more trouble in September, when the caisson walls began to pull apart on a horizontal line about 46 feet above the cutting edge, probably as a result of the increasing pressure from material outside the caisson. At some points, butt joints between the vertical timbers had opened up by as much as 3½ inches. The problem was above the level of the concrete in the caisson, and water and sand began running in through the open joints. The caisson walls began to show signs of stress and bulged in and out at various points along the side. Wooden strips were driven into the wider of the open joints, and all joints were recaulked. Iron straps and splice plates were spiked and bolted to the vertical timbers, and ¾-inch wire ropes attached to the upper wall timbers and embedded in the concrete over the deck. A number of 1-inch screw bolts were screwed into the wall timbers and embedded in the concrete. Diagonal braces were installed to square up the end of the caisson, and the inner crib timbers were reinforced. The repair work seemed to succeed, and no further problems were encountered.

The caisson reached bedrock below the riverbed during October, and concreting under the cutting edge was completed on November 3. Concreting of the working chamber began the next day, and by November 16, filling of the chamber and the access shafts had been completed. Grouting of the caisson to fill any cavities or fissures was completed on November 24, when work was shut down for the season.

Substantial progress was also made on other elements of the substructure during the 1912 season. Work had resumed on the north main pier on July 1. Tapering from a length of 168 feet and a width of 39 feet at the base to 160 feet, 8 inches by 32 feet at the top, the pier was constructed of concrete faced with granite. In order to prevent any cracking due to differential settlement of the two caissons, a total of thirty-eight 2-inch square steel bars were placed in the concrete backing of the first three courses of facing stone. By the time work ended for the season on November 20, eight of twenty-two masonry courses for the pier had been completed.

Work had begun in May for the north anchor pier, which was completed to a level about 50 feet above the base by the end of the season. Work was also begun and completed on the north shore during the season to build an intermediate pier required for the approach spans, and for the alterations required to adapt the original abutment for the new bridge. On the south shore, excavation for the south anchor pier had begun in April, and concreting of the foundation was substantially complete when work ended for the season on November 26.

Work continued throughout the winter and early spring of 1913 on the time-consuming cutting and dressing of the granite facing stone for the piers, with as many as 104 stone cutters at work in March. As soon as the weather permitted, work resumed on the various piers, and the substructure work was substantially complete by the end of the season. Work on the north main pier resumed on May 15, while the south main pier was started somewhat later, on June 1; but the last stone had been placed in both piers by mid-October. This was followed by careful dressing of the bridge seats on the top of each pier to assure an absolutely level bearing surface for the structure's enormous steel shoes. Both the north and south anchor piers and the alterations to the south abutment were also completed well before the end of the 1913 season. All that was left for the 1914 season was some cleaning and pointing of piers that had not been completed the year before, as well as removal of the old south shore anchor pier. All told, the construction of the new substructure piers and abutments represented a total of more than 106,000 cubic yards of concrete or stone masonry.

The St. Lawrence Bridge Company began work at the bridge site in the summer of 1912 with the construction of support facilities for the erection. A construction camp was built and erection plant and equipment were installed on the north shore. Because of the somewhat remote location, the camp included general offices, a kitchen and dining hall, bunkhouses for 250 men, a hospital, a store, and other facilities, including water and sewer

Dating to some time in 1913, this photograph shows the stonework nearing completion for the north main pier. The portion of the work platform that surrounded the outer side of the pier had already been removed. Smithsonian Institution (Neg. 98-2569).

On October 3, 1913, the stonework for the south main pier was almost finished. This view shows clearly the arrangement of headers and stretchers and the vertical bonding stones that were used in the upper courses. The last stone in the pier was laid just ten days later. National Archives of Canada (Neg. PA 108769).

This September 19, 1913, view of the completed south anchor pier shows clearly some of the support facilities that were required for the substructure construction. To the right of the pier is the boiler house that powered the compressed air plant. To the right of and above the pier are three of the typical stiff-legged derricks used for material handling. Beyond the pier and to the right are two of the chutes used to convey coal, stone, and other materials down to the shore from the bluff above. National Archives of Canada (Neg. PA 108768).

A view from the top of the bluff on the north shore shows the substructure construction nearing completion on both shores of the river, while an empty freighter steams down the river toward the Gulf of St. Lawrence and the Atlantic. Smithsonian Institution (Neg. 98-2574).

systems. Electric power and compressed air plants for operating the erection equipment, storage yards, and tracks and sidings for material and equipment delivery were installed on both the north and south shores. The boards of engineers also established its own offices and living accommodations for its engineers and inspectors on the north shore.

A short distance to the west of the camp, the firm established a large storage yard where the fabricated sections of the bridge were stored until needed in the erection sequence. The yard was equipped with elevated runways, placed at right angles to the railroad tracks into the site, for an 81-foot, 90-ton capacity overhead crane used to load and unload material from railroad cars. A similar installation was established on the south shore alongside the National Transcontinental Railway tracks about a mile from the bridge site.

In order to avoid any possibility of later changes that might affect the weight of the structure, the design for the entire bridge was worked out and shop drawings completed before any fabrication of the cantilever or anchor arms was begun. Because of this careful approach, the final weight of the structure was within 1 percent of the estimated weight upon which the dead load stresses had been calculated.

By the beginning of 1913, the detailed design work for the superstructure had reached the point at which fabrication could begin. Because of the great size and weight of many of the members that would have to be fabricated and the unusually stringent workmanship standards established by the specifications, no existing Canadian bridge plant could have done the work without extensive reconstruction and re-equipment. Instead, the St. Lawrence Bridge Company spent more than a million dollars to build an entirely new plant at Rockfield, near Lachine, Québec, that would be devoted exclusively to the Quebec Bridge project.

In order to fabricate the exceptionally large and heavy members required for the Quebec Bridge, the St. Lawrence Bridge Company built and equipped an entirely new plant at Rockfield, Québec, at a cost of more than a million dollars. This February 1914 view shows one of the portable vertical drills reaming rivet holes in the web of a floor beam. National Archives of Canada (Neg. PA 108791).

The main building of the new plant was a high-roofed structure of almost 140,000 square feet, arranged so that raw material entered at one end to pass through the building in a continuous process of fabrication into the structural members of the bridge. Reflecting the great size of these members, most of the machinery was of unusual size and capacity. In the area devoted to shearing, punching, and drilling, there were sixteen stationary and twenty-four portable radial drills and another twelve portable horizontal drills. In the section of the shop where the largest members were riveted, there were two 70-ton and one 35-ton traveling cranes, capable of handling sections up to 200 tons. At the finishing end of the shop, there was a horizontal boring machine that could bore a 45-inch hole 11 feet long. A duplex vertical and horizontal planing machine for finishing the ends of large compression members was capable of simultaneously planing both ends of a member 10 feet square. A duplex horizontal chord boring machine was capable of simultaneously boring the pin holes in each end of a member 90 feet long. A duplex eyebar boring machine had a bed 100 feet long. Installed in the finishing shed at one end of the shop was a large horizontal planing machine especially designed for planing of the large castings required for the main shoes that would rest on the bridge's two main piers.

In addition to mobilizing and staffing the entire organization required to operate the new plant, the St. Lawrence Bridge Company had to specially train the men to meet the extremely high standards of accuracy and detail required for the bridge. An unusually large inspection staff employed by the board of engineers helped to assure that these high standards were met. The new plant was designed and equipped to fabricate about 2,000 tons per month, but this capacity was substantially exceeded once the organization was running smoothly, with a maximum production in one month of 3,250 tons.

Virtually all of the carbon and nickel steel required for the bridge came from the plants of the Carnegie Steel Company at Pittsburgh. The pins for the entire bridge were forged and finished in the gun plant of the Bethlehem Steel Company. Tension eyebars for the structure were rolled at Carnegie's Pittsburgh plants but were upset, annealed, bored, and tested at the American Bridge Company's Ambridge, Pennsylvania, plant.

The work of fabrication began in the new plant early in 1913, and the first superstructure erection began on August 5, when work was started on the north shore approach spans, which were completed by November 7. Work on the main span began with the erection of the north anchor arm. This was accomplished with an enormous gantry crane traveler of the inside type, so-called because it traveled inside the line of the main trusses. This was a structural steel tower 190 feet high and weighing 920 tons in working order. Two trusses at the top of the tower, each 18 feet deep and 155 feet long, served as runways for two traveling cranes, each equipped with two 55-ton hoists. At each end of these traveling cranes were smaller auxiliary gantry cranes capable of a maximum lift of 10 tons, and there were four 70-foot, 20-ton derrick booms mounted one on each corner of the tower. The traveler was supported and moved on four six-wheeled trucks running on double lines of rails. The girders supporting the crane runway were part of the permanent floor system for the bridge. Material for erection was brought to the traveler on trucks carried on two railroad tracks that passed through the traveler on the main bridge floor.

Erection of the north shore traveler began in the fall of 1913 and continued through the winter. It was ready for operation on May 18, 1914, and three days later was moved out over the completed approach span to the north anchor pier. A week later the erection crew began moving the traveler out toward the main pier. As they moved outwards on this first pass, the erection crew installed the temporary staging that would support the anchor arm until it was complete, the main floor material of the bridge, and the girders for the traveler track. Next came the task of erecting the two main shoes, each of which weighed 420 tons. These were made up of four steel bed castings, each of 40 tons, followed by two additional tiers assembled in three pieces, with the largest one weighing 65 tons. These were then riveted up, and the 45-inch diameter sleeves and 30-inch diameter pins that would carry the anchor arm bottom chords were placed.

The two men give a sense of the enormous scale of this unusually complex member AL2, which would form one of the lower chord joints at the first panel point of the anchor arm, where four members intersected, all at angles. The member is shown here on the boring machine, where pin holes for a field connection were being drilled. Smithsonian Institution (Neg. 97-585).

Facing page:

(Top) This view in the Rockfield shop shows one of the main shoes for the bridge fully assembled, lacking only the diagonal side brackets on each side. Each of these enormous shoes was 21 feet long, 26 feet, 4 inches wide, and 19 feet high and weighed 420 tons. The steel 30-inch-diameter steel pins that linked the shoe to the cantilever and anchor arm bottom chords and to the main post would be driven into 45-inch diameter bushings in the shoe, while 20-inch-diameter pins in 30-inch bushings would link the web diagonals to the shoe. Once the bridge was complete, each of these shoes would support a total weight of 55 million pounds. Smithsonian Institution.

(Bottom) This view of the faced end of a bottom chord compression member shows the 45-inch-diameter half pin holes that would link the chord to the main shoe. This was one of the anchor arm chord members that would go into the panel next to the main pier. The section weighed 200 tons and would be disassembled into two halves for shipment to the bridge site. Smithsonian Institution (Neg. 98-2570).

Ready for shipment to Québec, a 72-ton segment of one of the main shoes was loaded on a flatcar at the Rockfield plant. Smithsonian Institution (Neg. 98-2571).

A gang of ironworkers gathered around one of the 145-ton top links that would go at the top of the main posts, with a man in each of the seven pin holes for the connections to the two rows of top chord eyebars, the main post, and the main diagonals in this view from the report of the board of engineers. Author's Collection.

Four engineers in a playful mood posed astride one of the 30-inch diameter steel pins for the bridge. From left to right they were the St. Lawrence Bridge Company's engineer of construction George F. Porter and Chief Engineer George H. Duggan, and board of engineers Chairman and Chief Engineer Charles N. Monsarrat and member Ralph Modjeski. Smithsonian Institution (Neg. 98-2577).

This 190-foot-high, 920-ton traveler was used to erect the north anchor and cantilever arms of the bridge. It is shown here on May 8, 1914, shortly before it was moved out over the already complete approach span, visible to the right of the traveler, to begin erection of the anchor arm. Smithsonian Institution (Neg. 98-2576).

This view of the top of the traveler used to erect the north anchor and cantilever arms of the bridge shows one of the two traveling cranes mounted on top of the traveler. Each of them was equipped with two 55-ton hoists. Smithsonian Institution (Neg. 98-2575).

Pages 137–142

The 575-foot-long north anchor arm of the bridge was erected in a carefully planned series of five passes of the traveler between the anchor and main piers over a period of thirteen months, with four and a half months off for the winter season.

On May 1, 1914, the traveler began its first outward pass from the anchor pier to the main pier, erecting temporary steel staging as it went that would support the anchor arm during erection. The main floor members of the bridge and girders for the traveler track were also installed at this time. This work had reached the fifth panel point of the anchor arm at the time of this July 8, 1914, photograph. National Archives of Canada (Neg. PA 61111).

By mid-July the bridge men had completed erection of the anchor arm scaffolding and flooring, and the traveler had reached the main pier, where it was used to assemble the castings and fabricated sections that made up the two 420-ton main shoes. Smithsonian Institution (Neg. 97-587).

Once the main shoes were in place, the erection crew began a return pass to the anchor pier with the traveler, erecting the main bottom chord and lateral members as they went. This view shows the first bottom chords being installed shortly after this phase of the erection began on August 1, 1914. Smithsonian Institution (Neg. 98-2572).

Erection of the bottom chord members had been completed in two of the seven anchor arm panels at the time of this late-August photograph. Smithsonian Institution (Neg. 98-2560).

Facing page:

(Top) With the aid of the two 55-ton traveling cranes mounted on the traveler, the erecting crew prepared to hoist two compression members for the lower web system into place on September 29, 1914. Smithsonian Institution (Neg. 97-590).

(Bottom) Installation of the anchor arm bottom chords was completed by the end of September, and the traveler was then moved back to the main pier to begin a second inward pass, during which the bottom half of the web members would be erected up to and including the "K" joints. Work had been completed in the first panel when this photograph was taken in October. Smithsonian Institution (Neg. 97-957).

Once the main shoes were ready, the erection crew began moving the traveler back toward the anchor pier, installing the main bottom chord members and lateral members as they went. These were enormous members 10 feet, 4 inches wide and 7 feet, 2 inches deep at their deepest point adjacent to the main piers. Four parallel web sections were each built up of two layers of $1^1/_8$–inch and two of $^{13}/_{16}$-inch-thick steel plates, with two 8-inch by 8-inch by 1-inch-thick steel angles and a continuous 20-inch by $^7/_8$-inch-thick steel plate at the top and bottom of each web. The four web sections were rigidly connected by a diaphragm system built up of steel plates and angles and a system of heavy lacing bars top and bottom. The total steel cross sectional area of the largest chord section was 1,902 square inches, compared with only 842 square inches in the corresponding chord members of the failed earlier structure. Each chord section weighed approximately 400 tons between main panel points. In order to ship and erect these huge members, they were fabricated in four pieces, each a half length and half width of the full chord section, which were then spliced and riveted together in place.

All of this work was completed by September 28, and the traveler was moved back to the main pier to begin another pass, this time erecting the lower half of the web system for the main trusses up to and including the middle or K joints. This was completed by November 9, and the anchorage eyebars linking the anchor arm to the anchor pier were then placed. On November 12 the erection crew began an outward pass with the traveler, erecting the upper web system and the top chord tension members as they went. These top chord members for both the anchor and cantilever arms were made up of steel eyebars 16 inches by $2^{13}/_{16}$ inches, with as many as thirty-two bars being required at the point of maximum loading adjacent to the main posts. The large number required made it necessary to arrange these eyebars in double rows, one above the other. Because of the length between main panel points, it was necessary to use two lengths of eyebars in each panel, with a pin connection at the midpoint in each panel as well as at the panel points. In order both to facilitate erection and to keep the bars properly aligned after erection, the eyebars were carried on supporting trusses, which remained permanently in the structure. Immediately behind the traveler as it moved outward, the lateral sway bracing system was installed between the two main trusses.

By December 3, when work ended for the 1914 season, all but the last two panel sections of the upper part of the anchor arm had been completed. It had been a remarkably productive erection season. Including the temporary staging, the erection crew and traveler had handled some 21,000 tons of steel between May 21 and December 2, with a best day's work of 411 tons. Work had begun that year, too, on the south bank, where the approach span had been completed and erection of a second traveler begun for the construction of the south anchor and cantilever arms.

Profiting from the experience of the 1914 season, the erection crews proved even more productive in 1915. Erection started again on the north shore on April 15, and by June 1 the main post at the main pier was erected and substantially riveted. "The main post, over the

---

Facing page:

(Top) By November 7, 1914, erection of the lower half of the web members on the fourth pass of the traveler was almost complete. Installation of the upper web system and top chord tension members would be completed on an outward pass of the traveler that would begin on November 12. Smithsonian Institution (Neg. 97-595).

(Bottom) On November 24, less than two weeks after they had begun, the erection crew completed erection of upper web and top chord members for three of the anchor arm panels. All but the last two panels would be complete by December 3, when work ended for the 1914 season. Smithsonian Institution (Neg. 98-2561).

piers," wrote H. P. Borden, the assistant to the board's chief engineer,[7] C. N. Monsarrat, "is probably the largest single member of this type ever built into a bridge."[8] Weighing 1,500 tons, and 310 feet long, center-to-center of pins, each main post was made up of four H type column sections, each 9 feet by 10 feet square and latticed together. Because of their great weight and size, each post was fabricated and shipped in twenty-four separate sections. The 130-ton main link at the top of each post, which incorporated pin connections for the top of the post, two rows of top chord eyebars, and a web diagonal from the anchor and cantilever arms, was 16 feet long, 10 feet wide, and almost 16 feet deep.

The traveler was then advanced outward from the main pier, erecting the cantilever arm by the usual cantilevering method as it went. During erection, each bottom chord member was temporarily supported from a movable "flying bridge" suspended from the completed structure, until a full panel was completed and the bottom chord became self-supporting. As on the anchor span, sway bracing was installed between the main trusses behind the traveler as it was moved outwards. This work proceeded smoothly, and the entire north cantilever arm was completed on November 12. The traveler was then disassembled and removed. About 200 men were at work on the structure every day, including anywhere from six to eight gangs of riveters. On several days during the 1915 season, the north shore erecting crews had put more than 600 tons of steel in place, with a record day's work of 670 tons.

Anywhere from six to eight gangs of riveters were at work as the erection of the north end of the bridge progressed. This gang was at work on the anchor arm on October 24, 1914. The man at left is holding a hot rivet with a pair of tongs. This will be inserted in a rivet hole and "bucked" at one end with a tool like that held by the man between the steel sections, while another will drive the rivet with a compressed air hammer that will form a head from the end of the hot rivet. The rivet will contract slightly as it cools, providing a tight grip to hold the metal sections firmly together. Smithsonian Institution (Neg. 98-2564).

Erection resumed on the north shore on April 15, 1915, and by June 1 the anchor arm members and the main post were substantially complete. This view shows a half section of the 130-ton main link being lifted into place at the top of one of the posts. Smithsonian Institution (Neg. 98-2573).

Once the anchor arm and main posts were in place, the north cantilever arm was erected outward from the main pier as a self-supporting cantilever. While a cargo ship steamed downriver below, one of the first bottom chord sections was lifted into place on June 10, 1915. At the left end can be seen the 45-inch-diameter half pin holes for the connection with the main shoe over the north main pier. National Archives of Québec (Neg. P302, P4).

2. QUEBEC BRIDGE. PLACING FIRST SECTION OF BOTTOM CHORD, CANTILEVER ARM.

(Above) In July 1915 the first bottom chord section for the north cantilever arm was guided into position at its link with the main shoe. The 30-inch diameter pin that provided the connection was already in place in the shoe. The metal structure in the foreground, supported by the inclined hangers on either side of the chord section, was the "flying bridge" used to support the bottom chord members until a full panel of the truss had been completed and the chord was supported by the web members above it. Author's Collection.

(Right) This July 13, 1915, photograph shows a completed post and top link over the north main pier. All seven pins connecting the top chord eyebars, both diagonals, and the main post to the top link have been driven. Just above the link is the traveler. Smithsonian Institution (Neg. 97-586).

This photograph, made from the south shore of the river near the mouth of the Chaudière River, shows the status of erection on July 15, 1915. The north anchor arm was complete, and erection had begun for the north cantilever arm. On the south shore, the erection crew with the second traveler has completed erection of the anchor arm falsework and floor members and has begun the erection of the anchor arm lower chords. National Archives of Québec (Neg. P302, P3).

Two eyebar bundles for the cantilever arm top chord were lifted into place on September 15, 1915. The tension loads in these members necessitated the use of two rows of eyebars, which were carried on the supporting trusses seen here to facilitate erection and to keep the bars properly aligned. Smithsonian Institution (Neg. 98-2563).

In a view downward from the platform of the traveler, the erecting crew is seen driving the pin to make a connection between two web members in the north cantilever arm. National Archives of Québec (Neg. P302, P2).

Over the summer and fall of 1915, the erection crew on the north shore completed the 580-foot-long north cantilever arm. Erection was in progress on the third of eight panels when this photograph was made. At the lower left can be seen the "flying bridge," which is supporting the bottom chord members of the panel until the web verticals and diagonal members are installed and can support the chord. Smithsonian Institution.

On the south shore the second erection traveler was complete and ready to begin work on June 1. Some of the temporary staging no longer required for the north anchor arm had been relocated to the south shore early in the year, and this and additional staging were fully erected by July 9, when erection of the south anchor arm began. This work went even better than it had for the north shore work, with the anchor arm being completed a month ahead of schedule and in about six weeks less time. The entire anchor arm and main posts were completed by November 8, when work was suspended for the season. Altogether, the south shore erecting crews had put some 20,000 tons of steel in place by the end of the 1915 season.

Work resumed on the south cantilever arm on April 1, 1916, and over the next ninety-two days the crews erected some 13,000 tons of steel. The south cantilever arm was complete on July 28, and the structure was now ready for what was to be the final step in building the great Quebec Bridge. This was to be the raising of the bridge's suspended center span into position. If all went well with this difficult task, the bridge could be in service by the end of the year, a season earlier than had originally been thought possible.

By October 6, 1915, the north cantilever arm was well along. Erection of the sixth of eight panels was in progress, and the entire arm would be complete a little over a month later. Work on the south end of the structure, which had started about fourteen months after erection began on the north shore, would be completed by the end of the following July. The bridge would then be ready for the final step, the lifting of the suspended center span into position between the two cantilever arms. Smithsonian Institution (Neg. 98-2562).

On August 1, 1916, the great bridge was ready for the dramatic final event of the erection, the lifting of the 5,000-ton center span into place from scows in the river. The devices hanging down from the outer end of each cantilever were mooring frames or trusses that would be used to moor the floating span and then to pull it directly under its final position in the center of the bridge. Smithsonian Institution (Neg. 97-592).

CHAPTER 9

AGAIN, DISASTER

AT THE END OF JULY 1916, THE ENORMOUS ANCHOR AND CANTILEVER ARMS FOR THE bridge were complete on both sides of the river. From each side, the 580-foot cantilever arms reached out toward the center of the river, waiting to grasp each end of the center span that would complete the bridge. This would be a substantial structure in its own right, 640 feet long and 110 feet deep at the center, weighing 5,000 tons. Floating this huge structure into position in the river and then lifting it into place between the two cantilever arms promised to be an exceptionally difficult undertaking.

In its tender for the Quebec Bridge project, the St. Lawrence Bridge Company had put forth just about every feasible method for erecting this suspended center span. In its erection plan for the board design, the company had proposed erecting the span by the usual cantilevering method, with the center span to be built outward from the end of each cantilever arm using a small top traveler. Once the two halves had been joined at the center, the temporary top chord links that permitted them to act as cantilevers would be removed; and the structure would function as a simple span. Two other erection schemes were also proposed for either the board design or the company's own alternate designs for the bridge. Both involved erecting the center span elsewhere and floating the completed structure into place. Under a "high floating" scheme, the center span would have been erected on high falsework that would have placed it at the correct height for inserting it into the bridge. This would have been set up along the shore at the bridge site, with the falsework abutting the anchor arm and at right angles to it, allowing a traveling crane used for the center span erection to take material from railroad cars on the completed portion of the bridge. Once the span was complete, eight large pontoons would have been used to lift the falsework off its foundations at high tide and to float the span into place in the bridge. The company's somewhat different "low floating" approach, and the one ultimately adopted, involved erecting the center span along the shore on piers, floating it into position on pontoons when complete, and then lifting it into place with hydraulic jacks.

It had been estimated that by building the center span elsewhere and floating it into position, close to a year could be saved over the time it would have taken to erect the center span in place by the cantilevering method. By 1916 this was an important consideration. The National Transcontinental Railway launched by Sir Wilfrid Laurier a little over a decade earlier had been completed the year before, lacking only the bridge at Québec to complete the new direct route between the Prairie Provinces and the Maritimes. In 1914 the NTR had acquired the car ferry *Leonard* to shuttle freight cars across the river as a

Adding urgency to early completion of the Quebec Bridge was the completion of the National Transcontinental Railway in 1915, which lacked only the new crossing of the St. Lawrence at Québec to begin operating its new, more direct route between central Canada and the Maritimes. In 1914 the NTR had acquired the car ferry *Leonard* as a temporary means of making the crossing. The Grand Trunk had done the same thing years earlier when the first Quebec Bridge had collapsed. This was the Grand Trunk's woodenhulled car ferry *Henry R. James,* which shuttled freight cars between Québec and Lévis. The unusual structure amidships on the vessel was a lift that could be raised or lowered to compensate for the 20-foot tidal range at Québec. The vessel was renamed *John S. Thom* in 1910 and was joined by a similar vessel, the *James R. Langdon,* in 1913. Andrew Merrilees Collection, National Archives of Canada (Neg. PA 166763).

temporary measure to complete the link until the bridge was open. The Grand Trunk had been operating its own car ferry ever since the collapse of the original bridge in 1907. This was a difficult crossing to make under the best of conditions, and completion of the bridge was eagerly awaited by the railroads on both sides of the river.

The great time savings lay in the builders' ability to complete erection of the center span itself even while the erection of the cantilever arms was still in progress. This work had begun a year earlier, during the 1915 season, when foundations for steel bents for the erection staging and approach tracks were erected at low tide in the shallow waters of Sillery Cove, about three miles downstream from the bridge site. During the fall and winter, some of the staging used for the erection of the north and south anchor arms was taken down and shipped back to the bridge company's shops at Rockfield to be reworked into the falsework bents that would support the center span and approach tracks during erection. These were erected at each main and sub-panel point of the span, and electric power and compressed air plants were set up to support the erection work. The traveler that had been used for erection of the north anchor and cantilever arms, minus its top trusses and traveling cranes, was set up to erect the staging and then the center span itself.

Erection was completed with two passes of the traveler. On an initial outward pass beginning on May 25, 1916, the erection crew installed the supporting staging, floor beams, bottom chords and laterals, and most of the web members for the trusses. On a return pass with the traveler, the crew placed the balance of the web members, the top chords and lateral members, and sway bracing to complete the structure. The crew averaged some 520 tons of steel in place per week; and by July 20 the entire structure was complete and "swung" from supports at the ends, and the intermediate staging was removed.

The entire operation of floating the center span to the bridge site and lifting it into place in the bridge was planned in meticulous detail. As the Montréal *Gazette* put it, "every precaution known to engineering science or thought of by the best minds among engineers has been taken to see that no untoward event shall happen."[1] The center span was moved to the bridge site in six large steel scows, each 32 feet, 5½ inches wide and 164 feet, 6 inches long, with a draft of 11 feet, 7½ inches. Three of these were placed under each end of the center span, with the load transferred from the trusses to the longitudinal bulkheads of the scows through a system of cross girders and I-beams. The scows were floated in under the truss and allowed to come to rest on concrete and timber beds placed on the bottom as the tide reached low ebb. Bottom valves were opened, allowing the scows to fill with water as the tide came in, keeping them on the bottom until they were needed. When it was time to float the center span, the water was allowed to drain out at low tide, and the valves were then closed. As they lifted with the tide, the scows would then float the span.

Preparations for the floating of the completed center span were finished on September 1, but the tides were not suitable for the operation. The waiting time was spent in training the men in the coming lift operations and in checking all of the equipment. Twice daily meteorological reports were received from the Canadian Meteorological Service at Toronto, while barometric readings and observations were made at the site to assess when the weather and tide conditions would be right for the operation. The next series of high tides suitable for the lift began on September 11. Weather conditions were favorable and at 3:40 a.m. on the 11th, the span was floated. By 4:40 a.m. the structure was on its way out into the river. Four small tugs and one large tug were attached to the downstream side of the tow, while two small tugs were on the upstream side. A large seagoing tug stood by to assist if needed. The tide was running in at a sufficient velocity that the tugs had little to do but guide their massive charge. The span reached the bridge site at 6:35 a.m., about a half hour after high tide. This had been carefully timed so that the delicate operation of hanging the span on the cantilever arms could be carried out during the slack water period.

Mooring frames or trusses, each 130 feet long, had been suspended from the floor beams at each end of each cantilever arm. These were designed to moor the floating span and then to pull it directly under its final position in the center of the bridge. This was accomplished with eight 1½-inch steel mooring cables from the mooring frame. Two of these cables were attached to each corner of the floating span while the tugs held it in place. Once it was in position, the center span was attached to lifting links or hangar chains suspended from the cantilever arm at each corner of the center span. Each of these links was made up of four strings of steel plate segments 30 feet long and connected by 12-inch pins. Each segment consisted of a slab of 30-inch by 1⅛-inch plate. Two of these links at each corner of the span were pin-connected to eyebar hangar links that were attached to lifting girders placed under each corner of the center span. At the upper end, the lifting links passed through lower and upper jacking girders, between which two 1,000-ton hydraulic jacks were installed, two at each corner of the span. During each lift the center span was supported by 12-inch pins

On July 25, 1916, just a few days after its completion, the 640-foot, 5,000-ton center span of the Quebec Bridge rested on its temporary supports in Sillery Cove. As soon as preparations for floating the structure were complete, and weather conditions favorable for the operation, the span would be floated out into the St. Lawrence and towed upstream to the bridge to begin the lift. Smithsonian Institution (Neg. 97-593).

Weather conditions were right early in September; and in the early morning hours of September 11, the center span was floated, and a flotilla of tugs took it upstream to the bridge. Despite the early hour, the surface of the river was alive with boats transporting sightseers to view the big lift. Notman Photographic Archives, McCord Museum of Canadian History (Neg. 5668 VIEW).

passing through diaphragms in the upper jacking girder and holes bored at intervals in the lifting links. As each jacking operation lifted the span 2 feet, the upper jacking girder moved upward with the lifting stroke of the jacks. At the end of each stroke, pins were placed through the diaphragms of the lower jacking girder and the lifting links, the pins through the upper jacking girder were removed, and the jacks and upper jacking girder were lowered to begin the next lift. As each 30-foot length of the lifting links passed through the upper jacking girders, it was disconnected and removed. In order to assure that the center span was kept level while it was being lifted, the jacking operations were carefully controlled with a system of "tell tales," which indicated the relative elevations of the four corners of the suspended span to the men operating the jacks. Throughout each lift the two corners at each end were never allowed to be more than a quarter- to a half-inch ahead of each other.

The lifting of the center span was an extraordinary public event for Québec. The night before the operation began, the bridge was outlined in electric lights. Cabinet ministers, deputies, senators, and members of Parliament arrived for the event in large numbers. The principal engineers from the board of engineers and the contractors were all there, and engineers from all over the United States and Canada had come to watch the largest operation of its kind ever attempted. The Canadian Society of Civil Engineers had arranged a special excursion of its members to witness the event. Every hotel in Québec was full; the Chateau Frontenac turned away five hundred people, and many spent the night in

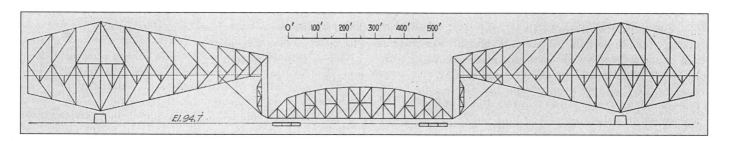

This drawing from the August 31, 1916, issue of *Engineering News* illustrates the general scheme for hoisting the suspended span into position. Author's Collection.

private homes. Every suitable steamship in the harbor had been chartered for the occasion. The Department of Railways and Canals had chartered the *Rapids King* to take members of the Senate and House of Commons and an Australian parliamentary delegation to the scene. The *Lady Grey* came down from Montréal during the night with a party of government officials. Guests aboard the *Lady Evelyn*, chartered by the mayor and city council of Québec, included former Prime Minister Sir Wilfrid Laurier.[2] Local residents by the thousands turned out to watch the lifting of the span. A crowd estimated at 50,000 began gathering on both banks of the river and on board the dozens of vessels, large and small, in the river in the early morning hours. A thick fog shrouded the tugs and the huge span as the operation began, but the morning sun soon broke through the haze. At 7:40 a.m. the lifting hangers at all four corners had been connected. The jacks began the lift at 8:50 a.m.; and during the third 2-foot lift, the scows floated clear, leaving the span suspended 20 feet above the water. One of the tugs gave a signal, and the rest quickly joined in a deafening chorus of whistles, joined by cheers from the shores, to mark the successful completion of the most difficult part of the operation. After one more lift the work was suspended for a time to allow the men a rest period and time for breakfast.

With the transfer of the span from scows to the cantilever arms successfully completed, several of the large vessels in the river returned to Québec and the crowd began to thin. By this time only a few thousand spectators remained at the bridge site. Jacking operations were resumed at 10:30 a.m., and one more lift was completed. By 10:50 a.m. the pins had been inserted connecting the lifting links to the lower jacking girders, and the jacks were being lowered in preparation for another lift.

Suddenly, what had seemed a day of triumph was shattered by a loud report as the southwest corner of the center span slid off its supporting lifting girder. Some described the sound as like the discharge of a cannon, followed by the cracking sound of other failures, and then slipping and roaring noises. As the southwest corner dropped into the water, the entire south end of the span began to twist, pulling the southeast corner off its support. The two north corner supports held briefly and then they, too, broke loose as the south end of the span disappeared into the water. In just a few seconds it was all over, and the 5,000-ton center span had disappeared beneath the surface of the St. Lawrence.

For the eighty men at work on the structure, it was a terrifying moment. Those at work on the center span itself went down with it. Some, who were working on the temporary wooden platforms at the outer ends of the cantilever arms, where the jacks and other lifting apparatus were located, jumped or were thrown into the river as the violent movement shattered the platforms. Others leaped to safety on the cantilever arm. As the great weight of the center span was suddenly released, the south cantilever arm sprang violently upward, setting up a series of vibrations and oscillations of perhaps 15 to 18 inches. The north cantilever arm was first pulled down and outward and then sprang up. Men on the two cantilever arms were thrown to the floor of the bridge by the violent motion. There was a moment of panic when many of the men, doubtless acutely conscious of what had happened in August 1907, thought the cantilever arms, too, were falling. "Foremen shouted savagely at a few of the men who seemed, quite excusably, to have lost their heads," reported the Montréal *Gazette*, "and order was restored quickly."[3]

All told, thirteen men lost their lives in this second Quebec Bridge disaster. Some had been working on the center span itself, while the remainder had been on the platforms at the ends of the cantilever arms. Most of the dead came from the nearby Québec communities along both banks of the river, while one was from Lachine, where the main plant of Dominion Bridge was located. Two Canadians from other provinces and two Americans were also among the victims. Mercifully, this time there were no lost Caughnawaga ironworkers.

A number of other men narrowly missed death. Nine were pulled from the river alive by nearby tugs and launches. A Pathé Moving Picture crew was filming the lifting operation from the tug *C. A. B.* about 100 feet away when the center span fell. The tug's Captain Bernier and his crew rescued three men who had fallen with the span. Unfortunately,

Among the many vessels transporting visitors to view the lifting of the center span was the *Lady Evelyn*, which had been chartered by the mayor and city council of Québec. As the center span was being connected to the lifting hangars in the background, the city's distinguished guests gathered on deck for a group photograph. At the center front was the former prime minister and National Transcontinental Railway proponent Sir Wilfrid Laurier. To his left was the Québec premier, Sir Lomer Gouin. National Archives of Québec (Neg. P560 (GH972-52)).

The center span was floated into position under the bridge as the tide turned, and the lifting hangers at all four corners had been connected by 7:40 a.m., completing the most difficult part of the operation. Within another hour the lifting operation would begin. National Archives of Canada (Neg. C 443).

Jacking operations began at 8:50 a.m., and the center span had lifted free of the scows during the third lift. A large crowd of sightseers had gathered on the south shore of the river at the Chaudière wharf and on boats in the river to watch. National Archives of Québec (Neg. P1000.S4 (PN1074-11)).

QUEBEC BRIDGE. SHOWING THE CENTRE SPAN JUST BEFORE IT COLLAPSED

Exclusive Rights

Thousands watched the lift of the center span from the high bluffs on the north shore at Sillery. At the time this view was made around 10:30 a.m., lifting operations had resumed after the men at work had taken time out for a rest period and breakfast. Author's Collection.

Without warning, disaster struck the Quebec Bridge for a second time at 10:50 a.m. on September 11, 1916, when the failure of a steel casting allowed one corner of the suspended span to drop, precipitating the collapse of the entire structure into the St. Lawrence. An alert news photographer captured this view as the 5,000-ton structure plunged into the river, taking 13 men to their deaths. National Archives of Canada (Neg. C 57787).

not among them was Captain Bernier's own son, who had fallen to his death from one of the platforms. Archie Cadorette jumped from the bridge and was rescued uninjured. Enoch McCann survived the fall of the center span and was pulled from the river. "I cannot swim," he said later, "and I thought I would never come to the surface again. When I did, I found two pieces of wood edged in tightly at the elbow joint of both my arms. How they got there I don't know, but they saved my life. I was carried down by the tide two or three hundred yards, it seemed to me, before I was picked up, and I was hardly conscious of anything until I found myself on a Government boat all swathed in flannels, and sweat just running out of me."[4] Eight-year-old Armand Hardin of St-Romuald was credited with saving one of the men who had fallen with the span. Seeing the man struggling to reach shore, young Hardin jumped into the river and managed to get the man safely out of the water.

Another fourteen men were injured in the accident, among them the board of engineers' chief shop inspector, Herbert W. McMillan, who broke his leg while attempting to jump to the end of the north cantilever arm from one of the jacking platforms. Others suffered broken bones, cuts, sprains, and shock.

A number of the visiting engineers narrowly escaped death or injury. A group of prominent engineers from the United States and Canada had been watching the lifting operation from the suspended span earlier that morning but had gone ashore during the pause for rest and breakfast. Still others had been watching from the cantilever arms; but, believing that the operation had been all but completed safely, many of these had left before the accident occurred. Even St. Lawrence Bridge Company President Phelps Johnson had left the span to assure friends by telephone that all was going well, when the terrible sound of the falling span brought him rushing back to the bridge.

Eyewitness accounts by the many highly qualified engineers at the scene and careful examination of the lifting apparatus quickly established the cause of the accident. The source of the failure was traced to a large steel casting that acted as a rocker or bearing supporting the southwest corner of the center span on the lifting girder. As the casting broke and the corner of the center span dropped, the lifting girder had been kicked back, allowing the span to begin its plunge into the river.

The center span had fallen into 200 feet of water, and it was quickly determined that no part of it could be salvaged. Soundings taken the afternoon of the accident by V. W. Forneret, superintending engineer of the ship channel, determined that no part of the wrecked span was within 50 feet of the surface, and the river was reopened to regular navigation. No attempt was ever made to remove the wreckage, and to this day 5,000 tons of steel from the second Quebec Bridge remains on the bottom of the St. Lawrence together with the wreckage of the first bridge. Inspection of the north and south anchor and cantilever arms established that the structure had come through the accident undamaged. The lifting apparatus, too, was largely undamaged, although several of the thirty-foot plates in the lifting links on the northwest and southeast corners of the center span proved to have been elongated by close to half an inch by the enormous overload they took when the southwest corner dropped.

Aside from the loss of life, the accident represented a monetary loss of at least $600,000. Within two days of the accident, the St. Lawrence Bridge Company announced that it took responsibility for the loss and would begin work at once on replacing the lost center span. But once again Québec had been frustrated in its long quest for a bridge across the St. Lawrence, this time when the goal had been so tantalizingly close. Now, it would be at least another year before the bridge could be completed.

On the morning of September 17, 1917, the bridge builders were ready to try again, as another flotilla of tugs towed the replacement center span up the river from Sillery Cove to the bridge site. Smithsonian Institution (Neg. 97-594).

CHAPTER 10

TRIUMPH AT LAST

THE ST. LAWRENCE BRIDGE COMPANY LOST NO TIME IN GETTING THE WORK OF replacing the lost center span underway. Despite the materiel demands of the great World War raging in Europe, the Carnegie Steel Company was able to supply virtually all of the steel needed for the replacement span by the end of 1916, while the specialized steel required for the pins came from the Cambria Plant of the Midvale Steel Company at Johnstown, Pennsylvania. The work of fabrication for the Quebec Bridge having been completed, the bridge company's plant at Rockfield, Québec, was in the midst of rearrangement: Special equipment for the manufacture of shells was being installed, and many of the large machines for bridge fabrication had been sold. Enough equipment was still on hand, however, and the old shop organization was re-established to fabricate the replacement span, and shop work for the new structure was completed during the first part of 1917.

The design of the center span was unchanged, except for minor details and a change to nickel steel for the top lateral bracing to give it greater flexibility. The design of the bearings in which the failure had occurred, however, was completely revised and the use of steel castings eliminated.

"No fundamental changes were made in the design of the lifting apparatus and mechanism," wrote the board of engineers in its final report. "The fall of the first span, bitter disappointment as it was, did not disturb in any way the confidence of the contractors or of the Board, or their belief in the efficiency of this scheme of erection which, notwithstanding the failure of one detail of the equipment, had given abundant evidence of its practicality. Any changes that were made were due largely to a sense of extra precaution rather than from lack of confidence."[1] Aside from these precautionary changes, the lifting links, many of which had been elongated by the severe stresses imposed during the fall, were replaced. Essentially, however, the design of the equipment and the operational procedures for raising the center span were unchanged.

Erection of the new span began at the same Sillery Cove site on June 4, 1917; and the structure was completed on August 27. Saturday, September 15, was the first date on which tidal conditions would be suitable for floating in the span. Weather reports received late the previous evening, however, were unsuitable, with rising winds and reports of an approaching gale. The operation was postponed until Monday, when the weather proved to be ideal for the work, with prospects for continued good weather over the following two days. The span was floated at 5:15 a.m.; and within half an hour, the armada of tugs and their huge charge began moving out into the river for the journey upstream to the bridge site, much as they had the year before.

Adding to the confidence of the workmen was the participation of Father A. E. McGuire, the priest of the Sillery parish church attended by many of them. It was Father McGuire who, ten years earlier, had administered last rites to dying victims of the collapse of the first bridge. Several days before the floating, Father McGuire had conducted a special blessing of the center span and both cantilevers. A special Mass was offered on the Sunday morning before the operation began, and on Monday morning the parish church bells rang out as the span floated by on its way to the bridge site. Father McGuire rode out on a launch to board the span and ride up the river with it, remaining with the men at the work over the next several days.[2]

By 7:25 a.m. the span was in its place under the bridge, and lines were quickly run out to the mooring frames. By 8:30 a.m. the lifting links had been attached at all four corners of the span, and the tidal current had shifted from upstream to down. By 9:00 a.m. conditions were right for beginning the 150-foot lift, and ten minutes later the jacks were started to begin the first of the seventy-five lifts that would be required to raise the span to its final position. At 10:28 a.m., at the end of the third lift, the scows came free and were carried downstream by the current, leaving the center span suspended above the river.

Lifting operations continued over the next three days. By the end of the day on Monday, twelve lifts had been completed. Jacking began again at 8:16 a.m. on Tuesday morning; and by the end of the day, another twenty-two lifts had been completed, raising the span by 68 feet. The work was delayed briefly in the afternoon by the only mishap of the entire lifting operation, when several bolts sheared off a support bracket, breaking the nose of one workman. Initially, each lift cycle had taken about fifteen minutes to complete, but as the men gained experience and confidence, some were completed in as few as nine minutes. Another twenty-six lifts were completed on Wednesday, leaving only fifteen to be made on the fourth and final day.

The splendid weather that had prevailed since Monday morning ended abruptly on Wednesday afternoon. The engineers had watched with alarm as the barometer fell steadily all afternoon, and just as work was ending for the day, a heavy thunderstorm swept the site, bringing in rising winds. The winds didn't amount to much, however, and the span rode through the storm without difficulty. Weather conditions were far worse the following morning. A nasty, gusting wind had risen to 25 or 30 mph and held the center span 5 to 7 inches off center when it was allowed to hang free.

Despite the weather, lifting operations began again at 9:05 a.m. By noon, when a break was taken for lunch, ten lifts had been completed, leaving only 8 feet to go. Work began again at one in an atmosphere of excitement and anticipation. The last few lifts went slowly,

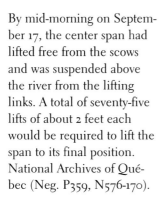

By mid-morning on September 17, the center span had lifted free from the scows and was suspended above the river from the lifting links. A total of seventy-five lifts of about 2 feet each would be required to lift the span to its final position. National Archives of Québec (Neg. P359, N576-170).

Late on the afternoon of September 18, as the lifting crew completed the thirty-second lift of the center span, the top of the truss had reached the level of the bridge deck. Visible at the left are the "tell tales" that indicated the elevations of the two corners to the men operating the hydraulic jacks. Author's Collection.

On Tuesday afternoon, September 18, at the end of the second day of lifting, the center span had been raised a total of 68 feet. Another forty-one lifts over the next two days would raise the structure to its final position in the bridge. National Archives of Canada (Neg. C 8082).

as work platforms and equipment were taken down to provide clearance for the span as it rose into its final position, and the eyebars that would link the spans together were guided into place. As the last lift began at 3:10 p.m., locomotive cranes were run out on all four corners with the equipment for driving the eight connecting pins. The first pin was driven as the jacks completed the last lift at 3:25 p.m. One by one the remaining pins were driven home through the eyebars by blows from a short rail swung by about ten men.

At 4:00 p.m. the last foreman shouted, "Right, here!" and the job was done. Almost seven decades after the idea had first been taken up, after seemingly endless struggles to finance and build it, and after two great construction disasters, Québec finally had its bridge across the St. Lawrence.

It was a happy moment of triumph. As soon as the last pin was safely driven, half a dozen workmen began a race to see who could be the first to cross the completed span, to the applause of onlookers. The Union Jack ensign of the Canadian Marine Department floated out from the span, signaling that the bridge was complete and the river again open for traffic. The river was soon alive with boats and steamers, all rushing to be the first under the bridge, the honor going to a disreputable-looking tug. Locomotive cranes on the floor of the bridge began whistling furiously, and the uproar was passed down the river to Québec by the whistles of steamers on the river. Thousands of whistles, bells, and automobile horns were soon sounding all across the city. Flags and bunting, held in readiness for the occasion, were quickly hung out. At the bridge, the engineers of the St. Lawrence Bridge Company and the board of engineers were surrounded by the bridge workers and loudly cheered as they left the span.[3]

There was more to be done. The next day wind struts and bracing between the cantilever arms and the center span were put in place, and over the next several days the lifting equipment was dismantled and removed. During the next four weeks, the floor of the center span was erected and one track put in place. The first train crossed the structure on October 17, 1917, transporting a party of officials and workmen in flag-bedecked open cars. One track was turned over to the operating department of the Canadian Government Railways on December 3, when a big 2-8-0 Consolidation took the first regular freight train across the bridge, marking the beginning of through operation of the new, direct route between the Prairie Provinces and Halifax. Work on concrete sidewalks and some additional riveting and painting continued into the next year. On August 21, 1918, two trains weighing some 7,000 tons were run out on the central span simultaneously in a final test; and the structure was finally fully complete and accepted by the Dominion government.

It was another year, after the end of the great war in Europe, before a final ceremonial event celebrated the completion of the great structure. On August 22, 1919, Britain's Prince of Wales—the future Edward VIII—formally opened the structure during his visit to Canada. Accompanied by the lieutenant-governor and premier of Québec, the mayor of Québec, the board of engineers, representatives of the contractors, and other dignitaries, the young prince arrived at the north portal of the bridge to unveil two commemorative bronze tablets. He then boarded a special train to cross the bridge to the south portal, where two similar tablets were unveiled and the bridge was declared open.[4]

Surely it was a triumphant moment for the engineers who had worked so long and hard to design and build this greatest of bridges. For Charles Monsarrat, chairman and chief engineer of the board of engineers, the Quebec Bridge would be one of the brightest achievements of a distinguished engineering career. Monsarrat continued in railway and bridge engineering work with the Department of Railways and Canals for several years; and in 1921 he formed a consulting civil engineering partnership with Philip L. Pratley, who had been one of the design engineers on the Quebec Bridge. Over the next 19 years, the two men were consulting engineers for such notable structures as the Jacques Cartier Bridge at Montréal, the Île d'Orléans suspension bridge at Québec, the Lions' Gate Bridge at Vancouver, and the Canadian National's new passenger terminal at Montréal. Monsarrat died in 1940 at the age of 69.

Following the successful lifting of the center span into position, another month's work was required to ready the bridge for its first train. On October 17, 1917, a party of invited guests and bridge workers boarded Union Jack–bedecked flatcars to ride the first train across the structure. Smithsonian Institution.

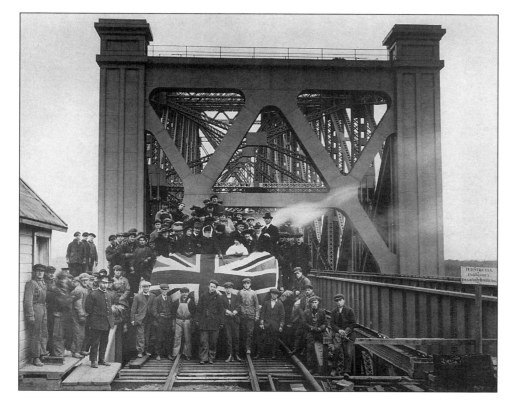

The first crossing complete, the group gathered at the south portal of the bridge for a photograph of the memorable occasion. Eugene M. Finn Photograph, Dominion Bridge Company, Ltd. Collection, National Archives of Canada (Neg. PA 148581).

Regular rail service over the bridge began six weeks later, when a Canadian Government Railways locomotive took a southbound freight train across the bridge on December 3, 1917. The locomotive for the historic occasion was 2-8-0 Consolidation No. 2900. G. A. Neilson Photograph, National Archives of Canada (Neg. P192, D11, P1).

On August 22, 1919, His Royal Highness the Prince of Wales, accompanied by a large party of political figures and the engineers and contractors for the bridge, formally opened the Quebec Bridge with appropriate ceremony. The youthful Prince—the future Edward VIII—unveiled bronze tablets at the north portal and then traveled over the bridge on a special train to unveil two more at the south portal. Author's Collection.

Ralph Modjeski, the only member of the board of engineers to serve from beginning to end of the project, went on to design such notable suspension bridges as the Ben Franklin Bridge over the Delaware River at Philadelphia (with Leon S. Moissieff) and the Ambassador Bridge between Detroit and Windsor, Ontario, and another long-span cantilever bridge, the Huey P. Long Bridge over the Mississippi River at New Orleans. Modjeski's last and greatest work was the double-suspension and cantilever truss San Francisco–Oakland Bay Bridge, which was completed in 1937, three years before his death.

For St. Lawrence Bridge Company President Phelps Johnson, who retired upon its completion, the Quebec Bridge was the capstone to a long and distinguished career in bridge engineering and construction. Johnson remained active as chairman of the Dominion Bridge Company board of directors until his death in 1926 at the age of 77. George Duggan, the bridge company's chief engineer and the principal designer for the Quebec Bridge, succeeded Johnson as president of the Dominion Bridge Company in 1918, serving in that position until 1936, when he became chairman of the company. He continued to serve in that position until his death in 1946 at the age of 84.

The Quebec Bridge was a source of enormous pride to Québec and Canada. It was built by Canadians, and it would rank as the longest bridge span of any kind in the world until completion of the Ambassador Bridge between Windsor and Detroit in 1929. It remains even today the longest cantilever span ever built. Open at last, the bridge began to fulfill its promise as a new gateway between central Canada and the Maritimes. In addition to completing the National Transcontinental Railway, the bridge provided a new line between the Grand Trunk and the Quebec Central on the south bank of the river and the Canadian Pacific, Canadian Northern, and Quebec & Lake St. John Railway on the north shore. Freight traffic across the bridge was soon approaching a thousand cars a week, and

The completed Quebec Bridge has stood astride the St. Lawrence for more than 80 years as a sturdy monument to the unflagging determination of the men who set out to build a great bridge at Québec so long ago. Canadian National.

A man standing at the highest point on the bridge, some 343 feet above high water level at the top of the main post, conveyed a sense of the enormous scale of the Quebec Bridge. To the lower right, visible through the steel work, is the bridge that crossed the Chaudière River at its confluence with the St. Lawrence. Smithsonian Institution (Neg. 97-588).

the Grand Trunk began operating Montréal-Québec passenger services via its south shore main line and the bridge.

But even as the bridge was nearing completion, the Canadian railroad landscape was being radically reorganized. Laurier's National Transcontinental Railway plan of 1903 had been only part of a frenzy of railroad building that would give Canada two new transcontinental routes over the next dozen years. While the government-owned NTR built east from Winnipeg, the Grand Trunk's subsidiary Grand Trunk Pacific, aided by government guarantees of its construction bonds, would build west from Winnipeg to Prince Rupert, British Columbia. Under the Laurier plan, the NTR would be leased to the Grand Trunk

Postcard views of one of the engineering wonders of the world became a popular item for Québec visitors. This one showed an early passenger train at the north portal of the bridge. Author's Collection.

LE PONT DE QUEBEC

QUEBEC BRIDGE. QUEBEC. CANADA

The bridge provided an impressive setting for photographs of ocean liners on the St. Lawrence. This was a view of the liner *Duchess of Athol* steaming up the river to Montréal in April 1934. National Film Board of Canada, National Archives of Canada (Neg. PA 44740).

Ever since it opened in 1917, the Quebec Bridge has provided a connection to Québec City for fast train services operating over Canadian National's main line south of the St. Lawrence. CN's westbound train 21, the Québec-Montréal *Rapido*, headed south across the bridge on a June morning in 1971. William D. Middleton.

Pacific for operation once it was completed. Meanwhile the privately owned Canadian Northern, which had begun operation in 1894 as a regional line in Manitoba, had begun building both east and west to complete a third transcontinental route. By 1915, when both the Grand Trunk Pacific and Canadian Northern had reached the Pacific, both lines were near bankruptcy, and much of the remainder of Canada's badly overbuilt railroad system was not much better off. The newly complete NTR—lacking only the crossing of the St. Lawrence that would be provided by the Quebec Bridge—was earning scarcely half its operating costs, and the GTP was unwilling to lease it as planned.

Unwilling to let the railroads simply fall into bankruptcy, the Conservative government began to move toward nationalization. The first step came in 1917, when the government took over the failing Canadian Northern. The NTR and other government-owned railways, which had been brought under common management as the Canadian Government Railways, were then amalgamated with the Canadian Northern as the Canadian National Railways in 1918. The acquisition of the bankrupt Grand Trunk Pacific and the Grand Trunk over the next few years completed the formation of the Canadian National System.[5]

This new order in Canada's railroads substantially altered the traffic patterns that the new NTR line across northern Québec and Ontario had been expected to create. An early move by the new CN management was the construction in 1923 of a connection between the former NTR at Nakina, Ontario, and the former Canadian Northern at Longlac, Ontario. This enabled CN to link a 500-mile segment of the much more direct NTR line east of Winnipeg with the more southerly former Canadian Northern route that led eventually to Toronto and Montréal. Reflecting Montréal's now well-established preeminence as the principal port city on the St. Lawrence, this new routing became the principal CN transcontinental line, while the former NTR was left with what little local traffic there was. Even traffic destined for the Maritimes was likely to take this route, crossing the St. Lawrence via the Victoria Bridge at Montréal and following the main line on the south bank of the St. Lawrence to a link with the NTR route to Halifax, bypassing both Québec and the Quebec Bridge. A 1948 CNR traffic density map reveals the low level of traffic on the former NTR. At some points the line was transporting little more than 1.2 million gross ton-miles per mile annually, no more than a branch line traffic level. In contrast, the CN's more southerly route through Capreol, Ottawa, and Montréal was carrying almost four times that level.[6]

Proponents of the northerly NTR route across Québec and Ontario had also seen it as a way to promote colonization of these remote areas. In this, too, the NTR had proved a disappointment. The inhospitable Canadian Shield could not support a significant population, and much of the area traversed by the NTR remains largely uninhabited to this day. In many ways Laurier's National Transcontinental Railway had proved to be the ill-advised venture his critics had said it would be.

If it had not assumed quite its anticipated role in rail traffic, the Quebec Bridge soon took on a new role in highway transportation. There was still no other bridge across the St. Lawrence anywhere below Montréal, and the decision to build the bridge without roadways had left the city with only the Québec City–Lévis ferry as a way across the river for motor vehicle traffic. By the end of the 1920s, however, the rapid development of a provincial highway system made a roadway crossing at Québec increasingly urgent. The Provincial Department of Public Works and Labor commissioned Montréal consulting engineers Monsarrat & Pratley to come up with a plan for a roadway on the Quebec Bridge. It was a good choice, of course. Charles Monsarrat had been chief engineer and chairman of the board of engineers for the bridge, while Philip Pratley had participated in some of the early design work.

As originally planned, the bridge was to have the two railway tracks at the center, spaced 23 feet center-to-center, with one roadway lane and a sidewalk on either side. With the decision to eliminate roadways on the bridge, the two tracks had been placed on 32-foot, 6-inch centers, which was as close to the trusses on each side of the bridge as clearances allowed. This was done to keep bending moments as low as possible in the long floor beams. This left room between the inner longitudinal plate girders supporting the track system only for a 15-foot, 2-inch wide roadway. The location between the two tracks also presented problems in linking the roadway to the access roads on the banks of the river. This was finally done with grade crossings over the east rail line at each end after it was determined that rail traffic required only a single track, and all trains were shifted to the west track. Construction of the reinforced concrete roadway began in May 1929, and the bridge was opened to highway traffic on September 23, 1929.[7] For almost forty years, the Quebec Bridge would remain the only road crossing of the St. Lawrence below Montréal.

The bridge took on a steadily growing role as a highway crossing as provincial highways and road traffic continued to develop. The narrow roadway confined between the two railroad tracks was soon overwhelmed by the growing traffic, and the demand for greater capacity brought another major change to the bridge in 1948. This time the east railroad track was removed entirely to permit widening of the roadway to 30 feet, allowing three lanes of traffic.

The Quebec Bridge's role as the principal highway link between the north and south banks of the St. Lawrence began to come to an end in 1968, when a bridge was completed at Trois-Rivières, some 60 miles upstream from Québec. Two years later the opening of the Pierre Laporte Bridge, a long suspension span, alongside the Quebec Bridge provided a new six-lane highway crossing of the St. Lawrence for Québec-area traffic. Since then, the great cantilever bridge has served only local road traffic.

As the Quebec Bridge's importance as a highway crossing declined, so too did its role as a link in Canada's railway system. If the one-time National Transcontinental Railway had never become the great artery between the Prairie Provinces and the Maritimes envisioned by its proponents, the line ceased to be a transcontinental route altogether in 1986, when Canadian National took up the former NTR line between Nakina and Calstock, Ontario, a distance of some 110 miles. Another section of some 150 miles between Calstock and Cochrane was sold to the Ontario Northland in 1993, while CN has since taken up still another segment of some 75 miles between Cochrane and Dupuy.

Today, railroad traffic across the Quebec Bridge is only a small part of what had once been envisioned for it. VIA Rail Canada, the national rail passenger operator, uses the bridge to reach Québec for four daily round trips in the Montréal-Québec corridor. Canadian National, which owns the bridge, makes little use of it. The railroad normally operates only two daily freight round trips over the bridge to link its main lines south of the river with the Limoilou Yard in Québec and the Québec Gatineau Railway, which operates the former Canadian Pacific line on the north shore of the river. "We use it because it's there," commented CN's Louise Filion recently.[8]

Over much of the last several decades, the declining importance of the Quebec Bridge seemed to be reflected in its upkeep. For a period of some twenty years from 1949 to 1969, no painting at all was done on the structure, and work was only sporadically accomplished over the next two decades. By the early 1990s, the bridge had accumulated a daunting volume of needed repairs and maintenance. With but little traffic using it, CN would have been happy to turn the bridge and its costly maintenance needs over to someone else.

But although its importance as a transportation link had diminished, the Quebec Bridge had come to assume an ever-growing symbolic significance to Québec and, indeed, to all of Canada. Reflecting both its enduring place as the longest cantilever span ever built and a growing recognition of the extraordinary engineering achievement represented by its design and construction, the bridge was designated an International Historic Civil Engineering Landmark in May 1987 by the American Society of Civil Engineers and the Canadian Society for Civil Engineering. In January 1996 the Department of Canadian Heritage declared the structure a National Historic Site. This widening recognition of the importance of the structure as a symbol of Canadian engineering achievement and determination helped to resolve what seemed an uncertain future for the bridge in the mid-1990s. Strong public and governmental interest in assuring its preservation led to a 1996 agreement among CN, the Province of Québec, and the federal government to jointly finance a comprehensive restoration of the structure.

Present-day Quebec Bridge
passenger services of VIA
Rail Canada, the national
passenger train operator,
employ Canadian-built low-
slung, tilting LRC (Light
Rapid Comfortable) rolling
stock. This was eastbound
LRC-equipped train 22, the
Citadelle, arriving at
Québec from Montréal in
September 1993.
William D. Middleton.

Westbound VIA Rail train 25,
the LRC-equipped Québec-
Montréal *Chaudière*, was
dwarfed by the immense
girders of the Quebec Bridge
as it headed south across the
river in September 1993.
William D. Middleton.

In 1994 Modjeski and Masters, the engineering firm founded by board of engineers member Ralph Modjeski, was commissioned to complete a detailed inspection and study of the structure and to develop a program for structural repairs and painting to fully restore and renovate the bridge. The needed work, the firm estimated, would cost $60 million and take ten years to complete. Under the 1996 agreement, CN agreed to invest $36 million, the Québec government $18 million, and the federal government $6 million in the work. Work began in 1997 under the overall supervision of CN engineers.[9]

During an initial three-year phase, the work was concentrated on structural repairs. Guardrails were repaired, some secondary members in both the main and approach spans were replaced or repaired, some of the main girders supporting the rail line were replaced, deteriorated rivets were removed and replaced by high tensile bolts, and all of the expansion bearings on the approach spans were replaced. Repair work for the piers included masonry joint repairs, injection of cracked stone, and replacement of a few broken stones. The most costly phase of the restoration is a complete cleaning and repainting of an estimated 7 million square feet of steel in the structure. The work began in 1999 and will continue from April through October each year through 2006. High-pressure water jets are being used to remove loose and deteriorated paint in preparation for applying a new coating of a flexible crystalline calcium sulfonate material in a greenish-grayish-beige color that CN calls "stealth."[10]

A tranquil park high on the bluffs along the north shore of the St. Lawrence at the Québec Aquarium provides a splendid vantage point from which to contemplate the looming majesty of the Quebec Bridge.
William D. Middleton.

In September 1993 this was
the view of the Quebec
Bridge from the south shore
vantage point of Chaudière
wharf at the confluence of
the Chaudière River and the
St. Lawrence. Just beyond
the bridge can be seen one
of the towers and the deck
of the Pierre Laporte Bridge
completed for highway
traffic in 1970. William D.
Middleton.

Chief among the supporters of the effort to establish a comprehensive restoration program for the bridge was a new organization formed in 1994 by more than fifty public,
business, and historic preservation groups in the greater Québec area called The Coalition for the Safekeeping and Enhancement of the Quebec Bridge (La Coalition pour le
sauvegarde et la mise en valeur de Pont de Québec). With the future of the bridge assured,
the Coalition then turned its efforts to an imaginative architectural lighting project that
would make the bridge a highly visible symbol of the city. Financed by Millennium project
grants from the federal and provincial governments, local government support, and private
contributions, the $1.5 million system designed by Yann Kersalé will include 252 1,000-watt
projectors that will bathe the structure in white, blue, and turquoise light at intensities that
vary with the tides in the St. Lawrence.[11] The Coalition plans to switch on the new lighting in elaborate ceremonies on October 2, 2001, 101 years to the day after the cornerstone
laying that marked the physical beginning to the long effort to bridge the St. Lawrence at
Québec.

Restored to sound condition and bathed in bright new colors, the Quebec Bridge stands
astride the St. Lawrence today as it has for more than eighty years now, a sturdy monument
to the unflagging determination of men who set out to build a great bridge at Québec so
long ago. It is a structure that has long since taken on a meaning transcending the purely
utilitarian purposes for which it was built. In the well-chosen words of the report that accompanied its nomination as an International Historic Civil Engineering Landmark:

> The Quebec Bridge has now become more than a rail and road link. It must be con-
> sidered as the primary symbol of Canadian engineering, recalling the strengths and
> weaknesses of the human spirit, the daring of Canadian builders and how tenacity
> can triumph over difficulties. This is why the governments must not only protect the
> bridge against too great a deterioration but must maintain it in a state worthy of the
> human, professional and national values which it symbolizes.[12]

Pleasure boats dot the surface of the Chaudière River
in this September 1993 view
of the Quebec Bridge from
St-Romuald, on the south
shore of the St. Lawrence.
William D. Middleton.

GLOSSARY

abutment: a support at one end of a bridge which carries the load of the bridge structure to the ground and, typically, restrains the earth fill adjacent to the bridge.

arch: a curved structural form in which the member acts principally in compression, producing both vertical and horizontal forces at its supports or abutments.

beam: a structural member, usually horizontal, which acts principally in bending and shear.

bearing: an assembly for transmitting the load from a bridge structure to the supporting piers or abutments.

bending: a force acting to bend a structural member, usually expressed as force times distance.

caisson: an enclosure, usually of timber and typically in the form of an inverted box, from which water is excluded by air pressure to permit the construction of deep foundations below water level.

caisson disease: the painful and sometimes fatal effect of dissolved nitrogen in the bloodstream, resulting from too rapid decompression after working under high air pressure in pneumatic caissons; commonly known as the "bends."

cantilever: a structural form in which a member is free at one end and restrained, or counterbalanced, at the support end.

cantilever bridge: a bridge form based upon the cantilever principal. In its typical form, cantilever arms projecting toward the center of the span from main piers are continuous with and counterbalanced by anchor arms extending between the main piers and anchor piers at each end. A simple span suspended between the two cantilever arms completes the structure. The weight of the suspended span and the cantilever arms is counterbalanced by that of the anchor arms and an anchorage embedded in the anchor pier.

chord: the longitudinal top or bottom members of a trussed structure which carry the principal tension or compression forces.

cofferdam: a temporary enclosure, usually of timber or steel, used to exclude water to permit the construction of bridge piers below the normal water level.

compression: a force acting on a member that tends to shorten it (the opposite of tension).

Cooper's loading: a widely used system of railroad live loads developed by Theodore Cooper which is based upon the axle loads of two 2-8-0 Consolidation steam locomotives of standard dimensions followed by a uniform loading representing the train. The actual loads used vary with the loading standard adopted for a structure. A Cooper's Class E10 loading, for example, is based upon driving axle loads of 10,000 pounds, with lesser loadings for the leading trucks and tender axles, and 1,000 pounds per foot for the uniform train load. Heavier loading standards are proportional; Cooper's Class E50 loadings, for example, are five times those for E10.

dead load: the loading imposed upon a structure by its own weight. Snow load is usually included in dead load.

erection: the process of assembling a bridge structure.

eyebar: a flat steel bar used as a tension member in chords or web members with a large "eye" forged at each end and drilled for the insertion of a connecting steel pin.

falsework: temporary staging installed to support a structure during erection until it is complete and self-supporting.

gantry: a raised platform supported by towers or side frames that runs on parallel tracks carrying cranes or derricks.

"K" Truss: a truss form in which each panel of the truss is subdivided by two diagonal web members meeting at the midpoint of a vertical web member at each panel point to form the letter "K."

latticing: a system of diagonal bars or angles used to connect two or more sections of a structural member to enable it to function as a unit.

live load: the external loading imposed by traffic moving over a structure. Other external loadings considered in design include the tractive or braking forces of trains, wind loads, and the effects of contraction or expansion resulting from temperature changes.

panel: an individual frame or segment of a truss structure defined by the arrangement of web members.

pier: an intermediate support for a bridge structure.

pin connected: a form of bridge erection in which members are connected by steel pins driven through pin holes drilled in the members. This method provides relatively simple and rapid erection compared to riveted, bolted, or welded rigid connections.

plate girder: a large beam built up by riveting, bolting, or welding, with a steel plate web connecting upper and lower flanges built up from steel plates and angles. The web is usually stiffened against buckling through the use of plate or angle stiffeners.

shear: a force acting across a structural member.

simple span: a structure spanning between two supports and unconstrained at either support.

steel: a refined form of iron alloyed with carbon that has greater strength, toughness, and wear resistance than either cast or wrought iron. Ordinary carbon steel is the usual form for structural steel. Nickel steel is alloyed with nickel for greater strength.

strain: the ratio of the change in length to the original length of a member under load.

stress: the intensity of loading on a member, usually expressed in terms of load per unit of cross-sectional area (i.e., pounds per square inch).

suspension bridge: a bridge carried on cables or chains that are continuous between anchorages at each end of the structure and supported from intermediate towers.

swung: a bridge erection term for a completed truss structure. When a truss span has been fully erected and temporary intermediate supports removed to allow the structure to carry its own weight, it is said to be "swung."

tension: a force acting on a member that tends to extend or elongate it (the opposite of compression).

traveler: a movable structure equipped with hoisting equipment used in bridge erection. Some travelers are designed to operate along temporary supports at the floor level of the structure being erected, while others travel along the top chords of a completed truss structure, erecting it as they go.

truss: a structure made up of a triangulated assembly of members designed to transmit loads in direct tension or compression with no bending.

voussoir: a wedge-shaped segment of an arch.

web: the vertical and diagonal members between the top and bottom chords of a truss; the vertical section of a rolled beam or plate girder separating the top and bottom flanges.

wrought iron: a form of iron with a very low carbon content that is tough, malleable, relatively soft, and much less brittle than cast iron.

SITES FOR A BRIDGE
AT QUÉBEC

Before the end of the nineteenth century, at least seven different alignments had been studied for a bridge over the St. Lawrence at Québec. In the end the engineers came back to the site at the river's confluence with the Chaudière River first proposed by Edward Wellman Serrell in 1852. — Map by David L. Waddington.

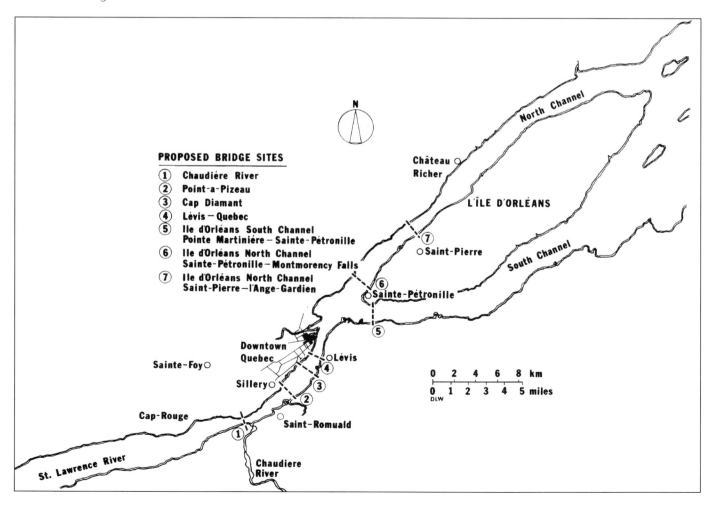

PROPOSED BRIDGE SITES

1. Chaudiére River
2. Point-a-Pizeau
3. Cap Diamant
4. Lévis — Quebec
5. Ile d'Orléans South Channel
   Pointe Martiniére — Sainte-Pétronille
6. Ile d'Orléans North Channel
   Sainte-Pétronille — Montmorency Falls
7. Ile d'Orléans North Channel
   Saint-Pierre — l'Ange-Gardien

RAILWAY LINES
CONTIGUOUS TO THE
QUEBEC BRIDGE SITE

Legend:

C. N. R.:	Canadian Northern Railway Co.
C. P. R.:	Canadian Pacific Railway Co.
G. T. R.:	Grand Trunk Railway Co.
I. C. R.:	Intercolonial Railway Co.
L. & M. R.:	Lotbinière & Mégantic Railway
N. T. R.:	National Transcontinental Railway
Q. C. R.:	Quebec Central Railway Co.
Q. R. L. H. & P.:	Quebec Railway, Light, Heat & Power Co.
Q. & L. St. J. Ry.:	Quebec & Lake St. John Railway Co.

This map from *The Quebec Bridge; Report of the Government Board of Engineers,* Vol. I, shows the railroad lines contiguous to the Quebec Bridge on the north and south shores of the St. Lawrence at the completion of the bridge in 1918. —Author's Collection.

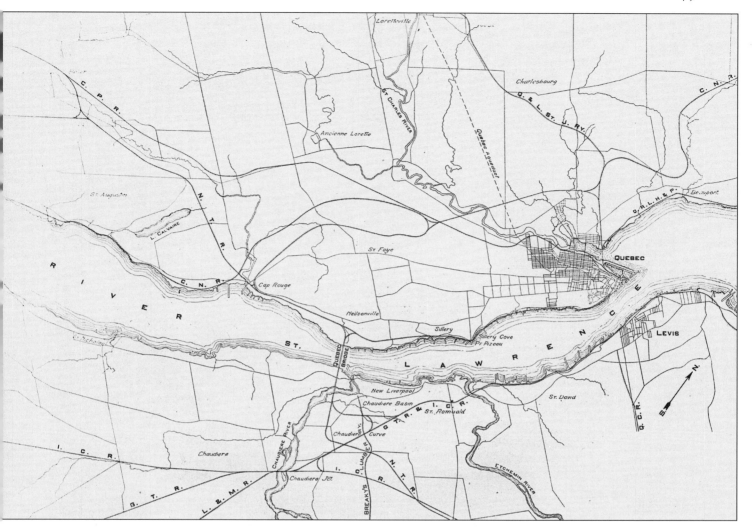

THE CONCLUSIONS OF C. C. SCHNEIDER

From the report of C. C. Schneider to the Deputy Minister and Chief Engineer, Department of Railways and Canals, dated January 1908.

Conclusions

The results of the writer's investigations and his recommendations may be briefly summarized as follows:

First.—The floor system and bracing are of sufficient strength to safely carry the traffic for which they were intended.

Second.—The trusses, as shown in the design submitted to the writer, do not conform to the requirements of the approved specifications, and are inadequate to carry the traffic or loads specified.

Third.—The latticing of many of the compression members is not in proportion to the sections of the members which they connect.

Fourth.—The trusses of the bridge, even if they had been designed in accordance with the approved specifications, would not be of sufficient strength in all their parts to safely sustain the loads provided for in the specifications.

Fifth.—It is impracticable to use the fabricated material now on hand in the reconstruction of the bridge.

Sixth.—The present design is not well adapted to a structure of the magnitude of the Quebec Bridge and should, therefore, be discarded and a different design adopted for the new bridge, retaining only the length of the spans in order to use the present piers.

Seventh.—The writer considers the present piers strong enough to carry a heavier structure, assuming that the bearing capacity of the foundations is sufficient to sustain the increased pressure.

FINDINGS OF
THE ROYAL COMMISSION

From the report of the commission to the Governor General in Council dated February 20, 1908.

Your commissioners find:

(a) The collapse of the Quebec bridge resulted from the failure of the lower chords in the anchor arm near the main pier. The failure of these chords was due to their defective design.

(b) The stresses that caused the failure were not due to abnormal weather conditions or accident, but were such as might be expected in the regular course of erection.

(c) The design of the chords that failed was made by Mr. P. L. Szlapka, the designing engineer of the Phoenix Bridge Company.

(d) This design was examined and officially approved by Mr. Theodore Cooper, consulting engineer of the Quebec Bridge and Railway Company.

(e) The failure cannot be attributed directly to any cause other than errors in judgment on the part of these two engineers.

(f) These errors of judgment cannot be attributed either to lack of common professional knowledge, to neglect of duty, or to a desire to economize. The ability of the two engineers was tried in one of the most difficult professional problems of the day and proved to be insufficient for the task.

(g) We do not consider that the specifications for the work were satisfactory or sufficient, the unit stresses in particular being higher than any established by past practice. The specifications were accepted without protest by all interested.

(h) A grave error was made in assuming the dead load for the calculations at too low a value and not afterwards revising this assumption. This error was of sufficient magnitude to have required condemnation of the bridge, even if the details of the lower chords had been of sufficient strength, because, if the bridge had been completed as designed, the actual stresses would have been considerably greater than those permitted by the specifications. This erroneous assumption was made by Mr. Szlapka and accepted by Mr. Cooper, and tended to hasten the disaster.

(i) We do not believe that the fall of the bridge could have been prevented by any action that might have been taken after August 27, 1907. Any effort to brace or take down the structure would have been impracticable owing to the manifest risk of human life involved.

(j) The loss of life on August 29, 1907, might have been prevented by the exercise of better judgment on the part of those in responsible charge of the work for the Quebec Bridge and Railway Company and for the Phoenix Bridge Company.

(k) The failure on the part of the Quebec Bridge and Railway Company to appoint an experienced bridge engineer to the position of chief engineer was a mistake. This resulted in a loose and inefficient supervision of all parts of the work on the part of the Quebec Bridge and Railway Company.

(l) The work done by the Phoenix Bridge Company in making the detailed drawings and in planning and carrying out the erection, and by the Phoenix Iron Company in fabricating the material was good, and the steel used was of good quality. The serious defects were fundamental errors in design.

(m) No one connected with the general designing fully appreciated the magnitude of the work nor the insufficiency of the data upon which they were depending. The special experimental studies and investigations that were required to confirm the judgment of the designers were not made.

(n) The professional knowledge of the present day concerning the action of steel columns under load is not sufficient to enable engineers to economically design such structures as the Quebec bridge. A bridge of the adopted span that will unquestionably be safe can be built, but in the present state of professional knowledge a considerably larger amount of metal would have to be used than might be required if our knowledge were more exact.

(o) The professional record of Mr. Cooper was such that his selection for the authoritative position that he occupied was warranted, and the complete confidence that was placed in his judgment by the officials of the Dominion government, the Quebec Bridge and Railway Company and the Phoenix Bridge Company was deserved.

THE TWO BRIDGES

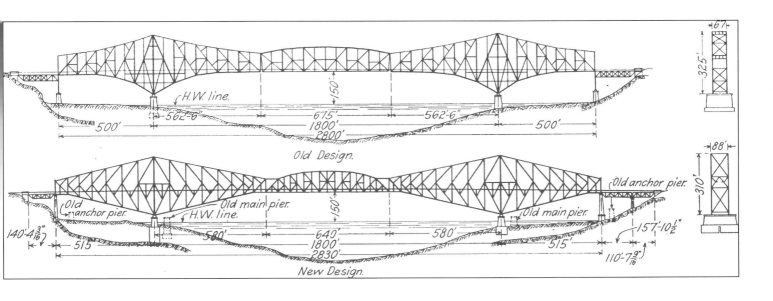

Principal Dimensions, Quantities, and Weights

	First Bridge (1900–1907)[1]	Second Bridge (1910–1918)[2]
Length of suspended span	675 feet	640 feet
Length of cantilever arms	562 feet, 6 inches	580 feet
Length of anchor arms	500 feet	515 feet
Total length of steel work	3,220 feet	3,239 feet
Distance center-to-center of main piers	1,800 feet	1,800 feet
Width center-to-center of main trusses	67 feet	88 feet
Width center-to-center of railway tracks		32 feet, 6 inches
Depth of suspended span at center	130 feet	110 feet
Depth of suspended span at hip	97 feet, 3 inches	70 feet
Depth of cantilever arm at end	97 feet, 3 inches	70 feet
Height of main post center-to-center of pins	315 feet	310 feet
Depth of anchor arm at anchor piers	96 feet, 10 inches	70 feet
Height of suspended span above high water	150 feet	150 feet
Height of suspended span above low water	172 feet	172 feet
Height of south main pier above foundation	110 feet	128 feet
Height of north main pier above foundation	82 feet	108 feet
Height of south anchor pier above foundation	62 feet	141 feet
Height of north anchor pier above foundation	61 feet	160 feet
Depth of south caisson below high water		101 feet
Volume of main and anchor piers	49,400 cubic yards	103,958 cubic yards
Weight of each anchor arm, including main post		17,000 tons
Weight of each cantilever arm, excluding main post		12,000 tons
Weight of suspended span		5,510 tons
Weight of approach spans		1,350 tons
Total weight of superstructure	38,500 tons	66,480 tons
Total number of field rivets	550,000	1,066,740
Maximum total stress in one member		29,583,000 pounds
Maximum reaction on one main shoe		55,200,000 pounds
Maximum load on base of main pier		192,000,000 pounds
Maximum uplift on one anchor pier		16,518,000 pounds
Weight of one anchor pier		65,000,000 pounds
Maximum chord section	842 square inches	1,902 square inches

Sources

1. Booklet, *The Quebec Bridge*, printed for E. R. Kinloch and N. R. McClure, ca 1907, and *Engineering News*, various dates.

2. *The Quebec Bridge: Report of the Government Board of Engineers*, Vol. I, 1919.

LIVE LOADINGS SPECIFICATIONS

	First Bridge (1900–1907)[1]	Second Bridge (1910–1918)[2]
Railway Live Load	*Floor system:* Cooper's E40 Class locomotive. *Trusses:* Continuous train of 3,000 pounds/linear foot on both tracks, a 900-foot train of two E33 Class locomotives followed by a load of 3,300 pounds/linear foot on each track, or a 550-foot train of one E40 locomotive followed by a load of 4,000 pounds/linear foot on each track.	Two Cooper's Class E60 locomotives followed by 5,000 pounds/linear foot on each track.
Roadway Loads	*Trolley stringers:* Loaded with cars weighing 56,000 pounds on two axles 10 feet apart. *Highway stringers:* Loaded with 24,000 pounds on two axles 10 feet apart.	
Sidewalk Live Load		500 pounds/linear foot on each walk. 500 pounds/linear foot of snow on bridge.
Impact Load		*Trusses:* 20% of railway load. *Floor beams:* 75% of railway load. *Stringers:* 100% of railway load.
Wind Load	*Suspended span:* Lateral wind force of 700 pounds/linear foot on top chord and 1,700 pounds/linear foot on bottom chord. *Anchor and cantilever arms:* Lateral wind force of 500 pounds/linear foot on top chord and 1,000 pounds/linear foot on the bottom chord, in addition to wind force on the suspended span.	30 pounds/square foot of the exposed surface of two trusses and 1½ times the elevation of the floor; plus a moving load of 300 pounds/linear foot applied 9 feet above the rail.

Sources

1. Royal Commission Report, Vol. I.

2. *The Quebec Bridge.* St. Lawrence Bridge Company, 1918.

NOTES

Prologue

1. *The Voyages of Jacques Cartier* (Toronto: University of Toronto Press, 1993), pp. 74–75.

2. Frances Brooke, *The History of Emily Montague* (Toronto: McClelland and Stewart, 1961), pp. 187–188.

1. A Bridge at the Narrowing

1. Edward William [*sic*] Serrell, *Report on a Railway Suspension Bridge Proposed, for Crossing the St. Lawrence River at Quebec* (1852), p. 12.

2. Ibid., pp. 57–58.

3. W. Marsden, M.A., M.D., *A Letter on the Subject of a Submerged Tubular or Tunnel Bridge under the St. Lawrence in Connection with the North Shore Railroad* (1872), p. 3.

4. *Le Canadien*, Québec, March 1, 1872, p. 2.

5. *Le Canadien*, Québec, October 5, 1872, p. 2.

6. Letter to the Editor of the Québec *Morning Chronicle*, A. L. Light, dated January 4, 1884.

2. A Project at Last

1. The *Chronicle*, Québec, April 1, 1887, report of meeting incorporated into Minute Book No. 1 of the Quebec Bridge Company.

2. Ibid.

3. Acts of the Parliament, 49-50 Victoria, Chapter 98, Ottawa, 1897.

4. Petition of the Quebec Railway Bridge Company to James Edmund Flynn, Premier, Province of Québec, dated November 14, 1896.

5. Report to Col. J. Bell Forsyth, President, Quebec Bridge Company, by E. A. Hoare, dated January 22, 1889.

6. Ibid.

7. Ibid.

8. Petition to Flynn of November 14, 1896.

9. 1889 report of Walter Shanly to the Quebec Bridge Company, reproduced in the minutes of the general annual meeting of the company on September 6, 1898.

10. Report to the Quebec Bridge Company, "Probable Cost of St-Lawrence Bridge at or near Quebec," by E. A. Hoare, dated March 6, 1890.

11. "Rapport sur le Pont de Quebec," par M. l'Ingénieur Bonnin, 21 Octobre 1890.

12. Report to A. P. Bradley, Minister of Railways and Canals, by Collingwood Schreiber, Chief Engineer and General Manager, dated February 28, 1891.

13. Letter to Honoré Mercier, Premier, Province of Québec, from Max am Ende, dated April 11, 1891.

14. *La Semaine Commerciale*, Québec, September 7, 1894, p. 3.

15. Report to Honoré Mercier, Premier, Province of Québec, "Considerations sur le Pont de Quebec," from Gustave Eiffel, dated July 21, 1891.

16. *La Semaine Commerciale*, Québec, November 20, 1896, p. 4.

17. Quoted by J. Bell Forsyth, President, Quebec Bridge Company, in his annual report to the general annual meeting of shareholders of the company on September 7, 1897.

18. Minutes of Quebec Bridge Company Board of Directors meeting of September 23, 1897.

19. Report of C. E. Gauvin, Civil Engineer, published as appendix No. 6 of the general report of the Commissioners of Public Works for 1896. Conclusions reproduced in the minutes of the general annual meeting of the Quebec Bridge Company on September 6, 1898.

20. Ibid.

21. *La Semaine Commerciale*, Québec, March 12, 1897, pp. 4–11, and *Engineering News*, October 14, 1897, p. 255.

22. Minutes of Quebec Bridge Company Board of Directors meeting of March 24, 1897.

23. Minutes of Quebec Bridge Company Board of Directors meetings of October 30, November 25, and December 9, 1897. Waddell was persistent in the extreme in pressing his services on the board. After having been informed at the November meeting that the board was unable to bind itself in any way at that time, Waddell responded by submitting a draft agreement that was taken up at the December meeting. According to the minutes, "the Secretary was instructed to acknowledge receipt of same and to inform Mr. Waddell that the Directors wish it to be distinctly understood that as it was plainly stated at the last interview between Mr. Waddell and the Directors, they were not in a position to bind themselves in any way at the present moment, and that it should be equally well understood that the present correspondence shall give Mr. Waddell no claim whatever against this Company."

24. Minutes of Quebec Bridge Company Board of Directors meeting of July 8, 1897.

25. Report of S. N. Parent, President, Quebec Bridge Company, to the annual general meeting of shareholders on September 6, 1898.

26. "Report Upon the Competitive Plans and Proposals for the Construction of the Quebec Bridge," by Theodore Cooper, dated June 23, 1899. Reproduced in Royal Commission Inquiry, Vol. 2, pp. 439–444.

27. Ibid.

28. Ibid.

29. "Supplementary Report," by Theodore Cooper, dated June 23, 1899. Reproduced in Royal Commission Inquiry, Vol. 2, p. 445.

30. August 23, 1899, letter from Parent to Deans, Royal Commission Report, Vol. I, pp. 23–24.

3. The Engineers and the Bridge Builders

1. Testimony of Edward A. Hoare to the Quebec Bridge Inquiry, Royal Commission Report, Vol. II, p. 50.

2. "Memoir of Theodore Cooper," *Transactions of the American Society of Civil Engineers*, Vol. 84 (1921): 828–830.

3. C. M. Woodward, *A History of the St. Louis Bridge* (St. Louis: G. I. Jones and Company, 1881), pp. 184–185.

4. Ibid.

5. August 4, 1903, letter from Cooper to Hoare, Royal Commission Report, Vol. II, pp. 546–547.

6. Thomas R. Winpenny, *Without Fitting, Filing, or Chipping* (Easton, Pa.: Canal History and Technology Press, 1996).

7. Data from directories of the American Iron and Steel Association included in Appendix A, "Shop Capacities in the 1890s," of Victor C. Darnell, *A Directory of American Bridge-Building Companies: 1840–1900* (Washington, D.C.: Society for Industrial Archaeology, 1984).

8. Winpenny, p. 49.

9. Ibid., pp. 49, 52–53, and *Engineering News*, December 28, 1893, pp. 517–521.

10. Winpenny, pp. 54–55.

4. The Great Bridge Underway

1. Testimony of John Sterling Deans to Quebec Bridge Inquiry, Royal Commission Report, Vol. II, p. 378.

2. May 1, 1900, letter Cooper to Parent, Royal Commission Report, Vol. II, pp. 446–447.

3. Quebec Bridge Company, Minute Book No. 2, p. 145.

4. August 23, 1899, letter Deans to Parent, Royal Commission Report, Vol. I, p. 24.

5. *The Globe*, Toronto, October 3, 1900, p. 2.

6. *Engineering News*, January 29, 1903, p. 94.

7. Official Report of the Debates of the House of Commons, 3 Edward VII, 1903, 7,658–7,697. Laurier's extraordinary address to Commons, which went on for close to three hours, appealed to Canadian fears of any dependency on rail routes that reached the ice-free Atlantic ports by way of the United States. "We ask parliament to assent to this policy because we believe—nay, we feel certain, and certain beyond a doubt—that in so doing we give voice and expression to a sentiment, a latent but deep sentiment, which is to-day in the mind, and still more the heart, of every Canadian," he said at one point, "that a railway to extend from the shore of the Atlantic ocean to the shores of the Pacific ocean, and to be, every inch of it, on Canadian soil, is a national as well as a commercial necessity."

8. *The Montréal Star*, January 23, 1904.

9. *The Gazette*, Montréal, January 1, 1904, p. 4.

10. The company had acquired the new name in July 1903 in yet another amendment to the original 1887 authorizing Act of Parliament, which now required completion of the bridge by July 1910.

11. June 19, 1903, letter, Reeves to Parent, Royal Commission Report, Vol. I, pp. 31–32.

12. Royal Commission Report, Vol. 1, p. 148.

13. July 9, 1903, letter Schreiber to Jones, Royal Commission Report, Vol. I, p. 42.

14. July 31, 1903, letter Cooper to Hoare, Royal Commission Report, Vol. I, p. 43.

15. August 3, 1903, telegram Deans to Hoare, Royal Commission Report, Vol. I, p. 45.

16. August 1, 1903, letter, Deans to Cooper, Royal Commission Report, Vol. I, p. 45.

17. Extract from a report of a committee to the privy council, approved August 15, 1903, Royal Commission Report, Vol. I, pp. 45–46.

18. August 21, 1903, letter Cooper to Hoare, quoted in Royal Commission Report, Vol. I, p. 20.

19. Testimony of Robert C. Douglas to the Quebec Bridge Inquiry, Royal Commission Report, Vol. II, p. 337.

20. Testimony of Theodore Cooper to the Quebec Bridge Inquiry, Royal Commission Report, Vol. II, p. 348.

21. Ibid., p. 414.

22. Royal Commission Report, Vol. I, p. 70.

23. Deans testimony, p. 19.

24. Mitchell, Joseph, "The Mohawks in High Steel," from *Up in the Old Hotel (and Other Stories)* (New York: Pantheon Books, 1992).

25. Deans testimony, p. 19.

26. Cooper testimony, p. 345.

27. Royal Commission Report, Vol. I, p. 73.

28. Ibid., pp. 73–75.

5. Countdown to Disaster

1. Testimony of Theodore Cooper to the Quebec Bridge Inquiry, Royal Commission Report, Vol. II, p. 356.

2. June 15, 1907, letter from McLure to Cooper, quoted in Royal Commission Report, Vol. I, p. 77.

3. June 17, 1907, letter from Cooper to McLure, quoted in Royal Commission Report, Vol. I, p. 77.

4. August 6, 1907, letter from McLure to Cooper, Royal Commission Report, Vol. I, p. 79.

5. August 8, 1907, telegram from Cooper to McLure, Royal Commission Report, Vol. I, p. 79.

6. August 9, 1907, letter from Cooper to Deans, Royal Commission Report, Vol. I, p. 80.

7. August 12, 1907, letter from Deans to Cooper, Royal Commission Report, Vol. I, p. 81.

8. August 13, 1907, letter from Cooper to Deans, Royal Commission Report, Vol. I, p. 81.

9. August 12, 1907, letter from McLure to Cooper, Royal Commission Report, Vol. I, pp. 82–83.

10. Ibid.

11. August 15, 1907, letter from Cooper to McLure, Royal Commission Report, Vol. I, p. 83.

12. August 16, 1907, letter from McLure to Cooper, Royal Commission Report, Vol. I, pp. 83–84.

13. August 26, 1907, letter from Cooper to Deans, Royal Commission Report, Vol. I, p. 85.

14. Testimony of E. R. Kinloch to Quebec Bridge Inquiry, Royal Commission Report, Vol. II, p. 232.

15. Testimony of D. B. Haley to Quebec Bridge Inquiry, Royal Commission Report, Vol. II, p. 127.

16. August 28, 1907, letter from Hoare to Cooper, Royal Commission Report, Vol. I, p. 88–89.

17. Ibid.

18. Haley testimony, p. 107.

19. Testimony of John E. Splicer to Quebec Bridge Inquiry, Royal Commission Report, Vol. II, p. 161.

20. August 29, 1907, telegram from Deans to Hoare, Royal Commission Report, Vol. I, p. 91.

21. Testimony of Edward A. Hoare to Quebec Bridge Inquiry, Royal Commission Report, Vol. II, p. 284.

22. August 29, 1907, telegram from Cooper to Phoenix Bridge Company, Royal Commission Report, Vol. I, p. 91.

23. *The Gazette*, Montréal, September 3, 1907, p. 1.

24. Blanchard, David, "High Steel: The Kahnawake Mohawk and the High Construction Trade," 1981. Manuscript in the library of the Kanien'kehaka Raotitiohkwa Cultural Center, Kahnawake, via Québec, pp. 13–14.

25. Unpublished manuscript in the papers of S. N. Parent, Québec National Archives, Québec.

26. Testimony of E. R. Kinloch to Quebec Bridge Inquiry, Royal Commission Report, Vol. II, p. 213.

27. *The Railroad Gazette*, September 6, 1907, p. 266.

28. *Engineering News*, September 5, 1907, p. 260.

29. Testimony of Ingwall Hall to Quebec Bridge Inquiry, Royal Commission Report, Vol. II, pp. 101–102.

30. Haley testimony, pp. 105–106.

31. Testimony of J. J. Nance to Quebec Bridge Inquiry, Royal Commission Report, Vol. II, pp. 156–157.

32. Testimony of Delphis Lajeunesse to Quebec Bridge Inquiry, Royal Commission Report, Vol. II, p. 186.

33. Testimony of Joseph Adolphe Huot to Quebec Bridge Inquiry, Royal Commission Report, Vol. II, pp. 75–77.

34. Testimony of Percy Wilson to Quebec Bridge Inquiry, Royal Commission Report, Vol. II, pp. 163, 166.

35. Testimony of Alexander Beauvais to Quebec Bridge Inquiry, Royal Commission Report, Vol. II, pp. 199–201.

36. Blanchard, pp. 13–14.

37. Testimony of Norman R. McLure to Quebec Bridge Inquiry, Royal Commission Report, Vol. II, p. 264.

6. Aftermath

1. August 28, 1907, letter from Hoare to Cooper, Royal Commission Report, Vol. I, pp. 88–89.

2. September 2, 1907, letter from Hoare to Cooper, Royal Commission Report, Vol. I, pp. 89–90.

3. *New York Times*, September 1, 1907, p. 3.

4. *Chicago Daily Tribune*, August 31, 1907, p. 5.

5. *New York Times*, August 31, 1907, p. 1.

6. *New York Times*, September 1, 1907, p. 1.

7. Ibid.

8. *The Gazette*, Montréal, September 13, 1907, p. 1.

9. Royal Commission dated August 31, 1907, reproduced in Royal Commission Report, Vol. 1, p. 5.

10. *Scientific American*, September 14, 1907, p. 182.

11. Testimony of Theodore Cooper to Quebec Bridge Inquiry, Royal Commission Report, Vol. II, p. 347.

12. Ibid., p. 350.

13. Ibid., p. 356.

14. Ibid., p. 352.

15. Ibid., p. 358.

16. Ibid., p. 351.

17. Ibid., p. 358.

18. Clipping dated October 31, 1907, in Phoenix Bridge Company news clippings held by the Chester County Historical Society, West Chester, Pennsylvania.

19. Testimony of David Reeves to Quebec Bridge Inquiry, Royal Commission Report, Vol. II, pp. 363–365.

20. Ibid., p. 16.

21. Ibid., p. 17.

22. Ibid., p. 390.

23. *Le Soleil*, Québec, November 22, 1907, p. 1.

24. C. C. Schneider's report to the Department of Railways and Canals of January 1908 is included in the Royal Commission Report, Vol. I, pp. 153–160.

25. Ibid.

26. Ibid.

27. Royal Commission Report, Vol. I, pp. 7–11.

28. Ibid.

29. Ibid.

30. *Engineering News*, March 19, 1908, p. 317.

31. David B. Steinman and Sara Ruth Watson, *Bridges and Their Builders* (New York: Dover, 1957), p. 308.

32. *The Bulletin of the American Iron and Steel Association*, April 1, 1908, p. 26.

33. "Notes from Mr. MacCornack on Quebec Bridge," unpublished manuscript at the Historical Society of the Phoenixville Area, Phoenixville, Pennsylvania.

34. *Of Men and Steel: Kahnawake and the Construction Industry*. Kahnawake, Québec, Kanien'kehaka Raotitiohkwa Cultural Center, and interview with Kanatakta, Director, Kanien'kehaka Raotitiohkwa Cultural Center, January 25, 2000.

35. Willa Cather, *Alexander's Bridge* (New York: The American Reprint Company, 1976).

36. Testimony of Peter L. Szlapka to Quebec Bridge Inquiry, Royal Commission Report, Vol. II, p. 392.

37. July 31, 1903, letter Cooper to Hoare, Royal Commission Report, Vol. 1, p. 43.

38. J. A. L. Waddell, *Bridge Engineering*, 2 vols. (New York, John Wiley & Sons, 1916), Vol. II, p. 1,546.

39. Royal Commission Report, Vol. I, p. 90.

40. *Engineering News*, March 19, 1908, p. 318.

41. Ibid., pp. 317–318.

42. Ibid.

7. Starting Over

1. *The Gazette*, Montréal, August 31, 1907, p. 1.

2. September 2, 1907, clipping in Phoenix Bridge Company news clippings held by the Chester County Historical Society, West Chester, Pennsylvania.

3. Royal Commission Report, Vol. I, p. 160.

4. Order-in-Council—P. C. 1787 of August 17, 1908, in *The Quebec Bridge*, Report of the Government Board of Engineers, 1918, Vol. I, p. 7.

5. Born Rudolphe Modrzejewska, Modjeski and his mother shortened their surname to ease her U.S. stage debut.

6. *Engineering News*, November 23, 1911, pp. 613–619.

7. *Engineering News*, May 19, 1910, pp. 577–578.

8. *Engineering News*, May 30, 1912, pp. 1,012–1,016.

9. *The Quebec Bridge*, Report of the Government Board of Engineers, 1918, Vol. I, p. 16.

10. Ibid., p. 18.

11. Ibid., p. 20.

12. *The Quebec Bridge: Notes on the Work of the St. Lawrence Bridge Company, In Preparing the Accepted Design for the Construction of the Superstructure*, by G. H. Duggan. Text of an illustrated lecture given at a meeting of the Canadian Society of Civil Engineers on January 10, 1918, p. 9.

13. Ibid. Duggan's paper gives an excellent and detailed account of this and the many other considerations that governed the design of the superstructure.

14. *Engineering News*, April 30, 1914, pp. 943–944.

15. *Railway Age Gazette*, September 26, 1913, p. 559.

8. Underway Again

1. *Engineering News*, November 10, 1910, p. 510.

2. Ibid., pp. 510–511.

3. *Engineering News*, September 8, 1910, pp. 262–263.

4. *The Quebec Bridge*, Report of the Government Board of Engineers, 1918, Vol. I, p. 43.

5. Ibid.

6. Ibid. p. 53.

7. In February 1916 Borden, who had been with the board of engineers since 1908, became the third member of the board, following the death of C. C. Schneider at the age of 72.

8. *Engineering News*, April 30, 1914, p. 944.

9. Again, Disaster

1. *The Gazette*, Montréal, September 11, 1916.

2. Ibid., and *The Globe*, Toronto, September 12, 1916, pp. 1, 3.

3. *The Gazette*, Montréal, September 12, 1916, pp. 1, 8, and *The Globe*, Toronto, September 12, 1916, pp. 1, 3.

4. *The Gazette*, Montréal, September 13, 1916, pp. 1, 9.

10. Triumph at Last

1. *The Quebec Bridge*, Report of the Government Board of Engineers, 1918, Vol. I, p. 33.

2. *Engineering News-Record*, September 27, 1917, pp. 580, 582.

3. Ibid., pp. 1, 5.

4. *The Gazette*, Montréal, August 23, 1919, p. 2.

5. Donald MacKay, *The People's Railway: A History of Canadian National* (Vancouver/Toronto: Douglas & McIntyre, 1992), pp. 5–32, provides an excellent account of the formation of CN.

6. Christopher Andreae, *Lines of Country* (Toronto: Boston Mills Press, 1997), p. 75.

7. Jaques Jobin, "Quebec Bridge Roadway Construction," *The Canadian Engineer*, August 26, 1930, pp. 261–264.

8. Interview with Louise Filion, Canadian National Public Relations, January 24, 2000.

9. Canadian National press release dated May 15, 1997.

10. Interview with Rocco Cacchiotti, Structures Operations Engineer, and Alain Martineau, Project Coordinator, Quebec Bridge, Canadian National, January 25, 2000.

11. Letter to the author from Jaques Jobin, President, La Coalition pour le Pont de Québec, February 16, 2000, and La Coalition web page: www.pontdaquebec.com.

12. International Historic Civil Engineering Landmark nomination to the Committee on the History and Heritage of American Civil Engineering, American Society of Civil Engineers, dated January 1987, and accompanying report.

BIBLIOGRAPHY

Books and Pamphlets

Andreae, Christopher. *Lines of Country: An Atlas of Railway and Waterway History in Canada.* Toronto: Boston Mills Press, 1997.

Brookes, Ivan S. *The Lower St. Lawrence.* Cleveland: Freshwater Press, 1974.

Browne, George Waldo. *The St. Lawrence River.* New York: G. P. Putnam's Sons, 1905. Reprint edition, New York: Weathervane Books.

Darnell, Victor C. *Directory of American Bridge-Building Companies, 1840–1900.* Washington: Society for Industrial Archeology, 1984.

Dawson, Samuel Edward. *The Saint Lawrence: Its Basin and Border-Lands.* New York: Frederick A. Stokes Company, 1905.

Duggan, G. H. *The Quebec Bridge: Notes on the Work of the St. Lawrence Bridge Company, in Preparing the Accepted Design for the Construction of the Superstructure.* Canadian Society of Civil Engineers, 1918.

Fournier, Leslie T. *Railway Nationalization in Canada: The Problem of The Canadian National Railways.* Toronto: Macmillan Company of Canada, 1935. Reprint edition, New York: Arno Press, 1981.

Hill, Richard. *Skywalkers: A History of Indian Ironworkers.* Brantford, Ontario: Woodland Indian Cultural Centre, 1987.

Hills, T. L. *The St. Lawrence Seaway.* New York: Frederick A. Praeger, 1959.

L'Hébreux, Michel. *Une merveille du monde: Le Pont du Québec.* Sainte-Foy, Québec: Les Éditions La Liberté, 1986.

MacKay, Donald. *The People's Railway: A History of Canadian National.* Vancouver/Toronto: Douglas & McIntyre, 1992.

Marsden, W., M.A., M.D. *A Letter on the Subject of a Submerged Tubular or Tunnel Bridge under the St. Lawrence in Connection with the North Shore Railroad.* Quebec: Printed by Middleton & Dawson, at the "Gazette" General Printing Establishment, 1872.

Moriarty, Catherine. *John Galbraith: Engineer and Educator.* Toronto: Faculty of Applied Science and Engineering, University of Toronto, 1989.

Proposed Bridge over the St. Lawrence, at Quebec [reprinted from *Engineering* of April 3, 1885]. London: Bedford Press, 1885.

The Quebec Bridge: At the Dawn of a New Millennium. Canadian National press kit. Montreal, May 15, 1997.

The Quebec Bridge: Carrying the Transcontinental Line of the Canadian Government Railways over the St. Lawrence River near the City of Quebec, Canada. Québec: St. Lawrence Bridge Company, 1918.

The Quebec Bridge: An Engineering Triumph in the World's History. Canadian Government Railways, ca 1918.

The Quebec Bridge: The Longest Single Span Bridge in the World Crossing the St. Lawrence River Seven Miles above Quebec, Canada—Building for the Quebec Bridge & Railway Company. New Liverpool, Québec: Printed for E. R. Kinloch and N. R. McClure, ca. 1907.

The Quebec Bridge over the St. Lawrence River Near the City of Quebec on the line of the Canadian National Railways: Report of the Government Board of Engineers. 2 vols. Ottawa: Department of Railways and Canals, 1919.

The Quebec Bridge, 29th August, 1901: Souvenir of a Visit to the Works by the Canadian Press Association. Québec: Daily Telegraph, 1901.

Royal Commission. *Quebec Bridge Inquiry Report.* 2 vols. Sessional Paper No. 154, 7–8 Edward VII. Ottawa, 1908.

Serrell, Edward William [*sic*]. *Report on a Railway Suspension Bridge, Proposed for Crossing the St. Lawrence River at Quebec.* Quebec: Augustin Coté & Company, 1852

Spanning Niagara: The International Bridges 1848–1962. Seattle: University of Washington Press, 1984.

Steinman, D. B. *The Builders of the Bridge: The Story of John Roebling and His Son.* New York: Harcourt, Brace, 1945.

Toye, William. *The St. Lawrence.* New York: Henry Z. Walck, 1959.

Triggs, Stanley, Brian Young, Conrad Graham, and Gilles Lauzon. *Victoria Bridge: The Vital Link.* Montreal: McCord Museum of Canadian History, 1992.

Winks, Honor Leigh, and Robin W. Winks. *The St. Lawrence.* Morristown, N.J.: Wayland/Silver Burdett, 1980.

Winpenny, Thomas R. *Without Fitting, Filing, or Chipping: An Illustrated History of the Phoenix Bridge Company.* Easton, Pa.: Canal History and Technology Press, 1996.

Periodicals

The railroad, engineering, and scientific press, particularly *Engineering News*, *Engineering Record*, and the merged *Engineering News-Record* after 1917, covered the development of both Québec bridges, as well as the two collapses, with exceptional thoroughness. Following are some of the most important articles:

The First Bridge

ENGINEERING NEWS

"The Substructure for the 1,800–Ft. Cantilever Bridge at Quebec, Canada." Vol. 49, No. 5 (January 29, 1903): 92–97.

"The 1,800 Ft. Span Cantilever Bridge across the St. Lawrence River at Quebec." Vol. 54, No. 11 (September 14, 1905): 272–274.

"Progress in the Erection of the Quebec Bridge." Vol. 55, No. 26 (June 28, 1906): 705–706.

"Progress of the Quebec Bridge across the St. Lawrence River." Vol. 57, No. 3 (January 17, 1907): 53.

"The Fall of the Quebec Cantilever Bridge." Vol. 58, No. 10 (September 5, 1907): 256–257, 258–264.

"The Quebec Bridge Failure: Our Deficient Knowledge of the Strength of Large Columns." Vol. 58, No. 11 (September 12, 1907): 284–289.

"The Fall of the Quebec Bridge." Vol. 58, No. 12 (September 19, 1907): 319–321.

"The Compression Members of the Quebec Bridge." Vol. 58, No. 14 (October 3, 1907): 364–366.

"The Quebec Bridge Wreck." Vol. 58, No. 15 (October 10, 1907): 388, with folding plate.

"Theodore Cooper on the Quebec Bridge and Its Failure." Vol. 58, No. 18 (October 31, 1907): 473–477.

"The Phoenixville Testimony in the Quebec Bridge Inquiry." Vol. 58, No. 22 (November 28, 1907): 576–586, 587–588.

"The Report of the Royal Commission of Inquiry on the Collapse of the Quebec Bridge." Vol. 59, No. 12 (March 19, 1908): 307–315, 317–318.

"The Wreck of the Quebec Bridge and the Stresses in the Bridge." Vol. 59, No. 16 (April 16, 1908): 421–423.

"Tests of Two Compression Chord Models: The Largest Column Tests Ever Made." Vol. 59, No. 17 (April 23, 1908): 454–459.

"The Theory of Latticed Columns, a Comparison of Cantilever Bridge Chords, and a Discussion of the Quebec Bridge Specifications." Vol. 59, No. 18 (April 30, 1908): 480–486.

"The Design of the Quebec Bridge: Report by C. C. Schneider, with Theodore Cooper's Specifications." Vol. 60, No. 6 (August 6, 1908): 153–154, 155–158.

THE RAILROAD GAZETTE

"The St. Lawrence River Bridge at Quebec, Canada." Vol. 39, No. 11 (September 15, 1905): 242–245.
"Progress of the Quebec Bridge." Vol. 42, No. 2 (January 11, 1907): 37.
"Collapse of the Quebec Bridge." Vol. 43, No. 10 (September 6, 1907): 266–269.
"Report on Quebec Bridge Failure." Vol. 44, No. 11 (March 13, 1908): 383.
"The Failure of the Quebec Bridge." Vol. 44, No. 12 (March 20, 1908): 407–412.
"The Wreck of the Quebec Bridge." Vol. 44, No. 17 (April 24, 1908): 580–581.

SCIENTIFIC AMERICAN

"The St. Lawrence River Bridge, Quebec." Vol. 93, No. 18 (October 28, 1905): 337–338.
"The Erection of the Quebec Bridge." Vol. 95, No. 13 (September 29, 1906): 225, 228.
"The Quebec Bridge Disaster." Vol. 97, No. 11 (September 14, 1907): 182, 185–187.
"Why the Great Bridge Failed." Vol. 97, No. 16 (October 12, 1907): 257–258.

The Second Bridge

ENGINEERING NEWS

"An 1,800–Ft. Steel Arch as a Quebec Bridge Project." Vol. 63, No. 20 (May 19, 1910): 577–579.
"Caissons for the Main Piers of the New Quebec Bridge; Launch of the North Pier Caisson." Vol. 64, No. 10 (September 8, 1910): 262–263.
Borden, H. P. "The Removal of the Debris of the Old Quebec Bridge." Vol. 64, No. 19 (November 10, 1910): 510–511.
"Resignation of Mr. H. E. Vautelet from the Board of Engineers for the Quebec Bridge." Vol. 65, No. 9 (March 2, 1911): 271–272.
"Designs for the New Quebec Bridge, and the Accepted Design." Vol. 65, No. 16 (April 20, 1911): 484, with two-page inset sheet.
"Tests of Nickel-Steel Details for the Board of Engineers, Quebec Bridge." Vol. 65, No. 18 (May 4, 1911): 526–531.
"Schemes of Erection Proposed for the Quebec Bridge." Vol. 66, No. 6 (August 10, 1911): 174–178.
Lindenthal, Gustav. "Notes on the Quebec Bridge Competition.—I." Vol. 66, No. 20 (November 16, 1911): 581–586.
———. "Notes on the Quebec Bridge Competition.—II. The Competitive Suspension Design." Vol. 66, No. 21 (November 23, 1911): 613–619, with two-page inset sheet.
Turner, C. A. P. "Remarks on the Quebec Bridge, and a Proposed Cantilever Design." Vol. 67, No. 22 (May 30, 1912): 1,012–1,016.
"The Construction of the South Main Pier of the Quebec Bridge." Vol. 68, No. 19 (November 7, 1912): 854–855.
Jost, L. G. "Contractors' Camp for Workmen on the New Quebec Bridge." Vol. 71, No. 10 (March 5, 1914): 498–499.
Borden, H. P. "Design of the Superstructure of the New Quebec Bridge." Vol. 71, No. 18 (April 30, 1914): 942–945, with inset sheet.
———. "Special Shopwork on the Heavy Members of the Quebec Bridge." Vol. 71, No. 20 (May 14, 1914): 1,070–1,076.
———. "Progress of Work on the Quebec Bridge during the First Erection Season." Vol. 73, No. 1 (January 7, 1915): 1–4.
———. "The Erection Traveler, New Quebec Bridge." Vol. 73, No. 9 (March 4, 1915): 417–422.
"Quebec Bridge Work in 1915." Vol. 74, No. 10 (September 2, 1915): 473–475.
"Quebec-Bridge Camp and Yards." Vol. 74, No. 16 (October 14, 1915): 748–749.
Borden, H. P. "Quebec Bridge Erection; Progress in 1915." Vol. 75, No. 1 (January 6, 1916): 20–22.
Meyers, A. J. "South Cantilever Arm of Quebec Bridge Completed." Vol. 76, No. 7 (August 17, 1916): 298–305.
"Quebec Bridge in Pictures." Vol. 76, No. 8 (August 24, 1916): 349–351.
Meyers, A. J. "Quebec Suspended-Span Hoisting Details Completed." Vol. 76, No. 9 (August 31, 1916): 420–425.

————. "Erection of Quebec Bridge Suspended Span." Vol. 76, No. 11 (September 14, 1916): 522–529.
"The Full Evidence on the Fall of the Quebec Bridge Span." Vol. 76, No. 12 (September 21, 1916):
    572–575.
"Computing the Stresses in the Quebec Rocker Casting." Vol. 76, No. 14 (October 5, 1916): 650–653.

ENGINEERING RECORD

Modjeski, Ralph. "Design of Large Bridges, with Special Reference to Quebec Bridge—Part I." Vol.
    68, No. 12 (September 20, 1913): 321–324, with insert.
————. "Design of Large Bridges, with Special Reference to Quebec Bridge—Part II." Vol. 68, No.
    13 (September 27, 1913): 354–356.
————. "Design of Large Bridges, with Special Reference to Quebec Bridge—Part III." Vol. 68, No.
    14 (October 4, 1913): 383–385.

ENGINEERING NEWS-RECORD

"Hoisting of Suspended Span in Progress at Quebec." Vol. 79, No. 12 (September 20, 1917): 570–571.
Barker, Harry. "Quebec Suspended Span Successfully Hung from Cantilevers." Vol. 79, No. 13
    (September 27, 1917): 580–589.
"The Men Who Built the World's Greatest Bridge." Vol. 79, No. 16 (October 18, 1917): 726–727.

RAILWAY AGE GAZETTE

Borden, H. P. "Construction of New Quebec Bridge Piers." Vol. 55, No. 9 (August 29, 1913): 365–369.
Modjeski, Ralph. "Adopted Design of the Quebec Bridge." Vol. 55, No. 13 (September 26, 1913): 559–
    563.
Borden, H. P. "The Erection Equipment for the Quebec Bridge." Vol. 57, No. 11 (September 11,
    1914): 463–466.
————. "Progress on the Erection of the New Quebec Bridge." Vol. 59, No. 26 (December 24, 1915):
    1,189–1,191.
Meyers, A. J. "The Season's Work on the Quebec Bridge." Vol. 60, No. 21 (May 26, 1916): 1,143–1,145.
————. "Erection Progress on the Quebec Bridge." Vol. 61, No. 7 (August 18, 1916): 275–277.
"Collapse of the Quebec Bridge." Vol. 61, No. 11 (September 15, 1916): 456.
"The Cause of the Quebec Bridge Disaster." Vol. 61, No. 12 (September 22, 1916): 487–492.
Meyers, A. J. "Quebec Bridge Central Span Successfully Hoisted." Vol. 63, No. 13 (September 28,
    1917): 569–573.

SCIENTIFIC AMERICAN

"The Design for the New Quebec Bridge." Vol. 102, No. 7 (February 12, 1910): 138, 148, 154.

Other Periodicals

Jobin, Jacques. "Quebec Bridge Roadway Construction." *Canadian Engineer*, Vol. 59, No. 9 (Au-
    gust 26, 1930): 261–264.
"Proposed Bridge over the St. Lawrence River." *Scientific American*, Vol. 52, No. 22 (May 30, 1885):
    335, 340.
Tarkov, John. "A Disaster in the Making," *American Heritage of Invention & Technology*, Vol. 1, No.
    3 (Spring 1986): 10–17.

Newspapers

La Semaine Commerciale, a French-language Québec City weekly whose editor, Ulric Barthe, also
    happened to be secretary of the Quebec Bridge Company, ran an extensive series of articles in
    1894, 1896, and 1897 describing most of the proposals for a Quebec Bridge up to that time:
"Le Pont du Québec." Vol. 1, No. 4 (September 7, 1894): 3–4.
"La Question de Pont." Vol. 5, No. 2 (August 28, 1896): 4.

"Le Pont de Québec." Vol. 5, No. 7 (October 2, 1896): 4–6.
"Les projets du Pont pour Québec." Vol. 5, No. 8 (October 9, 1896): 6.
"Les projets du Pont pour Québec." Vol. 5, No. 9 (October 16, 1896): 12–13.
"Projet de Pont de Chemin de Fer a Grand Portée en Acier Doux." Vol. 5, No. 13 (November 13, 1896): 9.
"Rapport sur le Pont de Québec par M. L'Ingénieur Bonnin." Vol. 5, No. 15 (November 27, 1896): 11–13.
"Étude de M. Hoare." Vol. 5, No. 16 (December 4, 1896): 9–10.
Shaw, Edward S. "Etude Descriptive d'un Plan de Pont Cantilever sur le St-Laurent, près de Québec." Vol. 6, No. 4 (March 12, 1897): 4–6, 9–11.

Other Newspapers Reviewed for Contemporary Reports Of Events

Le Canadien, Québec.
The Chicago Daily Tribune.
The Chronicle, Québec.
The Daily Republican, Phoenixville, Pennsylvania
The Gazette, Montréal.
The Globe, Toronto.
The New York Times.
The Press Post, Columbus, Ohio.
Le Soleil, Québec.
The Star, Montréal.

Biographical Sources

Sources for biographical information concerning the principal figures in the development of both bridges include A *Biographical Dictionary of American Civil Engineers*, published in two volumes by the American Society of Civil Engineers in 1972 and 1991; *The Canadian Encyclopedia*; the *Dictionary of American Biography*; the *Dictionary of Canadian Biography*; the *Dictionary of Canadian Biography, The Canadian Who Was Who, 1934; The Dictionary of National Biography* (Great Britain); *The Canadian Men and Women of the Time, 1898, 1912; The Canadian Who's Who, 1910; Who's Who and Why, 1914;* the Royal Commission *Quebec Bridge Inquiry Report; The National Cyclopedia of American Biography*; memoirs published in *Transactions of the American Society of Civil Engineers*; and profiles and obituaries published in *Canadian Transportation; The Daily Republican*, Phoenixville, Pennsylvania; *Engineering News-Record; The New York Times; The Peoria Star*; the American Public Works Association *Reporter*; and *The Times* of London.

Archival Sources

Hagley Museum and Library, Wilmington, Delaware. Records held include Phoenix Bridge Company field notebooks, letter books, and contract files for the Quebec Bridge.
National Archives of Canada, Ottawa. Records held include files of the Department of Railways and Canals and the Department of Indian Affairs; records of the Royal Commission, Quebec Bridge Inquiry; and Minute Books of the Quebec Bridge Company.
Québec National Archives, Québec. Records held include files of the Department of Public Works, Province of Québec; the papers of S. N. Parent.
Rensselaer Polytechnic Institute Archives, Troy, New York. Records held in the papers of John A. Roebling include the plans that accompanied Captain Edward Wellman Serrell's report for a railway suspension bridge over the St. Lawrence River near Québec and a Roebling cross-sectional sketch of a proposed 1,800-foot suspension span at Québec.
Smithsonian Institution, Museum of American History, Washington, D.C. Records held in the Division of Engineering and Industries include an extensive historical file on the Quebec Bridge and papers from the Modjeski and Masters firm founded by Ralph Modjeski.

INDEX

William D. Middleton is a 1950 civil engineering graduate from Rensselaer Polytechnic Institute and a professional engineer. He retired from the U.S. Navy's Civil Engineer Corps as a commander in 1979, and then served until 1993 on the general faculty and as the chief facilities officer at the University of Virginia. He remains active as a consultant in higher education facilities management. His professional career has also included work as a structural engineer and a bridge designer.

He has also been active for almost fifty years as a freelance journalist and historian on travel, engineering, and rail transportation topics. His published work includes more than five hundred articles for magazines and newspapers in Europe, the United States, and Asia, and seventeen books, among them *Landmarks on the Iron Road*; *South Shore: The Last Interurban*; and *"Yet there isn't a train I wouldn't take,"* all published by Indiana University Press.